全国14家国家特色服务出口基地（语言服务）联合推荐

新文科语言服务学术文库

走出象牙塔

翻译教育再思考

Beyond
the Ivory Tower

Rethinking Translation Pedagogy

Brian James Baer
Geoffrey S.Koby ● 编

吕世生 ● 导读

上海外语教育出版社
外教社 SHANGHAI FOREIGN LANGUAGE EDUCATION PRESS

图书在版编目(CIP)数据

走出象牙塔:翻译教育再思考:汉文、英文 /(美)布莱恩·詹姆斯·贝尔(Brian James Baer),杰弗里·S.科比(Geoffrey S. Koby)编;吕世生导读.—上海:上海外语教育出版社,2024

(新文科语言服务学术文库 / 王立非总主编)

ISBN 978-7-5446-7904-6

Ⅰ.①走… Ⅱ.①布… ②杰… ③吕… Ⅲ.①翻译—教学研究—汉、英 Ⅳ.①H059

中国国家版本馆 CIP 数据核字(2023)第 198273 号

图字:09-2022-0943 号

出版发行:**上海外语教育出版社**

（上海外国语大学内） 邮编:200083

电　　话:021-65425300 (总机)

电子邮箱:bookinfo@sflep.com.cn

网　　址:http://www.sflep.com

责任编辑:杨 洋

印　　刷:上海宝山译文印刷厂有限公司

开　　本:635×965　1/16　印张 18.25　字数 331 千字

版　　次:2024 年 1 月第 1 版　2024 年 1 月第 1 次印刷

书　　号:ISBN 978-7-5446-7904-6

定　　价:62.00 元

本版图书如有印装质量问题,可向本社调换

质量服务热线:4008-213-263

"新文科语言服务学术文库"专家委员会

张天伟（北京外国语大学）

张法连（中国政法大学）

张慧玉（浙江大学）

罗慧芳（当代中国与世界研究院）

屈哨兵（广州大学）

赵蓉晖（上海外国语大学）

胡开宝（上海外国语大学）

俞敬松（北京大学）

祝朝伟（四川外国语大学）

贺永中（美国蒙特雷高等国际研究院）

高明乐（北京语言大学）

高　霄（华北电力大学）

郭英剑（中国人民大学）

黄立波（西安外国语大学）

曹　进（西北师范大学）

崔启亮（对外经济贸易大学）

蒙永业（北京悦尔信息技术有限公司）

蔡基刚（复旦大学）

穆　雷（广东外语外贸大学）

Arle Lommel（美国 CSA 咨询公司）

前　言

　　语言服务兴起于 20 世纪 90 年代的欧美。2010 年，中国翻译协会首次正式在我国提出"语言服务"的概念。语言服务指以语言能力为核心，以促进跨语言、跨文化交流为目标，提供语际信息转化服务和产品，以及相关研究咨询、技术研发、工具应用、资产管理、教育培训等专业化服务的现代服务业。

　　根据统计，尽管全球经济不断受到挑战，但语言服务行业依然保持增长，2022 年，全球语言服务产值突破 600 亿美元。我国对外开放、中外人文交流和"一带一路"建设不断促进我国的语言服务市场增长。2022 年，我国的翻译公司和各类型的语言服务企业总计超过 42 万家，总产值突破 554 亿元人民币。语言服务发展的同时也带来巨大的人才需求。

　　语言服务教育在我国是一个新生事物，目标是培养行业需要的口笔译、语言技术和项目管理人才。2007 年，我国开办翻译硕士专业学位教育，为语言服务行业培养翻译人才。近年来，部分高校通过开设研究方向或独立设置二级学科点等方式，招收本地化管理、技术传播、翻译项目管理、医学语言服务、国际语言服务研究生，培养"语言＋技术""语言＋专业"和"语言＋管理"的复合型和应用型人才。部分高校成立了语言服务研究院所、应急语言服务基地（中心），召开语言服务论坛，编写语言服务研究报告等。2020 年，中国英汉语比较研究会批准成立语言服务研究专业委员会，出版《语言服务研究》集刊。2022 年，商务部、教育部、中国外文局等部委批准成立特色语言服务出口基地，国家发改委和商务部批准语言服务进入鼓励外商投资产业目录。以上举措有力地促进了语言服务的发展。

为了帮助广大师生了解国外语言服务领域学术研究和行业发展动态，满足高校语言服务学科建设、人才培养、教学科研的需要，上海外语教育出版社组织专家精心策划了"新文科语言服务学术文库"，从国外原版引进多种语言服务学术著作。本文库涵盖翻译及语言服务的职业技能和企业管理两个方面，包括翻译教学、技术文档写作、本地化技术、质量管理、服务管理、众包翻译管理等，体系完整，内容丰富，值得推荐。同时，为了方便读者理解重点，文库各书还专门配有中文导读和推荐阅读书目。

本文库可用作研究生教材，也适合语言服务行业人士和对语言服务感兴趣的广大社会读者作为参考书使用。希望文库的出版能为我国的语言服务发展贡献一份力量。

专家委员会主任

王泝邦

2023 年 12 月

导　读

一、本领域概述

翻译教学长期以来一直沿用传统的知识传递模式，由教师将自己的知识和技能传授给学生，教师是知识的来源，学生是知识的接受者。这种以教师为中心的知识传递模式随着认知科学、教育心理学和哲学思想的发展，开始受到质疑。翻译教学研究开始审视知识的本质，翻译教学理论出现建构主义转向。社会建构主义理论改变了传统翻译教学模式的理论假设，但传统模式的惯性依然强大，客观主义理论假设的翻译教学模式依然存在，似乎与社会建构主义理论假设下的教学模式并行不悖，翻译教学的建构主义转向仍有待完成。

客观主义与社会建构主义两种理论假设在翻译教学实践中分别体现为"传递模式"（transmissionist approach）和"转型模式"（transformationist approach）两种。两种模式反映了如下两种思想，构成了当前翻译教学研究的主要内容：

——视学习者为客户还是"全人"（a whole person）？学生是教室内的知识消费者，还是具有心理、生理特征及认知能力等属性的完整的个体？

——学习过程是教师主导，还是学生主导？学生主导的模式应包括教学内容、目标、学习程序和人际交流多方面的知识。

——知识是共有的还是私有的？学习者掌握的知识完全相同，还是因个体的不同而有所不同？

——学习过程是外在激励，还是内在激励？学习受外界激励，如教师或学习行为等影响，还是主要来自自我激励？

——知识是原子化的，还是整体化的？知识或技能可以分解为易于传递的片段，还是学习者接触的都是复杂现实的一部分并在其中发现自己的次级切分和秩序？

——学习过程是相同的，还是每个学习者都是独特的，有自己的方式和特色？

——学习过程是个体的，还是社会的？学习新的知识由个人单独完成，还是与他人合作完成？

——知识是内容，还是过程？学习意味着获知确定的事实，还是建构个人的意义（Miller and Seller, 1985）？

上述问题是当前翻译教学理论与实践普遍关注的问题，究其实质则是翻译教学研究"建构主义转向"以来两种理论范式共存的结果。无论哪一种选项表征的只是极端情形，具体的观点则在两者之间，或倾向某一端。然而，这些问题既是理论问题也是实践问题，因为它们出于不同的理论前提，又指向不同的教学实践。就此而言，不妨视其为理论与实践的接口，这是上述问题对翻译教学实践的意义。

翻译教学实践的探讨，目前主要聚焦于教学模式的转换。翻译教学模式探讨自 20 世纪 80 年代开始，经历了由"what"到"how"的转换过程（Introduction：V）[1]。所谓"what"指传授知识内容，"how"指传授知识建构的过程，两者可差拟授以"鱼""渔"之说。

在传统外语教学模式下，翻译教学中存在"教学空缺"（pedagogical gap）现象，主要表现为教学大纲中"缺乏清晰的教学目标、课程设计和教学法"（转引自 Introduction：VI）等内容。翻译教师往往套用外语教学法进行翻译教学，因此传统的翻译课堂教学与外语学习中的语法翻译教学并无明显区别（Introduction：VI）。随着二语习得的发展认知理论影响日益扩大，翻译教学也开始转向认知取向的教学模式。认知理论取向的教学模式"竭力使学生进入高级认知加工过程，Bloom 将其归纳为教室内外对词语意义的'阐释、表征和协商'（interpretation,

---

1　引自本论文集的"Introduction"部分。

expression and negotiation）三个过程"（Lee and Van Patten, 1995: 14）。区别于传统翻译教学模式，认知取向的翻译教学则"竭力将真实的世界带进课堂"（Krahnke, 1987: 57），但转向了"以学习者为中心的课堂"模式。这一模式下，教师的角色发生了根本变化，他是"一位学习促进者，指导学习者自己完成'真实世界'的翻译任务"（Introduction：Ⅵ）。他不仅要更好地激励学习者，让学习者更有效率；更重要的是，他应"创造真实世界中语言使用的语境，使学习者习得多种'语言外技能'（extralinguistic skill），包括特定的文化意识、非语言符号交际能力等"（Introduction：Ⅵ）。认知理论自 20 世纪 80 年代以来在外语教学以及其他应用性学科领域已得到普遍认同，其目标是揭示人脑认知的奥秘。受其影响，翻译教学也开始热衷于以认知理论来解释翻译过程，过程导向的翻译教学模式成为翻译教学的替代模式。该模式目前关注的主要问题如下：

（1）如何在传授陈述性知识（declarative knowledge）的同时也能传授程序性知识（procedural knowledge）?（两者又分别称为"信息"和"知识"。）

（2）如何使学生进入高级认知加工过程，使翻译教学更有效率?

（3）如何使学生能够模仿职业翻译行为，完成"译者自我形象"（self-image）的建构?

由于当下信息技术的发展，认知取向的翻译教学面临的挑战更为严峻，这使译者能力的概念又增加了技术的内涵，构成了翻译教学研究的前沿问题。

目前计算机的使用已成为译者必需的工作技能，"他们需要了解计算机桌面编辑程序，使用各种软件展示自己的翻译结果，与机器翻译互动，对机器翻译结果进行译后编辑等，因此职业翻译的能力构成中又增加了新的内容，他们需要具有翻译项目管理能力，要能使用机辅术语库，要能完成软件本地化，以及掌握语科库的管理、使用等技巧"（Introduction：Ⅶ）。信息技术在翻译教学中的使用又使翻译质量保证、评估方式及内容发生了变化，翻译质量评估随之发生了"过程评估转向"（Introduction：Ⅶ），与翻译教学的"过程转向"形成呼应。

然而，研究发现，技术的快速发展可能掩盖了翻译技能培养需要考虑的某些基本问题，主要表现为学习翻译技术弱化了对翻译基本能力的培养，如"文本研读"能力、写作能力、文本编辑及相关翻译研究能力等（Introduction：Ⅷ）。学习翻译技术还可能使教师更关注陈述性知识，局限于教会学生按键操作，而忽视了程序性知识。程序性知识能够保证学生及时掌握不断发展的新技术。此外，翻译培养方案中不仅要包括如何传授翻译技术，还应该包括翻译技术的一些基本原理，如术语管理、软件本地化等的技术原理（Introduction：Ⅷ）。翻译技术的发展使翻译教学研究与实践增加了新的内容，翻译能力的内涵也随之扩展。翻译技术在翻译教学中的应用使翻译教学研究的边界进一步扩大，这也成为翻译教学研究发展的显著标志。

综上，翻译教学是一种知识传授活动，对知识本质认识的发展带来了翻译教学模式理论假设的变化，产生了新的翻译教学思想和翻译教学模式，以及新的翻译手段和方式。翻译教学理论假设发生了建构主义转向，我们的知识观由客观主义转向了社会建构主义。社会建构主义改变了客观主义关于知识本质属性的认识，坚持知识是认知主体互动的结果，从根本上消解了传统翻译模式的理论基础。建构主义理论转向包括了认知理论转向和社会建构转向。认知理论揭示了人脑的认知奥秘，认为知识是人脑认知的过程，从一个新的视角揭示了知识的本质，这从根本上颠覆了对知识本质属性的认识。社会建构主义理论则从另一视角颠覆了对知识的本质属性的认识——知识是认知主体在社会环境下的互动过程。由此，两者共同完成了对客观主义理论范式的转换。翻译教学模式则确立了合作学习的思想，由结果取向转向过程取向，课堂教学中则表现为教师—学生课堂角色的变化，由以教师为中心的教学模式转向了以学生为中心的模式。信息技术的发展极大地改变了翻译教学的整体画面，机器翻译、机辅翻译、译后编辑和语料库技术等扩大了翻译教学研究的边界，改变了翻译能力构成和翻译质量评估理念及方式，这一切也都成了翻译教学研究的新内容和新挑战。

二、编者简介

本书的两位主编 Brain James Baer 和 Geoffrey S. Koby 均为美国肯特州立大学教授，讲授翻译理论和实践方面的本科及研究生课程，且都在翻译实践和教学上拥有丰富的经验。

三、内容概要

（一）本书概况

如果将翻译本体理论研究喻为象牙塔，那么翻译教学研究则可能是该塔之外的领域，这或是本书标题的所指。《走出象牙塔：翻译教育再思考》以翻译教学模式创新为取向，探讨翻译知识与技能课堂教学的理论与过程，涵盖了翻译教学的理论范式、翻译教学模式创新、课堂教学操作方案和信息技术在翻译教学中的应用、问题与解决方案等多个话题。本书运用社会建构主义理论，批评以教师为中心的翻译教学模式，提出了新的翻译教学思想：教师与学生的合作学习。本书的第一篇论文：《从教师讲授到合作建构：正在退场的范式还是翻译教学范式转换的前奏？》确立了全书的理论框架及研究基调。该文认为，社会建构主义本质上是关于知识本质属性的新认识，主张知识是人脑在社会语境下意义建构的过程，不能从一个主体转移到另一个主体。这一观点是在批判客观主义理论基础上建立起来的，认为传统的以教师为中心的翻译教学模式的理论基础不切实际。随着翻译教学理论范式的转换，翻译教学思想及相应的翻译教学模式的转换成为可能，于是，教师在翻译教学中的角色发生变化，他们不再是课堂的中心，学生才是；以翻译产品为基础的翻译教学转向了以翻译过程为中心的教学，学习者独自的认知过程变成了教师—学生合作学习的过程。本书所收录的论文以社会建构主义为理论范式，以合作学习为基本思想和课堂教学模式，从不同角度基于不同教学实践展开具体理论和实践的论证和演示，构成了一幅完整的社会建构主义理论范式下的翻译教学模式创新图景。

　　理论范式转换使翻译教学模式创新成为可能，信息技术的发展又进一步推动了这一过程，信息技术发展增加了翻译教学的内容，也带来了新的挑战。本书中研究翻译技术的三篇论文论述了软件本地化、语料库技术、术语管理等内容，这些内容的教学再次体现了合作学习的特征。

（二）本书结构

　　本书收录 12 篇论文，围绕翻译教学模式创新展开论述，涉及翻译教学模式的理论基础、翻译教学思想创新和模式创新。12 篇论文分为三个部分：翻译过程取向的研究、翻译结果取向的研究和翻译技术相关研究。第一部分（第 1—4 篇论文）是全书的基本框架和论证基础，论述了翻译教学模式的理论假设和相应的翻译教学指导思想，这是翻译教学研究领域具有里程碑意义的发展。这一部分回顾了传统翻译教学模式的理论基础——客观主义哲学思想，指出这一理论的不足，在此基础上推出了社会建构主义理论置换客观主义理论，以确立翻译教学模式的新的理论范式。依据新的理论范式，作者提出合作学习的思想，以改变传统的以教师为中心的教学模式，确立以学习者为中心的新模式，教师、学生的角色随之发生转换。基于过程取向的教学思想，作者提出以"真实世界"的翻译任务作为教学内容，培养学生的实际翻译能力。"教学工作坊"（workshop）为普遍的课堂教学形式。

　　第二部分（第 5—9 篇论文）结果取向研究聚焦于翻译教学评估的创新。该部分提出了一些新的方法，如综合评价法（portfolio approach)、成长评价法（formative approach）等，与传统的一次性结果评价完全不同。该部分的"译文修改"教学为翻译教学的一门独特的课程，以提高学生交际能力为目标，通过译文修改过程增强学生的"翻译意识"——以职业翻译为参照反思自己译文存在的不足。

第三部分（第 10—12 篇论文）论述了信息技术在翻译教学中的运用及相关问题。信息技术改变了翻译能力的内涵，翻译教学的内容因之改变，同时也带来了新的挑战，但这也为未来翻译教学指出了方向，翻译技术教学也充分体现了合作学习的思想。

（三）各篇概要

第一篇论文聚焦于翻译教学的理论范式转换。文章反思了传统翻译教学模式的理论基础——客观主义哲学思想，在此基础上提出了社会建构主义理论，尝试实现传统教学模式的理论范式转换。基于社会建构主义理论，文章详细阐述了"合作学习"的翻译教学思想，重新确定了新理论范式下的课堂教学模式和教师、学习者在教学过程中的角色定位、教学目标等，教学大纲、课程设计等是新的教学思想和实施方案的具体体现。这是一个从理论范式到教学思想再到课堂教学实践的、系统而完整的翻译教学创新方案，既包括理论阐释，又包括教学操作方案：从传统的"结果取向"（product）模式转向"过程取向"（process）模式，从以"教师为中心"的课堂教学转向了"学习者为中心的课堂教学"，从"教师讲授"转向"合作学习"，从"翻译能力"教学转向"译者能力"教学。

文章详细阐释了社会建构主义、客观主义、认知过程、翻译能力、译者能力、结果取向、过程取向等概念，围绕这些概念论证了具有理论深度且有可行性的翻译教学创新模式。

此外，文章还指出，为保证学习者发展实际的翻译能力，教师应使学习者处于真实的翻译环境、执行真实的翻译任务。这些都超越了传统课堂教学模式。

第二篇论文采用实证研究方法，以翻译交际能力培养为目标展开论述。"翻译交际能力"这一概念源于二语习得的"交际能力"概念。如何将二语习得的交际能力通过翻译教学发展成翻译交际能力，文章给出了理论解释及实际操作方案。文章将"翻译交际能力"定义为：完成交际翻译任务时，具有与目标语母语使用者一样恰当且充分地与目标语文本互动的能力。培养翻译交际能力是针对传统翻译教学的不足而提出的解决方案。传统翻译教学中，学习者往往表现出"只见树木不见林"的特征，采用单个词语语义取向（word-oriented）的思维方式，而忽略了"整体"的语义。针对这一问题，新的教学模式关注培养学习者理解"整体"语义的能力——将上下文语境纳入思考过程把握语用意义，即"意义取向"（sense-oriented）的能力。"意义取向"的能力是职业译者的能力特征。为实现这一目标，文章给出了相应的教学方案。

第三篇论文目标同样是培养学生的"意义取向"翻译能力。文章以日英翻译硕士生为被试，借助"有声思维法"（Think-Aloud Protocols, TPA）测试学习者翻译过程中存在的各种问题，并比较职业译者的翻译行为模式，以此探明初学者和职业译者行为模式的差异，再通过二者之间的差异，激励初学者尝试模仿职业译者的行为模式。这种教学模式的理论基础依然为社会建构主义。文章具体叙述了翻译过程各个环节上的初学者翻译行为模式特征和需要克服的问题，并给出了相应的解决方案。

第四篇论文从不同的角度阐释翻译能力培训，将翻译视为一种目标语写作，将译者能力培养等同于译者写作能力培养。文章回顾了关于翻译社会价值的一些观点和对可译性的一些看法，意在表述人们对于翻译活动的一般认识。无论是语言表述的艺术性、准确性，还是思想价值或美学价值，翻译本质上不可能达到原文的水平。一反通常的翻译创造性或跨文化交流价值的主张，文章从源语写作分析入手，通过母语记者的写作样本分析，指出即便同为母语写作者，被试记者对同一事件的写作在词汇选择、论证、思路等方面都表现出不同特征。因此，作为一种写作形式的翻译，与原文写作存在同样问题，不同的母语写作者对同一事件的同一命题写作也不可能完全一样。我们不能因译作与原作不同而得出其逊于原作的断言。译者的培训应确立翻译是一种写作形式的观念。

第五篇论文介绍了学生翻译能力评价方法——综合评价法，论证了综合评价法之于翻译教学的价值、特点，介绍了美国蒙特雷国际研究院（Monterey Institute of International Studies, MIIS，现更名为"明德学院蒙特雷国际研究学院"）翻译与口译研究院所采用的综合评价法的目标、内容、评估情况及其意义。这种评估方法在翻译教学中体现的是"以学习者为中心"的理念和教学模式，有助于培养学生的批判思维能力，有助于落实"以过程为中心"的教学理念，最终使学生具有熟练翻译能力、善于依靠直觉且勤于思考。要训练学生进行自我评估，保证完成的翻译作业能够达到职业翻译水平，文章介绍了两种不同类型的综合评估法：一种是课程综合评估，评估一门课程的翻译项目；另一种是职业综合评估，评估个人的职业发展，为就业做准备。

第六篇论文介绍了一项关于翻译质量评估的研究项目，研究内容包括：（1）确定并描述教学机构使用的翻译评估程序、标准及翻译行业使用的质量评估程序和标准；（2）对这些程序和标准进行比较分析；（3）对相关评估标准提出调整建议。项目提出了三个需要关注的问题：（1）翻译质量评估术语标准化；（2）基于不同理论的多种评估程序；（3）对翻译能力概念的界定。针对这些问题，文章提出了相应的解决方案，如建议成立专业人士组成的翻译术语标准委员会，制定统一的评估术语，系统地研究相关评估程序的理论依据等。该研究项目采用了问卷调查法。

第七篇论文探讨翻译教学中通常被忽略的重要环节——译文修改。文章介绍的课程为美国詹姆斯·麦迪逊大学开设的本科跨专业课程，学生来自不同学科、年级，但都具有双语能力，其专业都涉及双语转换，译文修改被视作提升翻译能力的一个重要环节。该门课程基于翻译能力培养的实际需要而设立，采用案例演示译文修改过程及要点，描述了课程设置、教学实践、这门课程的发现、相关的教训及教学理念等。此外，文章还介绍了该课程的历史发展过程及其掺杂的各种情感因素，定义了译文修改的术语。

第八篇论文讨论了文学翻译教学模式，通过三个文学翻译个案，对同一文本的多个译文进行比较研究，从而提升学生对文学文本翻译面临的特殊问题的意识。这些问题包括：阶级、性别、种族、宗教和民族等。文章对三个"翻译工作坊"使用的不同翻译教学模式或效果做了比较，期望以此培养学生对其翻译产品的反思意识，使学生能够对译文中意识形态的作用机制有所思考。文章指出三种方法各有长短，每种方法针对不同类型的文本有各自的优势或不足，在实际的文学翻译中，需要根据译者的经验加以选择。文学翻译教学的目标是确保学生对影响文学翻译方法选择的复杂因素有所认识。

第九篇论文旨在探讨如何通过恰当的翻译教学模式发展学生交际翻译策略。"交际翻译策略"概念来自"交际教学能力"概念，后者来自交际理论。文章对同一作家作品的多个英译文做了具体比较，以展示译文存在的多种交际翻译策略的各种欠缺和不足。此外，文章还指出翻译批评对提高学生的翻译能力具有重要作用，最后提出文本对比分析模式并不适用于各种文学文本翻译，只是提高学生交际能力的一种教学方法。

第十篇论文探讨了新技术，特别是语料库技术为翻译教学创新带来的多种可能性。在语言相关学科中利用语料库进行文本分析的重要性愈益明显，语料库已成为翻译教学的重要资源。文章首次提出基于语料库的翻译教学创新模式，并指出创建语料库仍需要坚持合作。为说明这一创新教学模式的可行性，文章介绍了创建目标语语料库所使用的几种不同的方法。这种基于语料库的翻译教学法坚持以学习者为中心的课堂教学模式，鼓励学生合作创建语料库，以此保证学生发展独立翻译学习能力和批判思维能力。

　　第十一篇论文提出在新技术大量应用于翻译过程的背景下，即便职业译者也面临挑战，如技术翻译、本地化翻译、项目管理等问题。处理这些技术相关问题时，他们也容易失败，或者往往需要耗费大量时间和精力。文章提出了"基于翻译任务教学法"（Task-Based Instruction, TBI），认为该方法适用于解决技术相关的翻译问题，因为这种教学法对学生的激励效果更好，可以复制真实翻译环境，有助于发展学生的高级认知加工能力，甚至不属于技术能力的其他能力也可尝试用这种方法来发展。文章利用几个软件演示了本地化案例的 TBI 翻译教学的具体操作过程。

　　第十二篇论文探讨与软件本地化教学相关的常见问题，以英—日软件本地化为例，分析了英译日的某些特征，分享了软件本地化教学的相关经验。文章认为目前缺乏高水平的软件本地化教师，但基于社会建构主义理论的合作学习模式可以缓解这一情况。基于这种模式，学生与教师能够充分分享相关知识和技能。此外，文章还介绍了美国蒙特雷国际研究院的软件本地化培训课程，这是一个英—日语的本地化软件，包括了图形和文字信息部分的本地化操作。作者使用了自我叙事的方法，详细介绍了文档、软件和 web 本地化的具体操作步骤和注意事项。文章针对如下三个问题进行论述：（1）翻译学生和教师对本地化的态度；（2）应为日语本地化翻译人员提供什么样的培训课程；（3）培训日语本地化学生应遵循的基本原则。

参考文献

Kiraly, D. 2000. *A Social Constructivist Approach to Translator Education: Empowerment from Theory to Practice.* Manchester: St. Jerome Publishing.

Krahnke, K. 1987. *Approaches for Syllabus Design for Foreign Language Teaching.* Englewood Cliffs, NJ: Prentice Hall.

Lee, J. K., and Van Patten, B.1995. *Making Communicative Language Teaching Happen.* New York: McGraw-Hill.

Miller, J., and Seller, W. 1985. "Transmission position: Educational practice". In *Curriculum: Perspectives and Practice*, J. Miller and W. Seller (eds), 37–44. New York: Longman.

Rorty, R. 1979. *Philosophy and the Mirror of Nature*. Princeton: Princeton University Press.

Spiro, R., et al. (eds.) 1992. "Cognitive flexibility constructivism and hypertext: Random access instruction for advanced knowledge acquisition in ill-structured domains". In *Constructivism and the Technology of Instruction: A Conversation*, T. M. Duffy and D. H. Jonassen (eds), 64. Hillsdale, NJ & London: Lawrence Erlbaum Associates.

推荐阅读

Abdel Latif, M. 2020. *Translator and Interpreter Education Research: Areas, Methods and Trends*. Singapore: Springer Nature Singapore.

Borodo, M., and Hubscher-Davidson, S. 2012. *Global Trends in Translator and Interpreter Training: Mediation and Culture*. London: Continuum International Publishing.

Deckert, M., and Bogucki, L. (ed) 2013. *Teaching Translation and Interpreting Advances and Perspectives*. Newcastle: Cambridge Scholars Publishing.

Gonzalez-Davies, M., and Enríquez Raído, V. 2018. *Situated Learning in Translator and Interpreter Training: Bridging Research and Good Practice*. London: Taylor & Francis.

Hatim, B. A. 2012. *Teaching and Researching Translation*（2th Edition）. London: Routledge.

Huertas Barros, E., and Vine, J. 2019. *New Perspectives on Assessment in Translator Education*. London: Routledge.

Kiraly, D. 2000. *A Social Constructivist Approach to Translator Education Empowerment from Theory to Practice*. Manchester: St. Jerome.

Laviosa, S. 2014. *Translation and Language Education Pedagogic Approaches Explored*. London: Routledge.

Tsagari, D., and Phlōros, G. 2013. *Translation in Language Teaching and Assessment*. Newcastle: Cambridge Scholars Publishing.

Venuti, L. 2016. *Teaching Translation: Programs, Courses, Pedagogies*. London: Taylor & Francis.

吕世生

Beyond the Ivory Tower

Rethinking translation pedagogy

EDITED BY

Brian James Baer
Geoffrey S. Koby

Beyond the Ivory Tower

Table of contents

Introduction

Translation pedagogy: The *other* theory

Brian James Baer and Geoffrey S. Koby

Much of the discussion of translation pedagogy today is drowned out by the endless debate over theory versus practice. Practitioners in the field typically see little value in academic theorizing on translation that is often the product of influences emanating from the humanities and social sciences. As Emma Wagner put it: "'Translation theory? Spare us...' That's the reaction to be expected from most practicing translators. Messages from the ivory tower tend not to penetrate as far as the wordface. (The wordface is the place where we translators work — think of a miner at the coalface)" (2002: 1). Translation theory is typically criticized as at best irrelevant to the professional translator and at worst distracting and misleading. "It is time," Douglas Robinson stated in *The Translator's Turn*, "to offer translators tools, not rules" (1991: xvi).

The prejudice against theory on the part of practitioners is understandable, for while translation may be "the world's second oldest profession," it has only recently been institutionalized as a unique discipline within the academy. Its position outside or on the margins of scholarship has helped to foster a profound skepticism toward translation theory, fueled by popular beliefs that translators are born, not made, or that translation is something that is learned on the job, not in the classroom. This view made its way into the academy in the concept of *natural translation*, proposed by Harris (1977) and Harris and Sherwood (1978), according to which translation was seen as a skill inherent in bilinguals. This effectively conflated translation pedagogy with that of language acquisition.

While there have been many significant attempts to think beyond the opposition of theory versus practice, the real loser in this debate — which is essentially a debate about curricular content — continues to be the whole question of *how* to teach translation. Is the challenge faced by translator trainers really just a choice between teaching tools or rules? We may hope to better prepare students for the workplace by offering them appropriate tools, but if our teaching methodology is of the traditional kind — the *performance magistrale* described by Jean-René Ladmiral (1977) in which the master passes on his/her knowledge to a passive apprentice — we may fail to produce translators who are capable of the flexibility, teamwork and problem-solving that are essential for success in the contemporary language industry, not to mention the creativity and independent thinking that have always been the hallmark of the finest translators. It may be, in fact, that the *how* is as important, if not more so, than the *what*: "If the translator has no formal training [in translation pedagogy]," writes Maria-Luisa Arias-Moreno, "the experience is more than chaotic and catastrophic for students" (1999: 335). Moreover, the very small number of doctoral programs in translation studies and the practical orientation of master's programs means that many instructors of translation have no formal training in pedagogy and must pick it up, if at all, on the job.

Throughout the 1990s, however, a growing number of translator trainers have addressed what Donald Kiraly has called the "pedagogical gap" in translation skill instruction, reflected in "the lack of clear objectives, curricular materials, and teaching methods" (1995: 5). Translator trainers interested in issues of pedagogy have looked to new methodologies developed for use in the teaching of foreign languages and various applied disciplines in order to challenge traditional classroom practice that "bears a strong resemblance to the antiquated grammar-translation method of foreign language teaching" (7).

Developments in foreign language pedagogy over the last twenty-five years that were engendered by the shift from behavioralist models (Skinner) to cognitive models (Bloom, Piaget, Vygotsky) of language acquisition, offer translator trainers a variety of new instructional methodologies.[1] These models seek to engage the student's higher-level cognitive processing — as elaborated in Bloom's taxonomy — involving "the interpretation, expression and negotiation of meaning, both in and out of the classroom" (Lee and Van Patten 1995: 14). The attempt to "bring the real world into the classroom" (Krahnke 1987: 57) is another common feature of these new pedagogical initiatives, as is the creation of more learner-centered classrooms, in which teachers function as facilitators, guiding learners in the completion of real-world tasks. In addition to producing more motivated learners and more effective learning, contextualization of language use in real-world situations also helps to develop a variety of extralinguistic skills in the learner, such as sensitivity to culture-specific issues and non-verbal means of communication (i.e., gestures, facial expressions, images).

Influenced by these trends in foreign language instruction and other applied disciplines that have adopted cognitive rather than behavioralist models of instruction, Jean Delisle, Daniel Gile, Donald Kiraly, F. G. Königs and Paul Kussmaul, among others, have called for a more process-oriented, learner-centered approach to translation training. Their work articulates challenges facing translator trainers that have little to do with the debate over theory versus practice so often articulated in our professional literature, where academics are unfairly pitted against practitioners.[2] Those challenges suggested by cognitive models are essentially threefold:

(1) How to impart both declarative knowledge (facts, rules) and procedural knowledge (conceptual understanding) — often referred to as information and knowledge, respectively;

(2) How to engage higher-level cognitive processing to make teaching more effective and learners more resourceful and flexible;

(3) How to encourage professional conduct and the development of the student's self-image as a translator.

These issues are especially relevant today as developments in various technology-related fields (i.e., telecommunications, the Internet, computer-assisted translation) are altering and expanding the skill sets that are expected of a professional translator, putting pressure on translator training programs to add them to the curriculum without increasing the credit hours needed for completion.

The traditional tasks that professional translators perform have been intensively modified by the language engineering industry and the recent development of highly sophisticated and customized computerized programs and tools. Increasing numbers of translators are already working with computer-assisted translation software, and are expected to know desktop publishers and other presentation software. It is also becoming increasingly common for translators to interact with and revise the output of machine translation software. Consequently, translators are expected to acquire a growing number of new translation skills as they build their professional profiles, such as technological project management, production of translated texts using computer-assisted terminology databases, ability to use localization software, as well as methodologies of corpus linguistics. Inherent in all these changes is the possibility that the language industry has modified the protocols for quality assurance and quality assessment, that is, the very process of translation evaluation.

Clearly, the greatest danger is that the pace of technological change will obscure important pedagogical considerations. First, training in technology may occur at the expense of other fundamental translation skills such as "learning how to read a text closely, writing, editing, researching" (Durban et al. 2003). Second, when introducing new technological skills, trainers may be tempted to impart only "declarative knowledge," showing students which buttons to press, rather than the "procedural knowledge" that will help them deal with the inevitable modifications and developments in that technology. A responsible translation studies program should not only teach technological skills, but should impart knowledge of the underlying principles in areas such as terminology management and software localization.

As suggested by the foregoing discussion, the present volume focuses on those pedagogical issues typically ignored within the theory vs. practice debate. All of the contributors are translator trainers working in various institutional settings in North America and Europe. Informed by both experience and theories of pedagogy, they offer critical discussion of pedagogical methods, together with sample lessons and exercises, confirming, we hope, Mildred Larson's observation that "as we look at the material that has been written on translation theory and practice, the books of particular significance are often written by persons who, in addition to being translators themselves, are also teachers of translation" (1991: 2). Moreover, it is our hope that such discussions of translation pedagogy can offer a way out of the impasse between theory and practice by suggesting different and perhaps ultimately more useful questions. Instead of "How relevant is what I'm teaching to the profession?" we might better ask, "How effectively am I teaching students to think about translation?"

This volume is divided into three sections. The articles in the first section explore various pedagogical interventions that are focused on the performance of translation, or translation as process. The articles in the second part discuss approaches to translator training that deal with finished translations, or translation as product, raising questions of assessment, evaluation, and text revision in both professional and academic settings. The articles in the third section of the volume address some of the pedagogical opportunities and challenges raised by developments in translation-related technologies. It should be noted, however, that the divisions here are provisional and the boundaries porous. For example, the approaches based on translation as product seek to influence translation as process, making students more aware of the ways in which they go about the translator's task, while many of the pedagogical initiatives mentioned in sections one and two are facilitated if not made possible by the advent of new technologies. And while Judy Wakabayashi's article on Think-Aloud Protocols has been placed in section one, we are aware that, using TAPs, "it is only *products* which are available, although products of a different kind and order" (Toury 1977: 65).

The volume opens with Donald Kiraly's discussion of process-oriented pedagogy. In order to displace the traditional objectivist approach to translator training, which is basically teacher-centered, Kiraly proposes the incorporation of an innovative social-constructivist approach that better reflects the multi-faceted activity of the contemporary language professional. He also encourages translator trainers to redefine translator competence in order to address the disparity between what is learned in the classroom and what is practiced in the field. After briefly describing social-constructivist educational epistemology, Kiraly asserts that fostering collaboration in the classroom is the key to shifting from a teacher-centered approach to a learner-centered approach. He argues that, by using a project workshop, students become more competent, reflective, self-confident and professional.

Sonia Colina addresses similar concerns in her discussion of the applicability of communicative competence as developed in the field of Second Language Acquisition to the translation classroom. The aim of communicative translational competence, Colina argues, is to encourage a more sense-oriented approach to translation that would address the traditional weaknesses of the beginning translator, such as the tendency to ignore "the global, textual, and pragmatic considerations used by professional translators." Colina then demonstrates how such translational competence can be fostered in the classroom by offering a well-structured lesson plan.

Sharing Colina's goal of encouraging more sense-oriented translation, Judy Wakabayashi explores the effectiveness of using Think-Aloud Protocols (TAP) in the classroom. TAPs can be used, Wakabayashi suggests, in order to highlight the differences between the processing performed by novices and that of translation professionals. TAPs can be performed by students in order to make them more aware of their general approach to translation. However, they can also be performed by the instructor in order to model professional translator behavior.

Alex Gross's contribution also aims at improving the student's self-image as a translator. By teaching translation as a form of target-language writing, Gross suggests that translator trainers can help dismantle the enduring stereotype of translation as an inevitably dim reflection of an authentic original text.

Section two's focus on translation as product begins with Julie Johnson's exploration of the ways in which portfolios can be used as an assessment tool in order to make the translation classroom more learner-centered. The proper use of portfolios, Johnson argues, can contribute to the preparation of translators who are skilled, intuitive, and self-reflective by fostering critical thinking and facilitating process-oriented learning. Moreover, they not only teach translators-in-training to evaluate their own work, they prepare them to present their work in a professional manner to potential employers. Johnson discusses two types of portfolio: the course portfolio, presented as a terminal project in a single course, and the professional portfolio, prepared as an exit project at the end of a course of study.

Fanny Arango-Keeth and Geoffrey Koby address the disparity between student evaluation in translator training and quality assessment as practiced in the translation industry. They report on a survey of such practices that they conducted in early 2002 which highlights these disparities, and argue for greater harmonization and coordination between the two.

Jonathan Hine discusses the challenges of teaching the important but often neglected skill of text revision within a multilingual environment, offering a case study of one such course. Born out of necessity, this course might serve as a model for meeting student needs when an insufficient number of students is working in a single language pair to meet minimum course enrollments. Monolingual and bilingual components were broken into modules and a protocol was developed for handling assignments outside the languages of the instructor.

Carol Maier continues the discussion of translation as product in her exploration of various ways in which the comparative study of translations can help literary translators become self-aware, more sensitive to issues of class, gender, race, religion and ethnicity in their work. Maier evaluates the effectiveness of the approaches she has used in translation workshops to encourage self-reflection and foster discussion among translators — professionals and students alike — concerning the general workings of ideology as reflected in the translation of gender.

Natalia Olshanskaya's contribution also makes use of evaluation of works of translation, but with the object of improving the student's communicative proficiency. Making reference to various translations into English of the works of Isaac Babel, a Ukrainian-born, Russian-speaking Jew, Olshanskaya isolates those moments in which the translations demonstrate communicative deficiencies. Like Maier, Olshanskaya suggests an important role for translation criticism in the teaching of translation competence.

Beginning section three, Lynn Bowker explores the pedagogical possibilities opened up by new technology, specifically for the building of corpora. Recognizing the growing importance of corpus creation and analysis in language-related disciplines and the value of using textual corpora as a translation resource, Bowker proposes an innovation to the pedagogical approach known as corpora-based translation instruction. Bowker advocates a collaborative approach to corpora building that allows students to build a corpus in the translation classroom. In order to demonstrate the viability of this proposal, she describes several different experiments she conducted in the building of targeted textual corpora related to the subject of computing. Bowker's learner-centered approach to corpus building encourages students to become independent learners and critical thinkers.

Geoffrey Koby and Brian James Baer address some of the challenges posed to translation pedagogy by the development and proliferation of new technologies. The urgent need for technical translators, localizers, and project managers may result in a failure to address fundamental questions of teaching methodology in an attempt to produce as many qualified professionals as possible in the least amount of time. Koby and Baer suggest that Task-Based Instruction (TBI) may be an appropriate methodology for teaching translation-related technologies in that it increases student motivation, replicates real world situations, engages higher-level cognitive processing, and addresses a variety of useful competences above and beyond technical proficiency. In order to demonstrate the applications of TBI to the translation classroom, the authors offer a number of tasks that can be used in the teaching of localization.

Takashi Kosaka and Masaki Itagaki also address general pedagogical issues related to the teaching of software localization, as well as specific problems involved with localization between English and Japanese. The authors dispel a number of myths surrounding translation of English text into Japanese and recount their own experiences as teachers of localization. Finally, Kosaka and Itagaki suggest that the dearth of qualified localization instructors can be remedied through a social-constructivist approach to teaching that offers a collaborative structure through which students and instructors can share knowledge and skills.

All of the phenomena discussed above — the development and implementation of new methods in foreign language pedagogy, pedagogical initiatives introduced in various applied disciplines, changes in the rapidly-expanding language industry, and the advent of new technologies for use in both the classroom and the workplace — are presently affecting the development of translation pedagogy, in both its content and its methods, leading it into new directions. They challenge teachers of translation to respond with a pedagogy that addresses not only the acquisition of new practical capabilities, but also the ability to re-conceptualize the translator's task and the evolving role of the individual translator. Moreover, it is our hope that this volume will further discussion of pedagogical methods among translator trainers, lending new visibility to the subject of translation pedagogy, which has been for too long the other, forgotten theory in translation studies.

Notes

1. While the theories of Bloom, Piaget and Vygotsky may all seem to be concerned with cognitive processes, there are fundamental epistemological differences among them. For Bloom and Piaget, there are innate structures in the brain designed specifically for language acquisition, while for Vygotsky, these structures do not exist *a priori*. Rather, they are constructed through the negotiation of meaning in language.

2. For a good discussion of the (often inaccurate) assumptions that structure the debate over theory versus practice, see Pym (2001).

References

Arias-Moreno, M.-L. 1999. "What? Teach translation?" In *Proceedings of the 40th Annual Conference of the American Translators Association*, A. G. Macfarlane (ed), 335–342. Alexandria, Virginia: American Translators Association.

Durban C. et al. 2003. "Translator training & the real world: Concrete suggestions for bridging the gap." *Translation Journal* 7 (1): <http://www.accurapid.com/journal/23roundtablea.htm> accessed on February 3, 2003.

Harris, B. 1977. "The importance of natural translation." *Working Papers on Bilingualism* 12: 96–114.

Harris, B., and Sherwood, B. 1978. "Translating as an innate skill." In *Language, Interpretation, and Communication*, D. Gerver and H. W. Sinaiko (eds), 155–170. New York and London: Plenum.

Kiraly, D. G. 1995. *Pathways to Translation. Pedagogy and Process*. Kent, Ohio: Kent State University Press.

Krahnke, K. 1987. *Approaches to Syllabus Design for Foreign Language Teaching*. Englewood Cliffs, NJ: Prentice Hall.

Ladmiral, J. R. 1977. "La traduction dans le cadre de l'institution pedagogique." *Die Neueren Sprachen* 76: 489–516.

Larson, M. L. 1991. "Editor's Note: The interdependence of theory and practice." In *Translation: Theory and Practice. Tension and Interdependence*, M. L. Larson (ed), 1–4. American Translators Association Scholarly Monograph Series, Volume V. Binghamton, New York: State University of New York at Binghamton.

Lee, J. F., and Van Patten, B. 1995. *Making Communicative Language Teaching Happen*. New York: McGraw-Hill.

Pym, A. 2001. "To localize and humanize... On academics and translation." *Language International* 13 (4): 26–28.

Robinson, D. 1991. *The Translator's Turn*. Baltimore: Johns Hopkins UP.

Toury, G. 1974. "The notion of 'native translator' and translation teaching." In *Die Theorie des Übersetzens und ihr Aufschlußwert für die Übersetzungs- und Dolmetschdidaktik,* W. Wilss and G. Thome (eds), 186–195. Tübingen: Gunter Narr.

————. 1977. *Translation Norms and Literary Translation into Hebrew*. Tel Aviv: Porter Institute for Poetics and Semiotics.

Wagner, E., and Chesterman, A. 2002. *Can Theory Help Translators? A Dialogue between the Ivory Tower and the Wordface*. Manchester, UK: St. Jerome.

1. Translation as process

From instruction to collaborative construction

A passing fad or the promise of a paradigm shift in translator education?

Donald C. Kiraly

Introduction

After some fifty years of a shadowy existence at the periphery of the emerging field of translation studies, translator education has reached a crossroads. Now that its parent field has matured to become a full-fledged area of study in its own right, there is increasing concern that the development of methods for educating professional translators has been neglected in favor of a "hand-me-down" principle, where each new generation of translators merely does unto their students what was done unto them. Over the past decade there have been some articles, a few books, and even some conferences on the teaching of translation, but so far there has been little concerted effort to either justify existing pedagogical models or create innovative ones for the education of non-literary translators.

This situation is finally beginning to change; witness the title of this volume, *Beyond the Ivory Tower: Rethinking Translation Pedagogy.* The question I have posed in the title of this paper is one that we, the community of translation teachers, need to answer for ourselves. There is a lively debate going on in other educational circles today that revolves around a family of concepts including "collaboration," "radical constructivism," "social constructivism," "empowerment," and "reflective practice." At the same time, job announcements in the language mediation field rarely fail to mention "the ability to work as part of a team" as a requirement for employment. The time is indeed ripe to ask ourselves if collaboration represents no more than a passing fad in educational jargon (and in job descriptions), or whether it might not serve as a key to innovation, allowing us to adapt our conventional hand-me-down approach in order to meet the exigencies of a much changed translation market and to address the challenges posed by contemporary views of the translator's craft.

In making a case for considering collaboration as a particularly valuable element in developing innovative methods for translator education, I particularly hope to demonstrate that the first step in the process of creating any educational approach must be the specification of the underlying epistemology, that is, our understanding of what it means to know and to learn. These philosophical underpinnings will form the essential conceptual foundation that will inform, justify and link together all subsequent stages of teaching, from curriculum and syllabus design to the creation of classroom techniques and methods of evaluation.

In this article, I will take the reader on a brief reflective journey through my own process of selecting and interpreting sources of inspiration from the extensive literature on collaboration, and through the development of my personal approach to translator education. Of course I understand that there is nothing absolute about my choices, interpretations or conclusions. Each teacher will draw on different sources and derive his or her own conclusions from them. However, if we tackle the philosophical, pedagogical and didactic problems of teaching as a community of practice, if we begin as a team to research and debate these issues, we can jointly develop collaborative approaches that can inform teaching on a systematic level throughout the field of translator education. My task here is to raise issues and incite debate that I hope will lead us far beyond my exploratory deliberations.[1]

Objectivism: A commonsense epistemology

Every educational method must be based on an epistemology: a theory, understanding or set of beliefs about what it means to know, and hence to learn. Of course, the shades of gray in this matter are infinite, but for the sake of argument, I will be presenting conventional epistemology as if it were monolithic so that it can be contrasted with its theoretical antithesis: social constructivism. I have no pretense to being impartial or "objective" in my portrayals here. I can only present and explain my interpretations, let you reflect on them, and encourage you to come up with your own.

Until recently, few authors of educational publications claimed to represent an "objectivist" viewpoint. The common sense view that teachers transmit truth about the world to their students has needed neither explication nor justification. It has been largely left to constructivists to define and specify the features and implications of this ubiquitous "common sense" epistemology. For example, in the words of the renowned linguist and cognitive scientist George Lakoff:

> Objectivism is a view of the nature of knowledge and what it means to know something. In this view, the mind is an instantiation of a computer, manipulating symbols in the same way (or analogously, at least) as a computer [...] Knowledge, therefore, is some entity existing independently of the mind, which is transferred "inside the mind." Cognition is the rule-based manipulation of the symbols via processes that will be ultimately describable through the language of mathematics and/or logic. Thus, this school of thought believes that the external world is mind independent (i.e., the same for everyone). (1987: 20)

From this viewpoint (also called "positivism" or "foundationalism"), meaning is believed to exist objectively in the real world independently of the observer, and the goal of learning is to come to know these objective meanings. In the objectivist classroom then, the teacher is privy in some sense to the right answers, that is, to truth, and the learners are there to find out what those answers are. Social constructivists claim that conventional teacher-centered instruction, where the teacher's knowledge is supposed to be passed on to students, is derived from the common sense positivist belief that:

> Experience plays an insignificant role in the structuring of the world: meaning is something that exists in the world quite aside from experience. Hence, the goal of understanding is coming to know the entities, attributes, and relations that exist. (Duffy and Jonassen 1992: 2)

Evidence for the prevalence of such beliefs about meaning, knowing and learning within the teaching profession can be found in instructional practice in classrooms "the world over, from the two Cambridges to Tokyo, from first grade to the Ph.D." (Bruffee 1995: 66).[2] Published accounts of anecdotal evidence[3] and my own informal survey of translation teachers and students at a number of translator education institutions in Europe over the past six years suggest that "didacticism" or knowledge transmission is the order of the day in translator education programs as it is in many, if not most, other institutionalized educational environments. A closer look at the "classical" didactic technique used in translation practice classes, as described by Christiane Nord (1996), reveals an underlying objectivist epistemology:

> The students have more or less thoroughly prepared the text to be translated at home, and then take turns reading their translation suggestions sentence by sentence. These suggestions are discussed by the class as a whole, with comments being made by the instructor, until an "optimal solution" is reached that everyone

can agree on. This solution is usually written down by the students. (320, my translation)

The chart in Figure 1 illustrates my interpretation of how learning is actually supposed to come about through such a classroom activity:

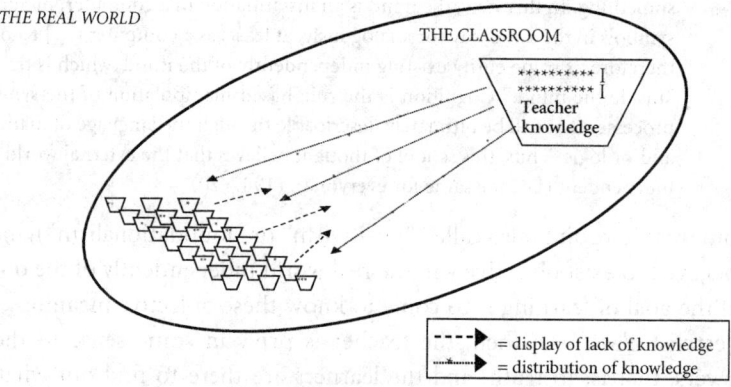

Figure 1. Interaction in a typical translator education classroom

Here, the primary teaching activity in the classroom involves the verbal "transmission" of some of the teacher's amassed knowledge to the minds of the learners in the form of the comments on the students' generally faulty suggestions. It is the learners' task to absorb this transmitted knowledge and commit it to memory. If students say anything at all in class, it is usually to display their lack of knowledge as they read off passages from their rough translations and ask questions so that the teacher can correct their errors and provide them with the right answers. Talk between students is generally considered disruptive to the transmission process. In decrying the evils of the collaborative classroom, a professor of history and dean of humanities and social sciences at an American college wrote recently:

> The teacher's role is to transmit [his or her] laboriously acquired assets to students and to open intellectual doors hitherto closed. The student's role is to pay attention, benefit from superior knowledge and experience, study diligently, and participate fruitfully when the moment is ripe. (Stunkel 1998: A52)

This statement eloquently illustrates Donald Schön's concept of "technical rationalism," the implication of the objectivist perspective that professional action is rational, rule-bound behavior predicated on the prior ingestion of ready-made cognitive tools. One question that comes to my mind immediately upon reading this statement is how does one know that "the moment is ripe" for fruitful participation, and when does the metamorphosis from being a passive recipient of knowledge to a competent professional occur? Is there actually a progression toward autonomy built into our curricula and teaching methods? Do we gradually wean students from dependence on our knowledge, as strongly recommended by Freihoff (1998):

> [...] it is the teacher's job to move to the background right from the beginning, and to eventually withdraw completely [...] Learning and teaching can thus be seen as an interactive process, in which learners become increasingly independent [...] (29, my translation)

Or, do we not in fact tend to treat students at all levels as if their main task were to absorb our knowledge right down until the moment when expertise and professionalism are conferred along with the diploma at graduation?

There are, of course, innumerable variations on the objectivist theme, but in my view, the model depicted here illustrates the most basic underlying assumption of the conventional approach to learning and teaching. In this type of classroom, "collaboration" is reduced to merely playing by the rules of the memorization game, which serves a largely passive secondary role to the main attraction, which is the instructor's display and distribution of amassed knowledge and experience. Here, there can be no team spirit, no lively interaction, and none of the negotiation of meaning that is the hallmark of more natural forms of discourse. Given the underlying understanding of what it means to learn and know, collaboration in such a classroom is a red herring. As Kenneth Stunkel has said:

> Virtually by definition, students are incapable on their own of exploring the topic at the same level. The reason is simple: A good teacher is an authority. He or she has more knowledge, experience, and insight into a subject than the student does. (1998: A52)

Decades ago, translation led but a shadow existence at the edge of the humanities, when translators were considered little more than bilingual scribes. Back then, it might well have been a viable educational approach to adopt an objectivist viewpoint and transmit the necessary knowledge about contrasting linguistic structures to students. Then, before researchers in translation studies had produced the wealth of research and literature on the cultural, social and professional aspects of interlingual mediation that is part of our community self-concept today, translation was surely seen as an essentially rational, rule-based, highly structured linguistic activity. As our earliest translator training programs were just emerging half a century ago, the teachers at that time had to come from other academic domains. They were not necessarily translators themselves; instead, they were philologists or linguists, and some were expatriates of other countries who found themselves employed as translation teachers because they happened to be native speakers of other languages. (This was in fact my own experience, although I was not hired to teach translation until 1983). In the absence of practical translation experience, teachers have little alternative but to deal with their subject matter as if it were primarily a pedagogical linguistic exercise rather than a multi-faceted professional activity.

If we believe in the efficacy of a transmissionist teaching approach, there is no real need for a debate on how to improve teaching. If students can acquire their teacher's expertise by listening to them talk about the subject at hand, so too can novice teachers learn from proficient ones by sitting in on classes and mimicking their mentors' behavior. In both cases, knowledge and experience can be distilled and communicated through verbal symbols and handed down from a better-stocked mind to less knowledgeable ones.

The training of translation teachers has in fact proceeded in a manner analogous to the training of translators themselves. It is only now that the first academic programs for the education of translation teachers are beginning to emerge.[4] I believe that this new interest is in part due to an increasing awareness that translation has become a full-fledged craft and profession, that there is far more to the translation teaching process than passing on acquired knowledge, and that direct transmission is certainly not the only (and perhaps not the most effective) way to help students acquire the wide range of skills and expertise that translators must have to complement their knowledge of contrastive linguistics.

Since translator education programs have now been around for decades, more and more representatives of the younger generation of translation teachers actually have academic training as translators and professional translation experience, which may encourage them to adopt a less ivory-tower and more praxis-oriented approach. As I will attempt to show later in this chapter, a focus on the actual practice of translation outside the classroom naturally leads away from a teacher-centered, transmissionist approach and toward one that puts the spotlight on students and (collaborative) learning instead. At this point I would like to introduce the social constructivist epistemology, which I believe can serve as a strong theoretical cornerstone for the development of student- and praxis-relevant teaching methods.

A family of alternative perspectives: The construction of reality

Constructivism is of course no more monolithic than the objectivist perspective. The two primary strains (around which are clustered numerous variants) are "radical constructivism," which derives primarily from Piaget's developmental psychology, and "social constructivism," which draws considerable inspiration from the work of Lev Vygostky, but also from John Dewey (1938) and Richard Rorty (1979). These two poles of the continuum share the fundamental idea that people construct their understandings of the world rather than reflect nature in their minds. In the Piagetian tradition, perhaps most vociferously defended by Ernst von Glasersfeld (1988), the "radical" variant focuses on the individual mind as the constructor of meaning and knowledge, whereas the "social" variant emphasizes the role of interaction between members of a community in coming to understand the world. My belief in a social constructivist perspective is a personal one, based on my own experiences as a learner and teacher. There is nothing inherently wrong or right about it, but it is viable for me. I see the best degree of "fit" between this viewpoint and my understanding of knowing and learning. The selection of a particular perspective is clearly one that will have to be made by each individual teacher. What is important, I think, is that the choice we make at this level will clearly have a profound impact on the implications we draw for our teaching practice, and specifically on whether we see learning as an essentially individual or collaborative process.

At the heart of the social constructivist perspective is the belief that there is no meaning in the world until we human beings make it — both individually and collectively. Learning and cognitive development — the lifelong creation of the mind — are seen to derive, first and foremost, from the interplay of communicative interaction and sense perception. In this view, while there is a reality outside of subjective interpretation and belief, we cannot come to know that reality in any objective way. Instead, we construct dynamic, viable understandings of the world on the basis of experience, the interpretation of our sense perceptions, and the resolution of conflicts with our existing beliefs.

> In this view, learning is a constructive process in which the learner is building an internal representation of knowledge, a personal interpretation of experience. This representation is constantly open to change, its structure and linkages forming the foundation to which other knowledge structures are appended. Learning is an active process in which meaning is developed on the basis of experience. Conceptual growth comes from the sharing of multiple perspectives and the simultaneous changing of our internal representations in response to those perspectives as well as through cumulative experience. (Bednar et al. 1992: 21)

An essential difference between a conventional, objectivist viewpoint and a social constructivist one, particularly for translator education, lies in the awareness that from the latter perspective, the teacher's experience and knowledge simply cannot be transferred to the learner. All input from the environment, including a teacher's utterances, will have to be interpreted, weighed and balanced against each learner's prior knowledge:

> [...] the argument is that meaning is imposed on the world by us, rather than existing in the world independently of us. There are many ways to structure the world, and there are many meanings or perspectives for any event or concept. Thus there is not a correct meaning that we are striving for. (Duffy and Jonassen 1992: 3)

The way Duffy and Jonassen have phrased the essence of constructivism points to a crucial realization for translator education: none of us, neither student nor teacher, can possibly have "the" right answers. When faced with translation decisions, we can come up with solutions that we believe are plausible and viable on the basis of our prior experience. But this experience has to be our own, not the distillation of someone else's experience handed down in an abstract, verbal form.

Of particular interest here is the finding of expertise studies that what the expert knows is neither separate nor separable from the professional activities in which that individual engages. In Donald Schön's words:

> I shall use *knowing-in-action* to refer to the sorts of know-how we reveal in our intelligent action — publicly observable, physical performances like riding a bicycle and private operations like instant analysis of a balance sheet. In both cases, the knowing is *in* the action. We reveal it by our spontaneous, skillful execution of the performance; and **we are characteristically unable to make it verbally explicit.** (Schön 1987: 25, my emphasis)

Schön sees the professional practice of lawyers, doctors, and engineers more as a matter of intuitive "artistry" in practice than of conscious, rule-bound decision-making. His realization that experts generally cannot express in words how they do what they do suggests that the transmissionist approach cannot accomplish what it purports to accomplish: the transfer of expertise from one mind to another. From a social constructivist viewpoint there is thus a need for extensive and intensive action (and interaction) on the part of each individual if learning is to be effective. Regardless of the domain involved, it entails actually using the tools of a profession to fashion and re-fashion one's own concepts and translational artifacts, strategies and procedures in conjunction with peers and experienced professionals. Hence, the collaborative undertaking of authentic tasks with the support of the teacher is at the heart of social constructivist teaching methods:

> Perhaps, then, learning *all* forms of professional artistry depends, at least in part, on conditions similar to those created in the studios and conservatories: freedom to learn by doing in a setting relatively low in risk, with access to coaches who initiate students into the "traditions of the calling" and help them, by "the right kind of telling," to see on their own behalf and in their own way what they need most to see. (Schön 1987: 17)

Over the past decade there has been a massive movement in many educational domains, from social studies to mathematics, from composition to distance learning, and from elementary school to teacher education programs, to devise and justify teaching methods on the basis of social constructivist principles. Nevertheless, while constructivism today is often portrayed as the dominant paradigm in contemporary educational philosophy and teacher training programs, didactic practice reflecting an objectivist viewpoint continues to persist in the classroom. The field of translation studies is starting to question the viability of the hand-me-down approach to translation pedagogy and is looking to collaborative methods for inspiration. It is ironic that this development is occurring while constructivist collaboration is both at its zenith in theory and under attack in practice in other educational domains. The main concerns seem to be that constructivist approaches are seen to fall short in the areas of academic rigor and classroom discipline, that they promote a chaotic, laissez-faire environment in the classroom where the teacher is no longer in control, and that they waste the teacher's laboriously amassed knowledge:

> [...] in much of higher education, no interactive model can substitute for a well-organized lecture that structures a mass of information, illuminates basic concepts, suggests applications, reviews relevant literature and major interpretations, and displays what it means for someone to care about learning, inquiry and teaching. (Stunkel 1998: A52)

I would not say that Stunkel is wrong; he is merely drawing logical conclusions from his underlying assumptions about the nature of knowing and learning. Interestingly, the article from which this quotation was taken is entitled, "We Want to See the Teacher: Constructivism and the Rage Against Expertise." It assumes that in a classroom based on constructivist principles, teachers set up learning environments and then withdraw to the sidelines, essentially leaving students to their own devices to make their way in the dark. This criticism may indeed be justified in the case of several other alternative educational movements, like the "discovery learning" or "autonomous learning" methods.

However, from a social constructivist perspective, the teacher in fact remains a key figure in the learning situation. One of the best-developed methods for teaching based on social constructivism is "cognitive apprenticeship" (Defalco 1995; Bednar 1992; Collins, Brown, Newman 1989), where groups of learners create pieces of work (rather than perform exercises) under the tutelage of and with the collaborative support of an expert practitioner. And while there is sure to be considerable conversation and interaction in a social constructivist classroom, one of the teacher's main jobs is to be attentive to those potential moments of developmental progress that Vygotsky called the "zone of proximal development" in the course of students' collaborative learning experiences. The teacher must also provide just enough assistance at those moments to help the group move to a new level of understanding.

Another key concept for social constructivists is "scaffolding" (see Fisher 1994), representing a framework of support for learning created by the teacher at the beginning of a program of study, a course or a lesson. It is a supportive intellectual framework that can be gradually dismantled as learners become more independent and assume more responsibility for their own learning. As for chaos, the social constructivist classroom may well be a less orderly place than many conventional, teacher-centered classrooms; but it can be a learning environment that is more full of life, marked by mutual respect and true team spirit among the learners as well as between the learners and their mentor. It is a place for authentic work and not just for exercises.

In educational circles in the English-speaking world, more and more voices like the one quoted above are calling the constructivist paradigm into question and plead for a return to traditional (i.e., teacher-centered and transmission-based) values in teaching. As the debate mounts in other applied fields, we in the field of translator education are only just beginning to become aware of the innovative potential that constructivism might have for our learning/teaching environments.

Preparing for the translator's craft: From translation competence to translator competence

For me, perhaps the most compelling reasons for considering a radical change in the way we understand the acquisition of translation-related skills and knowledge and the way we instruct novice translators can be found both in changes in the profession itself over the past half century and in recent findings of the extensive and multi-facetted academic work and research in translation studies. Today, the work of the professional translator extends far beyond "translation competence" or the ability to create an equivalent target text in one language on the basis of a pre-existing text written in another language. When I started translating professionally in Germany in the mid-1980s, I had no computer for word processing or terminology management, no e-mail, no modem or even a fax machine to send or receive original texts or translations, and Internet access at home was still a distant desideratum. Because of constraints on time and distance, translators often worked alone back then, painstakingly searching for terminology in printed dictionaries and glossaries, typing their translations on electric typewriters; they focused above all on their understanding of translation as a search for linguistic equivalence.

Of course, advances in technology have put a speedy computer with an Internet connection on the desk of most translators today. We have word processors and spell-checkers, on- and off-line dictionaries and a panoply of other software and resources to make the translation process more efficient. At the same time, however, the demands placed on us by the marketplace have increased exponentially. Turnaround time has been reduced to a minute fraction of what was once needed to complete a job. Any translator can now be expected to coordinate the translation of large projects with the help of colleagues in different cities, countries, or even on different continents. Now we are often expected to do extensive online research as the WWW places a universe of knowledge at our fingertips. We may also have to know quite a bit about things like desktop publishing, HTML editing, computer-assisted terminology management, and the intricacies of file conversion, compression, and transmission, to name but a few of the myriad skills translators must have today but which were the arcane knowledge of technical specialists just a few years ago. Translators can no longer be seen merely as bilingual scribes; they are multi-facetted inter-lingual mediators with a broad range of skills and capabilities that are essential to efficient text production.

Then there is the evolution in the field of translation studies, which, disseminated through a torrent of research and publications over the past 20 years, has clearly moved far beyond its previously predominant focus on linguistic "equivalence." Today, most translation scholars would agree that acts of translation involve an intricate interplay of social, cognitive and cultural as well as linguistic processes. Many of us now believe that the translator's basic tools include intuition, creativity, multi-cultural experience, and the awareness of his or her own mental problem-solving strategies, along with collaborative skills for negotiating with clients, coordinating and participating as a team member in large-scale projects, and seeking out expert assistance as necessary.

In short, both the study and the practice of translation have evolved from being well structured and narrowly defined domains (involving knowledge that many constructivists would agree can perhaps best be taught in a transmissionist mode), to being "ill-structured domains" encompassing an enormous range of skills and knowledge.

Today, with respect to both expertise and professionalism, and in both theoretical and practical terms, each act of translation can be seen as a unique event, dependent on the translator's dynamic ability to juggle prior knowledge with the particular constellation of factors involved in the task at hand. These can include idiosyncrasies of the text, the client's expectations, time constraints, the amount of terminological and background information available, and the amount of experience the translator has with the particular text type and topic at hand. The frequently lamented poor quality of many source texts adds an additional dimension to this complexity. In an ill-structured domain, there is no single way to reach a solution and no single correct solution to a particular problem. There are no rules governing how to translate (Peter Newmark's list notwithstanding) and there is no universal arbiter of right and wrong.

The authority that decides what makes a translation acceptable resides not in books of rules and regulations, not in the designated authority of translation teachers or any other higher instance, but within the norms of the community of translators itself. Rather than passively receiving this authority from their teachers, learners can be seen as active assimilators and co-constructors of their own emerging authority and autonomy as they enter the community of prac- tice. Certainly there is a need in education to ensure that the next generation of practitioners continues time-honored traditions that will guarantee continuity in professional practice. At the same time, however, there is an equally great need for each new generation to redefine itself and its norms. As I hope will become clearer in the remainder of this chapter, while only some aspects of standard practice could conceivably be transmitted to learners, both facets of learning can be thoroughly addressed through collaboration.

Moving toward collaboration: Building expertise in communities of practice

At this point, I would like to turn back to the academic domain to look briefly at another potential source of support for collaboration in professional educa- tion: the field of "expertise studies," which, over the past two decades, has been investigating the nature of expert behavior, skills and competence. It will, of course, be necessary for a new line of research to emerge within translation studies to investigate what constitutes expert behavior in the language mediation field, but the research already carried out on the nature of expertise in a variety of fields does provide initial arguments to help us propose viable pedagogies of translation.

The results of this research in fact tend, at least tentatively, to provide very strong support for non-transmissionist, collaborative learning in the development of professional skills. Donald Schön and Bereiter & Scardamalia (1993), for example, building on the pioneering work of Dreyfus & Dreyfus (1986), have outlined compelling arguments for non-transmissionist professional training based largely on their research into the nature of expertise and its development. Quoting John Dewey, Schön states:

> The student cannot be taught what he needs to know, but he can be coached; he has to see on his own behalf and in his own way the relations between means and methods employed and results achieved. Nobody else can see for him, and he can't see just by being "told," although the right kind of telling may guide his seeing and thus help him see what he needs to see. (1987: 17)

In studying the nature of expert behavior, Schön found, for example, that professionals in a variety of domains frequently have to work creatively and intuitively to solve new problems:

> Often, a problematic situation presents itself as a unique case […] Because the unique case falls outside categories of existing theory and technique, the practitioner cannot treat it as an instrumental problem to be solved by applying one of the rules in her store of professional knowledge. The case is not "in the book." If she is to deal with it competently, she must do so by a kind of improvisation, inventing and testing in the situation strategies of her own devising […] It is just these indeterminate zones of practice […] that practitioners and critical observers of the professions have come to see with increasing clarity over the past two decades as central to professional practice. (ibid: 8)

The evidence suggests that professionals do not amass a body of facts and rules that they then apply consciously as rational problem-solvers as they go about the business of professional practice. Instead, they seem to acquire an intuitive flexibility for dealing with the unique, unpredictable situations that seem to make up the bulk of their professional activity:

> […] as we have come to see with increasing clarity over the last 20 or so years, the problems of real-world practice do not present themselves to practitioners as well-formed structures. Indeed, they tend not to present themselves as problems at all but as messy, indeterminate situations. (ibid: 4)

A collaborative learning environment, where students work together with peers, more advanced students, and teacher-facilitators to resolve complex, authentic problems, would seem to offer an ideal setting for developing the type of cognitive flexibility and self-concept as a creative problem-solver that Schön depicts:

> When a practitioner sets problems, he chooses and names the things he will notice [...] Through complementary acts of meaning and framing, the practitioner selects things for attention and organizes them, guided by an appreciation of the situation that gives it coherence and sets a direction for action. So problem-solving is an ontological process, in Nelson Goodman's (1978) memorable word, a form of "world making." (ibid: 36)

From this perspective, translators do not merely discover translation problems that exist objectively in texts. Instead, they construct them on the basis of the specific situational factors they select and on norms extracted from their experience with both determinate and indeterminate zones of practice that they choose to apply to the situation. They work creatively and intuitively to decide what to focus on, which of the myriad potential factors impinge on what they see as a problem, and what weight to give these factors in coming up with a plausible solution.

Collaborative learning from a social constructivist perspective

Dovetailing with social constructivist ideology and the findings of expertise studies is the "collaborative learning" perspective that sees the development of professional skills in terms of enculturation into a "community of practice" (Bruffee 1995). Bruffee also draws on social constructivist ideas to illustrate how learners can best become competent members of a professional community by interacting with that community, by performing the actual work of that community, and by constructing understandings of behavioral norms and conventions that imply community membership. As Bruffee has put it:

> Non-foundational social construction understands knowledge in Richard Rorty's terms, as socially justified belief. It assumes that each authoritative community, each community of interdependent knowledgeable peers, each academic and professional discipline, constructs knowledge in the distinctive, local language or paralinguistic symbolic system that constitutes the community. (1995: 139)

From this collaborative learning perspective, learners become a "community of knowledge builders" (Bereiter and Scardamalia 1993: 210–211). In helping them enter and maintain the conversation that will lead them into the profession's inner circle, the teacher's role will change from attempting to package reality into neat, easily digested chunks for consumption and later regurgitation by learners, and into that of a member of a community who can help novices find and make their way into the community of practice. It is by working with peers who are also to become the next generation of the professional community, by engaging in "world making" with them and with members of the community of practice, that learners can gradually become full-fledged members of that community themselves. From this perspective, both expertise and professionalism emerge through praxis and conversation, not as the result of transmissionist interaction with a teacher, but through hypothesis developing and testing, through discussion and debate, and as a result of concerted effort exerted within a team of present and future members of the community in question.

Schön has taken a major step further with the idea of action and interaction as the basis for learning in proposing the concept of "reflective action," which suggests that learners must not simply perform authentic tasks if they are to learn from them, but that they must reflect on those actions to come to a higher level of awareness and abstraction. Law *et al* (1998: 6) lists four primary characteristics that can be ascribed to reflection as a tool for learning: consciousness, a contextualized problem, relevant experience, and action. In addition to the informal, impressionistic and self-regulatory types of knowledge that experts use to undertake professional tasks, learners must also reflect on what they are doing as they acquire expertise. There must be an awareness of problematic features of the task at hand; tasks must be contextualized rather than amputated from genuine experience; the experiences in which learning activities are embedded must be relevant to the learner's past, present and future scope of interests and knowledge; and learning tasks must entail active personal involvement. From this perspective then, having learners engage in learning activities goes far beyond rote exercises, drills and lectures, which essentially entail the committing to memory of pre-determined rules, patterns and facts.

Reflective action is thinking coupled with the undertaking of authentic tasks (that is, the normal activities of a professional community) within a learning domain. It can serve a variety of functions in the performance of such tasks, including the planning, implementation, and revision of actions taken. Reflection can lead to learning by providing a mental space in which the means, goals and implications of intelligent action can be consciously contemplated, revised and integrated into prior knowledge, ideally resulting in increased expertise. From a social constructivist perspective, reflective action also has a social dimension, not only because it enhances collaboration and communication, but also because it is the very act of collective reflective action that characterizes a professional community.

Putting constructivism and collaboration to work

I would like to move to another level of discussion at this point to discuss just a few of the implications I have drawn from the collaborative-constructivist paradigm for my own approach to translator education. In developing viable and useful teaching techniques, I have had to consider how I see the role of each individual course within the context of the overall curriculum. Keeping in mind the kinds of outcomes I am seeking to enhance over the course of my students' program of studies, I have found it most useful to move from the most abstract level to the most concrete, focusing first on the goals of the curriculum as a whole, and then moving step by step through course design down to the development of facilitative techniques to promote learning in individual lessons. Here I would like to illustrate how a social constructivist epistemology can inform each stage in the educational planning process.

Curricular goals

Borrowing the political concept of *empowerment* from Paolo Freire, I believe that the term "professional empowerment" can serve to depict a viable global objective of a modern translator education program that is designed to produce the kind of graduates that other professional translators would welcome as colleagues. By *professional* empowerment, I mean that graduates can be expected to have acquired enough self-reliance, authentic experience, and expertise to enable them to leave our institutions and make the final transition smoothly to full membership in the community of translation practice.

The political overtones of Freire's empowerment are implied in my use of the term as well. I see a primary goal of the institution as one of weaning learners from their initial dependence on it. We empower our students not by conferring upon them a diploma that states that they are authorized by the university to call themselves graduate translators, but by providing them with opportunities to participate in the activities of the profession, by helping them develop self-reliance and self-confidence, and by making them less dependent on our help as they move into the circle of the professional translators' community.

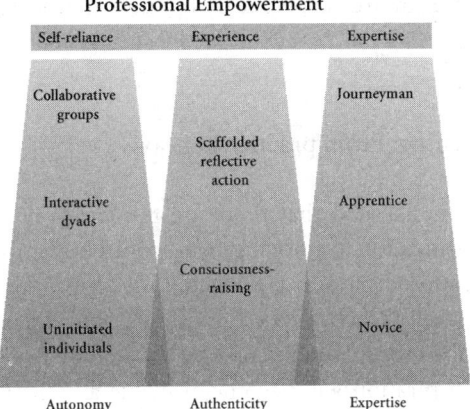

Figure 2. Dimensions of development toward translator competence

Figure 2 is my tentative depiction of how a principled approach to autonomy, authenticity and expertise can be interwoven to form a blueprint for curriculum design. Looking at the first pillar, that of autonomy, we can say that learners begin our programs as uninitiated individuals who are, in most cases, completely outside the community of professional translation practice. By encouraging them to work in pairs and then teams to jointly construct their understandings of the translator's profession, we can help them to break out of the deeply engrained habits of learning in isolation that they have acquired in school. By interacting with peers in discussing, debating, and world making, together they can better understand the concept of a community of practice and actually participate in one.

The dimension of authenticity, the second pillar, refers to the need to have learners increasingly do real work that is situated within activities very much like those they can expect to encounter once they complete their program of studies. I have divided the curricular focus into two parts: consciousness raising at the beginning of the program of studies so that learners as a group can define the community they are trying to join, followed by real work and collaborative reflection on the meanings they make as they progress.

We know from expertise studies that it takes years of professional practice for a person to become an expert and that in fact, many people do not make it beyond the journeyman stage.[5] Nevertheless, if we keep the idea of emerging, and then dynamically evolving, expertise in mind as a primary goal of our curricula, we can help ensure that graduates will have made considerable progress on the path towards expertise by the time they leave the educational institution.

Project-based learning: From practice to praxis

I hope to have demonstrated that there are numerous potential sources of inspiration and justification for moving away from a transmissionist, objectivist-based teaching approach towards a collaborative approach to learning. Each team of teachers as well as each individual within a team will naturally interpret and weigh the various sources of inspiration differently. And of course, many more sources of inspiration will become available as constructivist-oriented teachers begin to bring new sources of input to the topic, and as we begin to share our emerging understandings of and experience with collaborative teaching practice.

For my own teaching practice, I have found that the idea of the "collaborative learning project" can serve as a useful metaphor for course design based on a belief in social construction and the value of collaborative interaction in the classroom. Figure 3 illustrates a basic approach to undertaking authentic translation projects that I have used in a number of translation practice classes, which might better be described as "translation praxis classes."

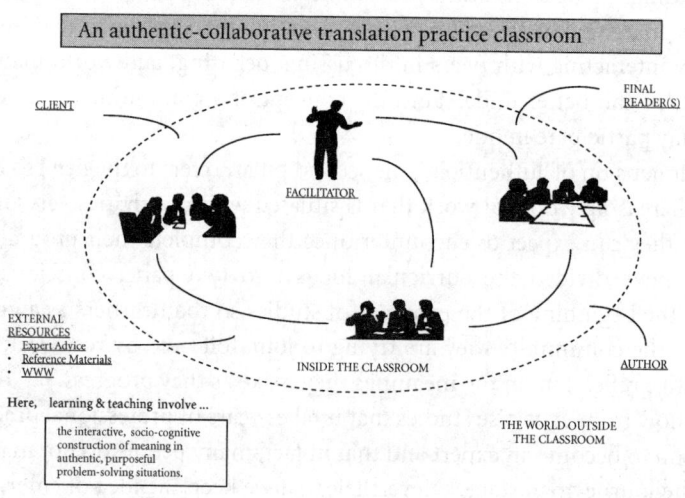

Figure 3. The project workshop: A collaborative framework for learning the translator's craft

The concrete objective of this class is for the entire group, with the assistance and participation of the teacher, to undertake and complete a real (rather than a simulated) translation project. The organization of the project is based on the principles underlying cognitive apprenticeship: authentic tasks, scaffolded teacher support, and learner responsibility for completing a piece of work that is acceptable to the client as an adequate translation. It is also compatible with Schön's idea of the "reflective practicum" (1987: 21). The teacher's roles in the undertaking of such projects can vary widely, largely depending on each teacher's personal stance with respect to the objectivism-constructivism dichotomy. It is important to note that the mere selection of "project" work as a global vehicle of classroom interaction need not be predicated on a social or radical constructivist view of learning. As Schön points out:

> If we see professional knowledge in terms of facts, rules, and procedures applied non-problematically to instrumental problems, we will see the practicum in its entirety as a form of technical training. It will be the business of the instructor to communicate and demonstrate the application of rules and operations to the facts of practice. (ibid: 39)

Pedagogical technique in the translation practice classroom

As a strong believer in social constructivism, I personally place great emphasis on working as a privileged member of the group along with the students, assuming a role much like that of a project coordinator working with a team of translators. My tasks may include: overall responsibility for project management; serving as a native speaker informant (as my students always translate out of their mother tongue into English); functioning as a mediator to facilitate negotiations between the students and the client; and also "reflecting in action" to model my own professional translation behavior as I work with small groups within the class to deal with translation problems as they arise. Rather than being a "guide on the side" (the controversial role often adopted by and attributed to constructivist teachers), I see myself more as a traveling assistant, moving from one nucleus of action and potential learning to another within the group to provide guidance, support and encouragement. Outside of class, I revise numerous rough drafts of the students' evolving work, providing proleptic feedback, that is, drawing attention to potential problems and hinting at ways to solve problems rather than distributing my ready-made solutions on a silver platter.

Learning in such a classroom environment is much more of a three-dimensional process than it can be in a teacher-centered classroom, because the learners are busy negotiating translation problems and solutions with each other and focusing on any number of other constraints and potential problems that may emerge from an authentic situation. These problems might include stylistic infelicities, grammatical and typographical errors in the source text, and uncertainty about the intended audience of the translation and what those readers can be expected to know — which might impinge, for example, on whether and how to make ideas that are implicit in a source text explicit in a target one. Working as they do in small groups, questions related to the standardization of style and terminology in the translation inevitably arise. While I sometimes take on the role of mediator between the students and the client, I let the students identify the need for such mediation themselves and encourage them to formulate the questions they wish to ask.

Language-related exercises can also play a major role within the global framework of our translation projects as students come to the realization that they lack an understanding of certain linguistic structures or translation strategies. Christiane Nord's (1996) list of instructional techniques (Figure 4) provides a panoply of tools that can be used against the background of situated projects to carry out the micro-instruction that is a major part of every class:

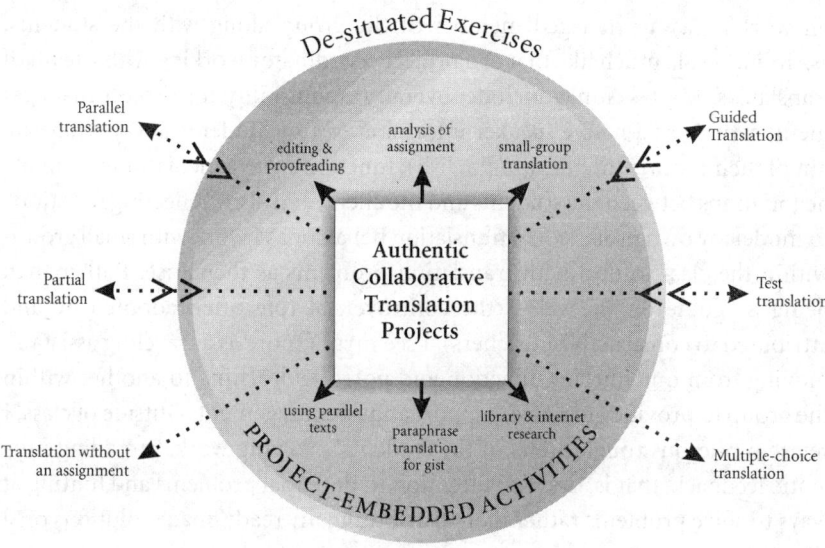

Figure 4. Embedding micro-instructional strategies in project work

In this manner, the project provides the context and justification for learning. Rather than having students engage in exercises to make sure that they amass the generic knowledge about translation that I feel they ought to know, I instead try to help them acquire competence in solving what they perceive as new translation problems that they cannot handle without assistance. Here, students see why we are focusing on pedagogical activities — so that they can proceed with their authentic project and accomplish it with competence and new awareness (learning!) that can serve them in their later work.

The variations on the project theme are infinite, of course. In one course, students lamented the need for more native speaker support than I could give during class, so I arranged to have other students, all native speakers of English, participate in a number of sessions to provide the necessary assistance. In another case, we asked an English speaker to come to class to do a think-aloud protocol while reading the students' all-but-completed translation. The students had agreed to discuss the problems the English speaker found in the text, and then go back to make final changes on the basis of those comments. In some cases, where money was being paid for the translation, I encouraged the class to hire outside proofreaders to check their work so that they could see the monetary value of doing a more careful job themselves.[6] While some teachers might balk at the task of finding suitable authentic work for students to carry out, the responsibility for project selection can also be shared with students and colleagues. Whereas most of the projects my students have worked on were originally offered to me on a freelance basis, in three cases so far, students have obtained commissions for projects that their entire class has completed. In other cases, projects have seemed to take on a life of their own. For example, the group decided to donate the proceeds from a book they had translated as a class project to a small charitable organization that has established a school in the highlands of Guatemala. When the organizers thanked us for our contribution, they also asked us if we were interested in translating the text for a perpetual calendar that would be sent out to contributors. That translation was the project for another semester-long course. A few months after that translation was submitted, the organizers appealed to us again, asking if we could arrange to have our English version translated into Italian and Spanish. Following a few inquiries via e-mail, willing colleagues and students at translator education programs in Italy and Spain were found to undertake those projects as well. Collaboration clearly need not stop at the classroom door.

In my experience, unfortunately, I have found that, as Schön has also noted:

> A reflective practicum is unlikely to flourish as a second-class activity. The professional school must give it high status and legitimacy or fall prey to the dilemma [...] where students are forced to choose between low status "relevance" or high-status "rigor." (Schön 1987: 171)

While I do get a solid core of highly motivated students in my project classes, only a handful of instructors offer such classes at my home institution. As a result, students often choose a parallel section that is run in a more conventional fashion precisely because project work is such an uncommon teaching approach. For students to see the value of working collaboratively on authentic projects, a focus on authentic practice and on the development of expertise through autonomy will have to be included in the mission of our educational institutions.

Many of the benefits of working on projects are self-evident. In these classes, the students are actively and continuously engaged in critical thought and debate for the better part of each session. Rather than focusing on one problem at a time that the teacher chooses to discuss, students find (or construct) their own problems and work toward resolving them in small groups. Reflection-in-action is also a major part of the students' work, as they must work together to compare alternative solutions with their fellow group members and justify the decisions they make. The project-based classroom serves as a constant reminder that my overriding goal as a translator educator is to help students become competent, reflective, self-confident, and professional colleagues; a goal that I believe can be better accomplished through participation in *praxis* rather than *practice*.

Action research: A tool for perpetuating innovation

The work that has been done on the development of collaborative approaches to translator education is clearly only the very tip of what I hope will turn out to be an enormous iceberg. However, it will be an uphill battle to establish a viable alternative paradigm as a counterweight to deeply ingrained objectivist beliefs and to generations of transmissionist teaching practice. Echoing my view of the "hand-me-down" nature of conventional, objectivist pedagogical practice, Michael O'Loughlin (1989) has said:

> Research suggests that the system is self-reproducing, and that if the cycle of didacticism is to be broken, it must be done by impacting on teacher beliefs about

> knowing and teaching, as well as by inducing teachers to engage in critical reflection on their practice. (9)

The very process of developing collaborative learning methods will have to be a collaborative one itself if it is not to fall by the wayside like a passing fad.

One way to promote the rapid generation of ideas and the formation of a community of constructivist teachers might be through a coordinated inter-institutional program of action research. Initially proposed by Kurt Lewin in the 1940s, participatory action research has become a powerful tool for change in education. It is based on the idea that teachers themselves can and should be researchers in their own classrooms. Starting with observations of what actually goes on in our own classrooms, followed by systematic plans and actions for change, we can create a groundswell of local research that can inform our common search for alternative teaching methods and techniques. Administrators cannot simply prescribe a teaching method, no matter how noble the aims or how plausible the approach, and hope that that one act will change the face of our profession. It is the teachers themselves who are tired of pulling old texts out of a drawer semester after semester, of sitting in front of group after group of passive students, and of dominating each and every class. They are the ones who must develop a veritable culture of innovation based on perpetual inquiry, through dialogue with other teachers, administrators and students. We need to start observing our own classes and effecting change in them rather than waiting for outside researchers to come along and put us under the microscope. We need to identify room for improvement in our own teaching practices and to devise our own viable remedies for change that we can continuously observe and modify as necessary. Instead of stagnating in a career of repetitive pedagogical practice that treads water while the translation profession and translation studies forge ahead, we need to turn our classrooms into experimental laboratories where innovation is the order of the day.

The translation profession will continue to evolve along with advances in technology, increased globalization, and changes in lifestyle and business practices. Society, and with it the translation profession, is programmed for permanent change. To keep pace, we need to infuse our classes and our curricula with the seeds of perpetual innovation and with a spirit of collaboration on many levels: between and among students, between teachers and students, and between and among teachers. Action research cannot be reserved for teachers alone. Students, too, need to get involved in the process of bringing change to translator education, since the next generation of translation teachers will come from the ranks of today's students. We need to encourage students to do seminar projects and write theses on experimental work in translator education, and we need to draw them into our research projects wherever possible so that they come to understand that education is not something that is merely done to them, but to which they can also make a significant contribution.

The creation of a culture of translation-education research through the joint efforts of administrators, teachers, and students would surely constitute a powerful force for catapulting pedagogical practice in translator education into the 21st century. Just as students cannot expect to be handed knowledge and skills on a silver platter, neither can teachers expect empowerment to be passed down to them by their institutional authorities. We must begin to work together toward the development of viable teaching methods and techniques that reflect the translation profession as we know it today and that can prepare all of us for the challenges that await us tomorrow.

Notes

1. The ideas summarized in this chapter are developed more extensively in *A Social Constructivist Approach to Translator Education*.

2. Similarly, Bereiter and Scardamalia (1993) write: "It is a fact that, even in the most intellectually barren of schools, students are expected to leave with more knowledge than when they arrived. But what schools do to bring this about has never been guided by theories of knowledge and knowledge acquisition, not even bad theories. Instead, it seems fair to say that at all levels, from kindergarten to university, education has been based on commonsense beliefs about knowledge..." (188)

3. I have discussed some of this evidence at length in *Pathways to Translation*.

4. For example, at the University of Rennes, the University of Stockholm, the University of Geneva and the Monterey Institute of International Studies.

5. See Klein, G.A. and R. Hoffman (1993) for a discussion of the stages of expertise.

6. The net proceeds of each paid project have been donated to charities of the students' choosing.

References

Bednar, A. K., Cunningham, D., Duffy, T. M., and Perry, J. D. 1992. "Theory into practice: How do we link?" In *Constructivism and the Technology of Instruction: A Conversation*, T. M. Duffy and D. H. Jonassen (eds), 17–34. Hillsdale, NJ & London: Erlbaum.

Bereiter, C., and Scardamalia, M. 1993. *Surpassing Ourselves — An Inquiry into the Nature and Implications of Expertise*. Chicago & LaSalle, Ill: Open Court.

Bruffee, K. 1995. *Collaborative Learning: Underlying Processes and Effective Techniques*. San Francisco: Jossey-Bass.

Collins, A., Brown, J. S., and Newman, S. 1989. "Cognitive apprenticeship: Teaching the craft of reading, writing, and mathematics." In *Knowing, Learning and Instruction: Essays in Honor of Robert Glaser*, L. B. Resnick (ed), 453–494. Hillsdale, NJ: Erlbaum.

DeFalco, A. 1995. "The learning process, apprenticeships, and Howard Gardner." *Journal of Cooperative Education* 30 (2): 56–67.

Dewey, J. 1938. *Experience and Education*. New York: Simon and Schuster.

Dreyfus, H., and Dreyfus, S. 1986. *Mind over Machine*. New York: The Free Press.

Duffy, T., and Jonassen, D. 1992. "Constructivism: New implications for instructional technology." In *Constructivism and the Technology of Instruction: A Conversation*, T. Duffy and D. Jonassen (eds), 1–16. Hillsdale, NJ & London: Erlbaum.

Fisher, E. 1994. "Distinctive features of pupil-pupil classroom talk and their relationship to learning: How discursive exploration might be encouraged." In *Language, Literacy and Learning in Educational Practice*, B. Stierer and J. Maybin (eds). Clevedon: Multilingual Matters.

Freihoff, R. 1998. "Curriculare Modelle." In *Handbuch Translation*, M. Snell-Hornby, H. G. Hönig, P. Kussmaul and P. A. Schmitt (eds), 26–31. Tübingen: Stauffenburg Verlag.

Kiraly, D. C. 1995. *Pathways to Translation*. Kent, Ohio: Kent State University Press.

Kiraly, D. C. 2000. *A Social Constructivist Approach to Translator Education*. Manchester: St. Jerome.

Klein, G. A., and Hoffman, R. R. 1993. "Seeing the invisible: Perceptual-cognitive aspects of expertise." In *Cognitive Science Foundations for Instruction*, M. Rabinowitz (ed), 203–226. Hillsdale, NJ: Earlbaum.

Lakoff, G. 1987. *Women, Fire, and Dangerous Things. What Categories Reveal About the Mind*. Chicago & London: University of Chicago Press.

Law, L. C., Mandl, H., and Henninger, M. 1998. *Training of Reflection: Its Feasibility and Boundary Conditions*, Research Report #89, Munich: Ludwig Maximilian University.

Nord, C. 1996. "Wer nimmt denn mal den ersten Satz? Überlegungen zu neuen Arbeitsformen im Übersetzungsunterricht." In *Übersetzungswissenschaft im Umbruch*, A. Lauer, H. Gerzymisch-Arbogast, J. Haller and E. Steiner (eds), 313–328. Tübingen: Narr.

O'Loughlin, M. 1989. "The influence of teachers' beliefs about knowledge, teaching, and learning on their pedagogy: A constructivist reconceptualization and research agenda for teacher education." Eric Reports 339 679; Paper presented at the Annual Symposium of the Jean Piaget Society (Philadelphia, June 1989), 1–25.

Rorty, R. 1979. *Philosophy and the Mirror of Nature*. Princeton: Princeton University Press.

Schmitt, P. A. 1998. "Marktsituation der Übersetzer." In *Handbuch Translation*, M. Snell-Hornby, H. G. Hönig, P. Kussmaul and P. A. Schmitt (eds), 5–13. Tübingen: Stauffenburg Verlag.

Schön, D. 1987. *Educating the Reflective Practitioner*. San Francisco: Jossey Bass.

Stunkel, K. R. 1998. "The lecture: A powerful tool for intellectual liberation." *The Chronicle of Higher Education*: A52.

von Glasersfeld, E. 1988. "The reluctance to change a way of thinking." *Irish Journal of Psychology* 9 (1): 83–90.

Towards an empirically-based translation pedagogy

Sonia Colina

To date, translation pedagogy has been largely dominated by anecdotal evidence and case studies. While this situation may be unavoidable in very young disciplines where the theoretical and empirical foundations are still mostly nonexistent, this is no longer the case in Translation Studies (TS); there is at this time no reason why translation pedagogy should remain in the unscientific, anecdotal stage.[1] Therefore, after reviewing empirical and theoretical evidence relevant to classroom teaching (Sections 2, 3 and 4), this article will demonstrate how this knowledge can be applied to lesson and curriculum design (Sections 5 and 6). More specifically, and following the lead of Second Language Acquisition (SLA), I argue that in order to acquire the necessary communicative translational competence (Kiraly 1990; Bell 1991) it is necessary to ascertain who possesses it (cf. Toury 1986), what subcompetences it comprises, what the stages of its acquisition are, and what factors contribute to its development (Shreve 1997) (Section 1). Although we still do not know much about what fosters acquisition, we do have a significant body of evidence, obtained through the use of think-aloud protocols (TAP), about the descriptive aspect of translational competence, i.e., features of professional versus student behavior. For instance, we know that students tend to have difficulty isolating problems and recognizing weak points in their translations (Kussmaul 1995; Jääskeläinen 1996; Tirkkonen-Condit 1992); they also ignore the global, textual, and pragmatic considerations normally taken into account by professional translators (Tirkkonen-Condit and Jääskeläinen 1991; Jääskeläinen 1993; Kussmaul 1995; Colina 1997), and often show evidence of sign-oriented translation, focusing on words rather than meaning (cf. sense-oriented strategies of professional translators) (Kussmaul 1995; Lörscher 1991, 1992; Königs 1987; Krings 1987; Lörscher 1997; Colina 1999); students are also excessively dependent on bilingual dictionaries (Krings 1986; Hönig 1988; Kussmaul 1995), and make improper use of world knowledge (Tirkkonen-Condit 1992; Kussmaul 1995; Kiraly 1995). This paper reviews the empirical evidence summarized above and presents concrete examples of ways in which it can be applied to curriculum and lesson design in order to facilitate acquisition of professional translation competence.

1.   Establishing a goal for translation teaching

I propose here that the goal of translation teaching is to facilitate the acquisition of *communicative translational competence*. Donald Kiraly defines *communicative translational competence* as the "ability to interact appropriately and adequately as an active participant in communicative translation tasks" (1990: 215). In other words, it includes the ability to take into account a source text (ST) in its context, the requirements for the translation assignment, and the participants in the process (commissioner of the translation, author, intended audience, etc.) in order to produce a target text (TT) that is adequate to the needs of the assignment and the target context. To Kiraly's definition, I would add that translation is a special type of communicative competence that requires interlingual and intercultural communicative competence (cf. Wilss's supercompetence, 1976) in addition to separate communicative competences in L1 and L2.

Roger Bell proposes a model of "translator communicative competence" which he defines as "the knowledge and ability possessed by the translator which permits him/her to create communicative acts — discourse — which are not only (and not necessarily) grammatical ... but socially acceptable" (1991: 41).

Communicative competence is defined by Second Language Acquisition (SLA) theory as the ability to interpret, express, negotiate meaning. Sandra Savignon (1983) proposes that communicative competence consists of four competences: grammatical competence (knowledge of the structure and form of language), discourse competence (knowledge of the rules of cohesion and coherence across sentences and utterances), sociolinguistic competence (knowledge of the rules of interaction: turn taking, appropriate formulae for apologizing, appropriate requests), and strategic competence (knowing how to make the most of the language that you have, especially when it is deficient) (cf. also Bachman 1990 for similar categories; within TS, cf. Bell 1991: 41). Why, one might ask, should *translation be described as a type of communicative interaction?* Does the interpretation, expression, and negotiation of meaning have anything to do with the translation task? Although the translator did not produce the meaning contained in the ST, he/she is responsible for the interpretation of ST meaning, which involves the negotiation and expression of meaning in accordance with task specifications, translational conventions, and target language conventions. In other words, in order to achieve the purpose of the translation, the translator has to interpret meaning in the source text, express it in the target text, and negotiate it between source and target linguistic and cultural communities so that it satisfies the requirements of the translation brief. The translator's work is guided by the communicative purpose of ensuring that the target reader can access those components of the source message that are necessary to accomplish the communicative goal of the translation. In order to illustrate this point, suppose that someone asks you to convey a particular message to a third person. In doing so, you are attempting to fulfill a particular communicative purpose: that of the person who left the message. The fact that the actual content did not originate with you does not disqualify the interaction as an instance of communication. The translator plays a similar communicative role in translation tasks, with the added difficulty of having to convey the message to a person who does not share the culture and language of the sender of the message.[2]

Gregory Shreve adds a cognitive dimension to the communication-based definition of translation competence above by defining translation ability as "a set of schemata for remapping across culturally bound form-function sets" (1997: 130). From the point of view of what happens in the translator's brain, translation ability consists of a series of knowledge structures, i.e., knowledge of relevant facts and procedures, that allow the translator to transfer form and function associations (meaningful linguistic material as presented in the source) into other form and function associations in a different culture. The communication-based definitions of translational competence focus on the social context of the translation task — the external factors — while the cognitive definitions focus on the translator as an individual, on the internal elements. Both the social and cognitive dimensions are essential to communicative translational competence.

2.   The acquisition of translation competence: Theoretical models

Given that the goal of translator training is to facilitate acquisition of communicative translational competence, we need to consider several issues:

1. Who possesses communicative translational competence? In other words, what is the equivalent of the native speaker in translation?
2. What subcompetences exist?
3. What are the stages in the acquisition/development of translational competence?
4. How does the translator manage to move from one stage to another, and what factors contribute to the development of translational competence?

In first and second language acquisition, full communicative competence is embodied in the educated native speaker. Within translation studies, Gideon Toury (1986) proposed the concept of the native translator. Just as a child equipped with some innate ability to acquire language will develop into a native speaker when placed in a particular linguistic and cultural environment, a translator, equipped with the basic innate ability to transfer between two or more languages and with communicative competence in both languages, will develop into the native translator if placed in a particular socio-cultural environment where he/she performs acts of translation.

Native speaker competence is defined by most specialists in language acquisition as consisting of various subcompetences (e.g., phonological, grammatical, discourse, pragmatic). Regarding translational competence, however, there is less agreement on what competences and subcompetences make up the cognitive system of the native translator. On a theoretical level, translation scholars have presented various models of translation competence (Cao 1996: 328; Hatim and Mason 1997: 205). Deborah Cao's (1996) model is adequate for communicative translation because it clearly reflects the components of communicative language as described by Lyle Bachman (1990) (in a proposal very similar to Savignon's), according to which language competence, strategic competence, and knowledge structures are the basic elements involved in communicative language use. By analogy, communicative translation consists of the following subcompetences: translational language competence, translational knowledge structures, and translational strategic competence (Figure 1). Figure 2 lists the subcomponents of the first of these three modules. Translational knowledge structures include knowledge of the world and the specialized knowledge necessary for performing a translation task. Translational strategic competence enacts the language and knowledge competence necessary to perform a communicative translation task; furthermore, it relates the other two submodules of competence to the context of the translation, thus enabling interlingual and cross-cultural communication.[3]

Figure 1. Components of translation proficiency (Cao 1996: 328)

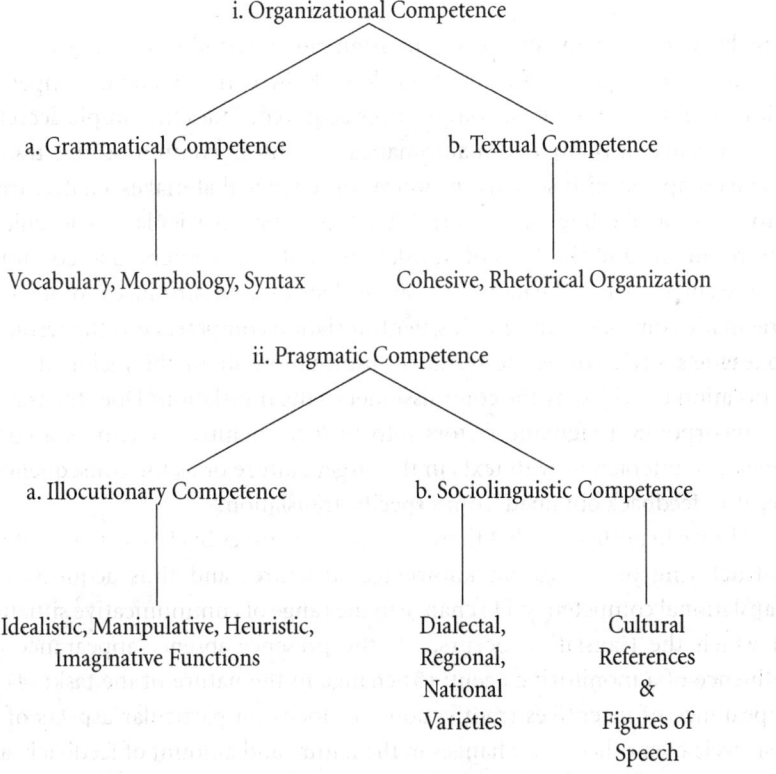

Figure 2. Components of translational language competence (Cao 1996: 330)

The developmental stages in the acquisition of translational competence must also be considered: what steps does a language student and/or a bilingual go through before becoming a professional translator? Wolfgang Lörscher proposes three main stages:

1. The rudimentary ability to mediate observed in bilingual children; it takes place in authentic communicative contexts and is a sense-oriented approach to translation.
2. The mediation ability of foreign language learners: a form (sign)-oriented approach; mostly occurring in non-communicative situations (artificial situations); it involves the presence of a mother tongue and partial competence in a foreign language.
3. The mediation ability of professional translators: mostly, a sense-oriented approach, which takes place in real communicative situations, involving quasi-bilingual proficiency. (1997: 80–82)

Finally, we need to investigate the environment and conditions that are conducive to the emergence of translation skills. How is translational competence with all of its attendant subcompetences acquired? Does the simple accretion of experience or bilingualism automatically result in communicative translational competence? If so, what produces the change that makes a native translator out of a bilingual speaker? What are the "particular socio-cultural environment" and the "acts of translation" that Toury refers to as conditions for the emergence of the native translator? Does a translator incorporate use of pragmatic considerations into his/her translation competence as the result of a colleague's advice or as the result of information about the recipient of the translation provided by the commissioner of the translation? Does the translator incorporate pragmatic factors into his/her cognitive system as a consequence of interaction with texts in the target culture or as the consequence of negative feedback obtained from a specific translation?

Shreve hypothesizes that there are various sources of change that motivate restructuring of translation knowledge structures and thus acquisition of translational competency: (1) change in the range of communicative situations in which the translation occurs; (2) the presence/absence/appearance and influence of a monitoring agent; (3) change in the nature of the task; (4) the appearance of incentives (motivations) to focus on particular aspects of the task cycle over others; (5) changes in the nature and amount of feedback; and, perhaps most importantly, (6) changes in the goals and expectations of the translator (1997: 133–134). He suggests that, as observed in the literature, novices fail to consider global factors, e.g., textual markers, cohesive markers, etc., because they are not paying attention to the relevant cues. Although the necessary cues are available to both novices and professionals, the frequency with which they are encountered in professional tasks makes them more noticeable (i.e., valid) for the professional. Rarely exposed to professional tasks, the novice is not aware of the relevance of textual cues in translation. Shreve's hypotheses could be tested in the classroom, for instance, by helping students to focus on the relevant information (cues) and by exposing them to various communicative situations and professional tasks (changes in the nature of the task), to see if this has any effect on the results of instruction.

The model of second language acquisition shown in Figure 3, when applied to the acquisition of translational competence, can throw some light on how acquisition of translational competence might proceed:

a. Input → b. intake → c. developing system → d. output

Figure 3. A model of second language acquisition (Lee and Van Patten 1995: 95)

For acquisition to occur, the right input (a) must be present and salient (the learner needs to focus on it). In a translation task, for instance, the student needs to see textual markers as a relevant feature of the assignment. After processing the raw data of the input, learners end up with the intake (b), which the translator then uses to restructure his/her translational structures in a way that will allow him/her to "to interact appropriately and adequately as an active participant in communicative translation tasks" (Kiraly 1990: 215), and to obtain "a set of schemata for remapping across culturally bound form-function sets" (Shreve 1997: 130). In other words, the intake is used to create the developing system (c), which will in turn be tapped to produce the output (translated texts that respond to the specifications of the assignment) (d). Shreve's model could therefore be modified by saying that, in order for the acquisition of translational competence to take place, the subject has to be exposed to *acquisition-rich* input (i.e., the type of input that will lead to acquisition). *Acquisition-rich* input — the data that translation students are exposed to in their classes — must contain the following (based on Shreve's list of change factors): (1) a varied range of communicative situations; (2) a monitoring agent; (3) tasks of various kinds; (4) incentives/ways to focus on particular aspects of the task cycle over others; (5) varied and frequent feedback; and (6) indications of a professional translator's goals and expectations.

Although no empirical evidence is yet available to confirm the theoretical propositions above, I propose that a sound teaching methodology should aim to create materials and teaching methods that work with this hypothesized process of acquisition. Researchers can then use classroom data to test the validity and instructional effects of the model and the corresponding methodology.

3.   Describing translation competence: The empirical evidence

Most data on translator behavior are taken from TAP experiments in which translators are asked to verbalize their thoughts as they translate, although evidence from production, translated corpora and error analysis can also be used. Discussion of translator behavior often refers to Paul Kussmaul's 1995 protocol study, probably the most comprehensive empirical research on translation pedagogy available today.[4] It has been argued that a great percentage of TAP experiments use language students as their subjects and are therefore not valid for the study of translation competence. While this is an important variable and one must be careful to discriminate between student TAPs and those of professional translators, the TAPs of language students are extremely relevant to the study of the acquisition of translational competence because of the nature of translational competence as a continuum (note also that many translators are not raised as bilinguals, but start out as language students).

Referring to the issue of interference, Kussmaul notes that the students in his study had *difficulty isolating problems* as well as recognizing weak points in their translations (1995: 17). In most cases they were not aware of the danger of interference or of the complexity of the issues involved because they were busy solving another problem in the immediate context. One probable cause for this is the amount of processing in progress, which makes it difficult for the subjects to attend to a number of different things at the same time. Another possible explanation has to do with a lack of experience and subject area knowledge: "Novices are blissfully unaware of their ignorance" (Jääskeläinen 1996: 67). In a TAP study, Tirkkonen-Condit found similar results concerning unaware translators: "The professional is more modest, and more sensitized to noticing those areas in her translation that may need checking. The non-professional, in contrast, seems to be more arrogant in her approach and does not voice a need to have her translation checked" (1992: 439). As in any discipline, previous exposure to similar problems helps the professional identify areas of difficulty faster, thus freeing up processing space for other problems. In addition, students may transfer patterns of expectations from the language classroom, therefore failing in the identification of translation-specific problems.

The above features of student translators provide justification for introducing the following elements in the translation classroom:

1.   A revision component would not only improve solutions, but more importantly, would locate problems that have been overlooked on a first pass (due to limitations in processing capacity). For instance, systematically

incorporating instructor and/or peer feedback into translation tasks could be required in the form of a final portfolio that would include drafts and final versions of translations. Although the motivation for the revision component may be more relevant to beginning students, the need for revision remains a part of the professional practice of translation.

2. Activities and short contextualized lectures that focus exclusively on specific issues and problems (cf. samples of translation activities in section six) would help raise students' awareness of the possibility of overlooking problems due to limited processing capabilities and translation experience. It must also be pointed out to them that these problems are different from the ones encountered in their language classes.

Kussmaul notes that semi-professionals exhibit an *excessive fear of interference* absent in the professional translator. The subjects in Kussmaul's TAPs avoided formally corresponding words and desperately tried to find a solution that had no formal similarity with the source word, even when a formal equivalent would have been the most adequate translation in the target language (1995: 18–19). Hönig (1988: 12) reports similar behavior, and both Kussmaul and Hönig attribute it to the effects of the foreign/second language classroom, where students have probably been warned repeatedly about the dangers of *false friends.*

The instructor can deal with these issues by teaching professional awareness, focusing on the differences between professional translation and translation in the language classroom; by discussing with students the nature of false friends, explaining that a false friend in translation is not determined by formal similarity but by contextual and meaning factors; and by making students aware that not all mistakes involving false friends are equally serious in translation.

Overreaction to false friends, particularly in cases in which consideration of the surrounding and situational context points towards the formally similar term as the best solution, is one of various manifestations of deficient or *unbalanced application of bottom-up/top-down processes* in semi-professionals.[5] The same imbalance was also detected by Tirkkonen-Condit (1992: 439). In the case of false friends, the translation processes of semi-professionals show heavy bottom-up orientation, usually at the cost of top-down strategies such as consideration of pragmatic features (e.g., genre, audience, function) that could help in making translation decisions.

Other forms of bottom-up (or misuse of top-down) processing were observed by Kussmaul (1995) and Riita Jääskeläinen (1993), who found that the global strategies or pragmatic approaches used by professional translators and advanced students are absent in novices. Along the same lines, Tirkkonen-Condit and Jääskeläinen (1991) report that student and professional reactions to *situational features of the translation task* differ: the professionals paid attention to this information immediately and used it in a global way to guide specific translation decisions; the students either ignored the information or went back to it only when they encountered problems in the translation. Further support for labeling the use of pragmatic, text-type and stylistic considerations as professional behavior comes from Lörscher (1993) and Jääskeläinen (1993) who found that professionals check their work for pragmatic factors, such as text type, audience and stylistic adequacy. In a 1997 study I also report that, although the students were familiar with features of recipes determined by text type, they did not make use of this knowledge in their translations until explicit discussion of text type features became part of the lesson (Colina 1997). It thus appears that failing to make proper use of global, contextual, and pragmatic information is a widespread form of student behavior that manifests itself in various unsuccessful translation processes. Consequently, empirical research provides ample justification for making the understanding and use of pragmatic approaches an essential part of translation pedagogy.

Students also show evidence of sign-oriented translating — a feature typical of language learners (Kussmaul 1995; Lörscher 1991: 272–274, 1992: 153; Königs 1987: 168ff.; Krings 1987: 271) and indicative of excessive reliance on bottom-up processes. Lörscher (1997: 78) reports that non-professional translators take a mainly sign-oriented approach to translation, and professional translators, a sense-oriented approach. Related findings in Jääskeläinen (1990) indicate that weak translators approach the translation task at a purely linguistic level, while more adept ones attend to the factual content of the source and the needs of the potential readers. I also found that language students and beginning translators exhibit greater percentages of transfer, i.e., sign-orientation, than professionals, even when dealing with low-level linguistic structures such as prepositional phrases (Colina 1999).

Because many translation students reveal behavior typical of language students, Kussmaul (1995) concludes that improvement of second/foreign language skills is necessary. However, deficiencies in the students' knowledge of the source language may be only one cause of this behavior. It is reasonable to hypothesize that the language teaching methodology students were exposed to may also be a factor determining their behavior when confronted with a translation task. One of the reasons for disproportionate reliance on bottom-up processing may lie in the bottom-up, sign-based approach predominant in traditional translation teaching, which views translation as a linguistic replacement operation instead of a communicative activity, as well as in traditional, grammar-based approaches to the teaching of language and reading comprehension.

The nature of the task presented to the students (i.e., the instructions, if any, provided with the translation) could also influence student behavior. Another explanation for sign-oriented behavior in students is that, as suggested in Wilss (1993), the skills and behavior of translators differ in nature from those of language students (cf. also Colina 1999, where the differences observed could not be ascribed to linguistic competence). Lörscher cites two additional explanations: the widespread view among laymen that translation is an exchange of signs between two languages and the artificiality of the mediating situations encountered by students in language classrooms and in other non-professional situations (1997: 78–79).

The above observations suggest the need to develop teaching methods that incorporate a translation brief and information relevant to the situational context into translation assignments, as well as activities that focus on these aspects and that help students understand the communicative, global nature of professional translation (cf. samples of translation activities in Section 6; cf. also Vienne 1994).

Hans Krings describes some rather *unorthodox* strategies used by students in their dictionary searches, such as the principle that says that "If all the equivalents concerned are in the dictionary, take the one that precedes others" (1986). Further use of ineffective, irrational strategies was found by Hönig, some of whose subjects adhere to the principle: "Never use the word which precedes the others" (1988). Kussmaul (1995: 22–25) and Hönig (1988: 1991) found that, although their subjects were able to guess the right meaning of a word through context, they ended up discarding it when they could not locate it in their dictionaries. In addition to indicating misuse of dictionaries, in particular bilingual dictionaries, this behavior constitutes evidence in favor of a typical stick-to-the-word attitude in students of translation, who often consider the dictionary to be the final authority on the meaning and translation of individual words. Furthermore, the behavior reported by Kussmaul and Hönig is indicative of the students' preconceived concept of word meaning as lists of synonyms associated with the source term rather than as potential meaning activated within a specific context (cf. Section 4.1). This view is (tacitly) reinforced by the bilingual dictionary.

Students also tend to allow preconceived ideas and experiences of the world (world knowledge) to dominate, obliterating the information actually present in the text unless counterbalanced by bottom-up information.

Kussmaul's protocol data provide evidence for improper use of world knowledge in students (1995: 25–28). Although this type of mismatch can also be found in other types of activity such as reading comprehension, it becomes especially damaging in translation. One way to foster *proper use of world knowledge* would be to make students aware of their processes of understanding and of how excessive reliance on what they already know (top-down processes) over what is present in the text (bottom-up processes) can result in defective comprehension of the ST and an inadequate TT. Such an approach is suggested by Kussmaul and Kiraly (1995: 113) (cf. Section 4 for models of reading comprehension and word meaning that can help us understand and explain these processes to the student). In relation to the use of world knowledge, Tirkkonen-Condit (1992) also found that professional translators attend to textual knowledge and rhetorical structure, whereas non-professionals activate irrelevant extratextual knowledge.

Improper use of top-down processes and global strategies, as well as a preference for sign-based translation, result in incomplete and unsuccessful paraphrasing. Paraphrasing is a common technique in translation, used to help the translator free himself/herself from source forms in order to come up with target language equivalents. Kussmaul found that his subjects had an ambivalent attitude toward paraphrasing: while they revealed the mental ability to separate words from their meanings, they did not use this skill to produce their translations. They did not trust the solutions found through paraphrasing, preferring solutions found in the bilingual dictionary.[6] Here again, the individual word seems to be the focus of attention, revealing a lack of understanding of communicative translation on the part of students.

Most of the features listed above (incomplete paraphrasing, strong reliance on the authority of the dictionary, excessive fear of interference) point towards — among other things — a lack of self-awareness and self-confidence. Kussmaul argues that the better informed the student translator is about the processes involved in translating and the more he/she knows about translating, the greater the degree of self-awareness. Once self-awareness is developed, self-confidence follows as a natural consequence (cf. Kiraly 1995: 113 for a related term: *the translator's self-concept*). Johanna Laukkanen (1993) found in her protocol study that confidence resulted in a critical attitude, which in turn resulted in better quality. Insecurity, on the other hand, resulted in heavy reliance on source text structures, which lowered the quality of the translation product. Tirkkonen-Condit and Laukkanen also report, in their investigation of the translator's self-image, that there seems to be a positive relationship between confidence and translation quality (1996: 56).

Since, as empirical evidence seems to indicate, *self-confidence and self-awareness* — necessary conditions for professionalism — are lacking in many students, translation teaching needs to incorporate them as goals into curriculum and course design. These qualities can be developed by teaching about translation-relevant processes (comprehension, bottom-up and top-down processes, meaning and meaning potential realized in texts; cf. Section 4 for the relevant models) and about techniques of textual and pragmatic analysis dealing with, for instance, text types and genres, textual cohesion and coherence, the informational structure of texts, etc. Once the student translator is equipped with these tools, it will be easier for him/her to defend translation choices in a professional, informed manner, which is another way to foster self-awareness and self-confidence. An alternative method for fostering these attitudes involves exposing students to professional behavior, which justifies incorporation of electronic resources into course design, such as electronic mailing lists for professional translators.

Translation teaching needs to integrate *expert behavior* as one of its goals. If translators are supposed to be experts in cross-cultural communication, their education must provide them with the skills to act as such. Expert behavior develops out of *self-awareness and self-confidence*, the ability to discuss translations in an objective way, and an understanding of translation processes and skills. The need to acquire expert behavior also justifies the use of such techniques as discussion/defense of translation solutions in front of peers or in translation teams, e-mail discussions, and a student-centered classroom that moves away from the traditional teacher-centered "performance magistrale" (Kiraly 1995; Ladmiral 1977).

The features described above have been isolated through the study of unsuccessful or less than ideal behavior. However, it is also important to examine *successful behavior* in order to design teaching methods that encourage its development (Kussmaul 1995; Jääskeläinen 1990). TAP research has shown the existence of two types of translation processes — conscious and automatized. While the first can be studied through TAPs, the second are not verbalizable and are thus more difficult to observe. Nevertheless, they have been examined by Tirkkonen-Condit and Jääskeläinen (1991) by comparing the protocols of non-professionals and professionals, the underlying assumption being that the same processes would not be automated and therefore would be verbalized in the non-professionals. Although unconscious processes are essential to translation activity, and translation pedagogy and methodology should devise ways to help the student automate processes that appear to be routine in the professional, there will always remain a considerable percentage of translation activity that requires conscious effort at all stages of development. Kussmaul's protocol data (1995) examine conscious translation strategies that require *creativity* (cf. also Wilss 1997 on creativity and intuition in *translator awareness*). Below I review some of the successful processes he observed and show how they can be integrated into translation teaching methodology.

Fluency describes the ability to produce a large number of thoughts, ideas or solutions for a problem in a short period of time (Guilford 1975). In Kussmaul's data, for instance, when trying to come up with a translation for "murmuring machos," the subjects produced a number of alliterative solutions in German, focusing first on form and then on meaning (Kussmaul 1995: 42). *Brainstorming* is a technique that trains fluency and should therefore be incorporated into the translation classroom. *Relaxation* is also important in facilitating creative activity. One technique used by the students in Kussmaul's data consisted of what he calls "parallel-activity technique," i.e., putting a task aside for a while, thereby producing the necessary relaxation to solve the problem. In translation classes, this could be done by giving the students a break and/or by having a small workshop atmosphere with food or drinks available. Kussmaul's protocols also provide evidence for *divergent thinking and transformations* in the translation process, that is, the consideration of a broad range of possible solutions instead of focusing on just one. Divergent thinking and transformations are also associated with creative activity.

While these processes need not be conscious in translating, teachers may need to call the students' attention to them in order to help students use them efficiently and to activate them when a translation problem presents itself. It should also be noted that the fluency and flexibility (i.e., ability to perform transformations, to abstract meaning from linguistic form) observed in the protocols could be the result of teamwork, as Kussmaul suggests, since the protocols were dialogue protocols. This provides justification for introducing teamwork in the communicative translation classroom in order to jumpstart these creative processes.

4. Non-translation-specific research

Translation teaching can benefit immensely from theoretical and empirical research in related disciplines. In this section, I offer a brief overview of some theoretical models that may be helpful for students and teachers of translation, such as reading comprehension research and models of word meaning in text understanding. I would emphasize that it is not so much mastery of a particular model, but an understanding of the processes involved in translating that needs to be emphasized in the classroom. Such understanding is likely to lead to increased awareness and self-confidence in students of translation.

4.1   Reading comprehension research

In the 1970s and 1980s, researchers demonstrated that readers are an active part of the comprehension process (Bransford 1979; Rumelhart 1977, 1980), understood as an interactive process in which readers contribute their schemata (i.e., the units that contain the reader's knowledge and experience),[7] while the text provides new information to modify the schemata. In other words, comprehension consists of the interaction between existing schemata and the information present on the written page (Anderson and Pearson 1984). Different schemata result in different comprehension processes. Take, for instance, the case of two students, one in linguistics (a native speaker of English) and the other in chemistry (a non-native speaker of English). Each one has specialized schemata, the consequence of their training and background, and thus the chemist's comprehension of, for example, an article on linguistic identity will be significantly different from that of the linguist, even if the text remains invariant. Schemata also help make up for deficient linguistic ability. For instance, when reading a chemistry article, our chemistry student can compensate for his deficient linguistic ability with specialized content knowledge and may therefore have fewer comprehension problems than the linguistics student, despite his/ her being a native speaker of English.

Comprehension is built up from various knowledge sources (syntactic, lexical, semantic, letter analysis, feature analysis, world knowledge) that interact with each other on the input page (Lee and Van Patten 1995: 191) through a combination of bottom-up (feature analysis → letter analysis → letter cluster analysis → lexical, syntactic, semantic knowledge → world knowledge) and top-down (opposite order) processes. Comprehension is achieved by relating new information to information already existing in the schemata. When creating texts, writers have particular audiences, with their own schemata, in mind; on that basis, they make assumptions about which facts are known to the readers and which are not. Difficulties arise, however, when the audience is not the one anticipated by the writer, or, in other words, when the audience's schemata (the old information) and the new information contained in the text do not coincide with those assumed by the writer. In such cases, comprehension fails. This accounts for the fact that technical texts are difficult to translate when a translator lacks relevant knowledge of the specialized domain.

There is an especially high risk of miscomprehension in translation insofar as translation makes a text available to an audience not necessarily imagined by the author of the ST, an audience (potentially including the translator) with different schemata from the ST audience. In translation, possession of the right schemata, or the ability to construct them in time for the production of the TT, is an essential condition for successful completion of the translation task. Making students aware of the schemata necessary for the comprehension of a text and filling in domain-specific schemata through contextualized lectures and/or exercises (cf. reading comprehension activities in 6.1.2) can be extremely useful in moving from student to professional behavior (in this case, fostering proper use of world knowledge).

4.2   Word meaning and textual comprehension: Scenes and frames

Another important theoretical model for understanding textual comprehension is *scenes and frames semantics* (Fillmore 1976, 1977). This model shares with schemata theory a grounding in people's experiences and knowledge of the world. *Words* are the *frames* that activate mental pictures or *scenes* related to past experiences and *world knowledge*. For comprehension to take place, frames must activate the proper scenes. In this context, words (frames) have only potential meanings (scenes) which are realized through activation in a specific context. In other words, the context activates the relevant meaning(s) of a word to fit a particular scene; this particular meaning is foregrounded and others are suppressed (or never activated). One of the difficulties encountered by language learners or translators when reading in the L2 is that they often have no scene for a particular frame. The dictionary usually offers little help because the reader does not have the knowledge necessary to determine whether the frame provided by the dictionary matches the scene created by the text.

Consider an example of how unawareness and defective use of comprehension processes affect translation (Figure 4). The data in this case comes from translations made by beginning translation students and collected by the author over a number of years. A common mistake among the students, all non-native speakers of Spanish, who translated the text in Figure 4, was to translate *comprendido* as 'known.' Error analysis allows us to compare the students' comprehension processes to those of a native speaker. For a native speaker, the only scene activated by *comprendido* in the text provided is that of a time period between two points; others, such as the achievement of understanding or knowledge, are never activated because they are unrelated to the scene created by the text. The students' comprehension processes are quite different. They do not involve foregrounding or suppression of the feature or scenes associated with *comprendido* at all. Instead, they consist of retrieving from memory a list of English frames that have been linked to the Spanish *comprendido*, the most frequently occurring of which activates the meaning 'known,' probably due to the way *comprendido* was learned. From this, we can infer that the students' comprehension process involves the replacement of linguistic signs rather than the creation or restructuring of schemata as they make their way through the text. If comprehension had proceeded success-fully, the fact that *comprendido* was an unknown term would not have been an obstacle to translation (that is, to the selection of the appropriate scene), since the presence of a date both before and after would have been sufficient to activate the idea of a time period.

Dos piezas que datan del   período comprendido entre
Two pieces that date   from-the period enclosed   between

300AC y   800 son especialmente notables,   y   cada una
330BC and 800 are especially   noteworthy, and each one

representa un   símbolo mítico.
represents one symbol   mythic

'Especially valuable are two pieces [dating] from the period between 330BC and 800, each representing a mythic symbol.' [Saboia 1990: 59]

Figure 4. Student translation illustrating comprehension processes

As noted above (cf. section three), empirical evidence shows that student translators do not interact with the text in the same way as professionals do. Their application of top-down and bottom-up processes, as well as their view of word meaning, results in unsuccessful translation. One way to obtain better results — as suggested by Kussmaul — would be to make the student aware of the existence of such processes by briefly explaining models like the ones presented here.[8]

5. Developing a research-based translation pedagogy

In a research-based model of translation pedagogy, empirical and theoretical research findings, e.g., awareness of pragmatic factors in translation, are used to identify and justify areas that need pedagogical intervention. Subsequently, methods, activities, and classroom implementation are devised to produce the desired educational goals, such as guided activities that force the student to consider these factors by focusing and asking questions about them. The choice of methods is also influenced by the process of acquisition (e.g., guided activities help the student focus on relevant aspects of the translation process). Finally, classroom data collection and analysis serve as empirical support for the effectiveness of the methods and teaching materials employed. The empirical studies of student and professional translators reviewed above (section three), as well as the theoretical proposals on the acquisition of translational competence (section two) and on reading comprehension and word meaning (section four), serve as justification for this methodology: I propose that they be used as the basis for the development of new teaching methods (course design, syllabus, lesson plan, activities). The concrete procedure proposed for the design of teaching materials and methods is discussed in section six.

It should be noted here that, while linguistic competence (L1 and L2) is unanimously considered an essential component of translational competence, I do not explicitly address linguistic subcompetencies. While it is clear that translational competence supersedes linguistic competence, not much is known about the nature of the relationship between these two types of competencies and/or their interaction. Translation studies long ignored the issue, concluding that because linguistic proficiency is required of any translator, language acquisition must always precede translational competence acquisition. Obviously, a certain degree of bilingualism is necessary for translation skills to be possible; however, there is no empirical evidence to suggest that language acquisition and translational competence acquisition are always separate (i.e., that language acquisition is complete before the onset of translational competence acquisition). Furthermore, when studying the acquisition/development of translational competence, we cannot ignore the early stages of the process, no matter how deficient.

In sum, more needs to be known about the nature of the relationship between linguistic and translational competence before an explicit methodological approach can be created. For now, I address translational competence in general without making any assumptions about the degree of bilingualism or the direction of translation. Note, however, that I am *not* claiming that these are variables to be ignored; rather, that they are to be treated on a case-by-case basis until more data on the interactions between translational and linguistic competencies becomes available.

6. Developing teaching materials

Although easily adaptable to other contexts, the teaching materials presented in this section are particularly suitable for students with little or no translation experience/training, who exhibit typical student behavior (vs. professional behavior). Courses appropriate for these activities would be designed to introduce students to various approaches to translation and to a variety of translation tasks.

6.1 Translation activities

6.1.1 *Preliminaries*

A set of activities should be developed around each translation task in order to emphasize the procedural aspect of translation; to bring to the foreground the pragmatic, functional, and textual considerations neglected by beginners (cf. section three); to guide students through the translation process; and to help them attend to relevant information (Shreve 1997). The design of these activities would be based on the assumption that the acquisition of translational competence does not occur by observing teacher performance and imitating it by osmosis; rather, the acquisition of translational competence is a slow and gradual process through which students must be guided. Furthermore, translation activities allow the teacher to focus on particular aspects of translational competence that have been identified by research as requiring pedagogical intervention. For instance, teachers can write questions that focus on textual features in order to focus the student's attention on the role they play in making translation decisions (e.g., the omission of objects in recipes in English, no omission in Spanish); or they can extract particular instances where problems such as sign-orientation, negative transfer, etc. are likely to occur (likelihood would be based on data collected from previous translations produced by students in the class). Finally, under an activity/process approach, it is also possible to incorporate the linguistic basis of previous methods in a *Focus on Language* section, and the theoretical level in a post-translation section. This last section has the advantage of contextualizing translation theory.

In general terms, the purpose behind the use of sequenced, guided activities in the translation classroom is to facilitate the process of acquisition by means of guided translation tasks. Such tasks provide quality input and force students to focus on information that is relevant to both translation and acquisition processes.

The activities proposed share a common organizational framework that is shaped by the requirements imposed by the text under consideration and that places a different degree of emphasis on each of the various components of translation competence. This organizational framework consists of the following elements:

1. A set of pre-translation activities that allows for consideration of pragmatic factors in the ST and TT, a translation brief (complete or partial) to help in determining contextual factors for the TT, transfer issues (how do the pragmatic factors studied relate to the transfer process? what are the consequences for textual features and organization?), and parallel text analysis.
2. A section on reading comprehension that would help to make up for difficulties in comprehension, incomplete schemata, and unclear terminology; in addition, such a section could aid in the understanding of reading and its role in translation and could teach the students how to work with these processes in order to facilitate translation processes.
3. Language exercises that would focus on smaller units of translation, language use, and well-known linguistic problems, e.g., negative transfer, sign-translation, translation difficulties, and lower level — word or phrasal level — linguistic issues as they relate to the brief and global translation decisions.

The particulars of the design of the activities, and their selection and sequencing, are determined on the basis of research in translation, reading comprehension, writing, and second language acquisition, as well as on the basis of the specific constraints and features imposed by the particular text under study.

In addition, each component of a sequence of activities responds to specific objectives/purposes which are detailed below:

Pre-translation activities
—   to force students to consider pragmatic factors; and to do it at the right time in the translation process, so that pragmatic considerations will guide global and local translation decisions
—   to help students understand translation as a communicative activity that goes well beyond its linguistic basis
—   to start undoing the effects of traditional (sentence-based, formalistic) approaches to translation teaching
—   to encourage top-down processing and the use of global processes
—   to discourage sign-translating and encourage sense-translating

Reading comprehension activities
- to encourage global comprehension
- to help students understand the process of reading comprehension and how it affects translation
- to teach students to make better use of context
- to teach the nature of meaning and meaning potential, and more adequate use of dictionaries
- to teach the importance and role of world knowledge and background knowledge and schemata in reading and in translation
- to demonstrate that terminology is only one aspect of technical translation
- to undo the influence of traditional approaches to reading in the language classroom (approaches that viewed reading as the decoding and replacement of linguistic units)
- to help students develop strategies to deal with the diverse range of requirements imposed by specific translation tasks

Focus on language
- to help students avoid sign-translating and unjustified transfer
- to remind students of the importance of accuracy (grammar, spelling, in addition to form and content), and to ensure that matters of detail do not get lost among global considerations
- to direct student attention to lower-level structures and to show how global decisions made earlier become apparent at these levels

Post-translation activities
- to develop a more principled account of the translation process
- to develop the translator's self-concept and self-confidence
- to foster professional awareness and behavior; to teach how to effectively and professionally support translation decisions

With regard to implementation and sequencing of the components, it is recommended that pre-translation activities be assigned one or two class periods before the date scheduled for the start of the task so that they can be done outside of class and the results brought to the next meeting for discussion and review. One reason for this is that some of these activities require access to research materials that are often not available in the classroom. In addition, valuable and limited class time needs to be used efficiently by devoting it to tasks that could not be carried out elsewhere (i.e., tasks that require feedback and input from teachers and peers).[9] As for the subsequent activities, most are to be done simultaneously with the translation, which means that they will be done at home and then discussed in class.

The extent and depth to which pre-translation activities are reviewed in class depends on where students are in the acquisition process. During the initial stages of training, more time will have to be spent on the pre-translation component, for obvious reasons, but also because this is a non-traditional approach to translation teaching with which many students may not be familiar. As students advance in their training, changes will be made in the emphasis placed on certain aspects of the pre-translation activities. In other words, although pragmatic factors must always be considered, not all of them should be given the same amount of attention at all times. The purpose is not to go through a checklist, as some approaches suggest (cf. Nord 1991), but to facilitate acquisition of translation competence by helping students modify translation-specific schemata. Such modification requires attending to cues/input that vary among translation tasks. The ability to adapt to different translation contexts and focus on the information relevant to the task at hand has been claimed to be a key factor in the acquisition process (Shreve 1997).

In-class discussion of pre-translation activities can be justified on the basis of the global nature of the tasks involved. Since many of the activities focus on pragmatic factors that will affect translation decisions later in the process, ensuring that students are on the right track before they start translating will save time and avoid frustration. This will also help them to automate the communicative dimension that shapes the translation task.

6.1.2   Sample activities[10]

The following sample activities are based on the text sample provided in Figure 5. Explanations and teacher annotations appear in brackets.

Reading comprehension
[May be done before *pre-translation activities*]
[This text should not involve many comprehension problems if the students are residing in the U. S. It could prove fairly difficult, however, for those unacquainted with U. S. culture. The student audience is very important in the design of reading comprehension units; it determines whether the purpose of the activity is to call attention to natural reading processes (use of background knowledge, etc.) or to the creation of new schemata. The teacher must learn to work with these issues, to call attention to them, and to instruct students in ways of compensating for missing background knowledge.]

Figure 5. An advertising poster sample

[The activities below will be most helpful for non-native speakers of English.]

1. [*Teacher:* If necessary, provide some background knowledge on sales, discounts, and department stores in the U. S. (e.g., sales before busy seasons, early hours, people wait for the store doors to open to get the best deals, etc.).

Another alternative is to let the students offer their knowledge of the topic and share it with the class.]

What do you think *doorbusters* means? Do not provide a translation equivalent, but only a paraphrase or explanation at this point. What does it refer to? If you don't know, ask your teacher or classmates for help.

[*Teacher:* Don't give a translation; tell the students about the early hours, people waiting for the doors to open, and then rushing into the stores.]

Once you have obtained the key piece of information, explain why knowing this is essential to your translation. Is this the type of information that you'd find in an average dictionary?

2. Look at the list of items that are discounted. What main categories do they fall into? Use this information as well as cognates and brand names to guess the meaning of the words you don't know.

Pre-Translation Activities

[*Teacher:* Day 1: introduce *Activity* 1 and *Activity* 2, *Steps* 1, 2, 3 (or let students work on them for a while); assign *Steps* 4 and 5 to be done at home. Day 2: go back to *Steps* 3, 4, 5.]

Activity 1. Pragmatic Factors in the ST and the TT
   Step 1. ST Analysis:
          What is the function of the ST?
          Who are the addressees?
          What is the:
              time of reception?
              place of reception?
              medium of transmission?
              motive for production?

[*Teacher:* This will be fairly simple for an American audience because it is a text produced within their contemporary culture and most students will have encountered similar texts. For other audiences, one might select a more culturally familiar text, although if the purpose of the exercise is to introduce cultural differences, no replacement is necessary.]

Step 2. Translation Brief: the text below is to be translated for Hispanics living in the US. It is to be published concurrently with the English text (not necessarily side by side or in the same newspaper), e.g., the week of December 9–15.

Step 3. TT Analysis:

What is the function of the TT?

Who are the addressees?

What is the:

time of reception?

place of reception?

medium of transmission?

motive for production?

[*Teacher:* Notice that the addressees, time, and place of reception become extremely important now.]

Activity 2. Pragmatic Factors and Translation Decisions.

Step 1. Compare the situational factors in ST and TT. Note the differences in the pragmatic factors of the TT imposed by the translation brief. Think about how these changes will affect translation strategy, e.g., text function remains the same (to inform and attract customers); however, the addressees and place of reception are different. How does this affect translation decisions? Bear this in mind as you translate the text.

[*Teacher:* Consider, for instance, the advertising slogan *Doing it Right*. Under the current brief, a translation may not be necessary, since many Hispanics will encounter the English more often in monolingual street signs and TV stations. However, if we were dealing with an advertising campaign in Spain, the slogan would have to be replaced by a Spanish one. Notice also that, given the communicative purpose of the translation, *Doing it Right* cannot, in most cases, be translated literally. If a Spanish version exists that buyers have been exposed to, this must be used (it is possible that Spanish-speaking radio/ television stations may have produced their own in Spanish). A similar case is that of *No Fear Apparel.*]

Step 2. Text Types and Genres: structural, organizational and syntactic features. Take five minutes to analyze the ST and list as many features as you can that identify it as an instance of an instructional (operative) text type belonging to the advertising genre. [After time is up, ask students for their ideas and provide a summary on the board; ask someone to copy it for you.]

Step 3. Using your experience with Spanish ads (for instance in newspapers and magazines), try to list as many features of the advertising genre as you can.

[*Teacher:* Allow students to brainstorm; as in *Step 2* above draw a map on the board and keep a record of it for the next day of class.]

Step 4. Parallel Text Analysis. You may have had some difficulty coming up with a list of features in *Step 3*, if all you have to rely on is your memory. It is even more difficult when you are dealing with textual features in the foreign/ second language. Try using some data: study examples of Spanish ads as you did with the ST in English above. Collect a few of these examples and bring them (two copies of each) to the next class. This procedure is called parallel text analysis in professional translation. Professional translators often resort to it to do exactly what you have done (they also look at terminology and usage).

[*Teacher:* In the next class collect copies of the students' parallel texts; provide the summary from the previous day and ask students for their new data-based lists; modify the summary accordingly; if you are aware of applicable research, modify the summary to allow for this as well.]

Step 5. How might the differences in the pragmatic factors surrounding the ST and TT and in the textual features of advertisements in both language communities affect your translation of this text?

Activity 3. Research and Documentation.

Step 1. Parallel text analysis is one form of translation-related research. What are other types of research and documentation necessary for this translation assignment? [*Teacher:* Clothing terminology.] [*Teacher:* Remind students that they can share results of research.]

Step 2. Prepare a glossary for this ad. [*Teacher:* Remind students that glossaries are important not only for the translator's current and future work in a particular area, but also to assure consistency of terminology when more than one person is involved in the translation job.]

Focus on language

Activity 1. Provide TT correspondents for the following terms and expressions:
    Focus on Structure:
    "For your holiday shopping *convenience*"
[*Teacher:* Purpose: to encourage students to move away from sign-translation that would produce the formally similar, but unacceptable *conveniencia*]
    "Sleepwear"
[*Teacher:* The linguistic replacement approach would favor replacement with a single word. Entrenchment of such attitudes will make it difficult for the student to come up with longer translation solutions, e.g., *camisones y pijamas* 'nightgowns and pajamas'; *ropa de dormir* 'clothes to sleep in']
    Focus on Accuracy/Usage:
    "Values"
[*Teacher:* Purpose: to encourage students to move away from sign-transla-

tion that would produce the formally similar, but unacceptable *valores*]
>Focus on Structural and Cognitive differences:
>>"Doorbusters"
>Focus on Prepositions and Low-Level Structures:
>>"40% off"

Activity 2. Share your glossary with your group. [*Teacher:* Have students share their glossaries in groups of four or five; collect their answers and produce a common glossary on the board; guide discussion of terminology, checking accuracy and usage.]

Post-translation activities
Given the context, does this assignment raise any issues concerning dialectal variation across Spanish-speaking communities? Discuss. How would the language/cross-cultural expert deal with them?

7.   Conclusion

This paper has taken a step towards establishing closer ties between research and pedagogy in translation teaching. Teaching materials were included mostly for illustration purposes, since many other formats and exercises are possible, and to demonstrate that translation pedagogy does not have to be divorced from research. In fact, any sound pedagogy and methodology for teaching translation should be based on empirical and theoretical research findings. The findings of future empirical and theoretical research should be used to modify and refine pedagogical and methodological principles. Furthermore, classroom research on the effectiveness of teaching materials can also be an invaluable source of data to advance our knowledge of the field and to produce teaching methodologies and materials that will be increasingly useful in facilitating and accelerating the acquisition of translational competence.

Notes

1. In this paper, I use *translation studies* to refer to the discipline that investigates translation in all its aspects (e.g., social, cultural, linguistic, cognitive, etc.) and *translation pedagogy* to allude to the subfield of translation studies devoted to the study of the teaching of translation. Although the terms are related, they are not interchangeable, since much translation

studies research that is relevant to teaching does not deal with pedagogy *per se* (e.g., think-aloud protocol (TAP) studies).

2. These observations are valid for all translation activity that results from an actual need to communicate across languages; hence we refer to it as *communicative translation*. This excludes translation activity that does not respond to communicative purposes, e.g., the need to study linguistic structure (interlineal translation) or to evaluate understanding of grammar rules (grammar-translation). Note that the concept of communicative translation is functionally equivalent to Nord's instrumental translation (Nord 1997); the only difference is in emphasis and presentation. We believe, however, that the term *communicative* is more adequate because it is more in tune with work in related areas such as second language acquisition, and because it stresses communication as the purpose behind translational activity.

3. Theoretical models of translational competence such as Cao's need to be confirmed and modified by empirical evidence. Data-based research such as TAP studies and error analysis constitute efforts in this direction. In section three, I review the findings of empirical studies that are relevant to translational competence.

4. This section is not intended as an exhaustive review of all empirical literature in translation studies, but a review of major findings and studies.

5. *Bottom-up* and *top-down* are terms used to describe the mental processes involved in comprehension. In top-down processing, sources of knowledge such as world knowledge, semantics and syntax take precedence over others, such as feature analysis, letter analysis, morphological and lexical analysis; bottom-up processing operates in the opposite direction (see 4.1.). To illustrate: when readers use what they know about a topic to understand a text in a foreign language, rather than trying to look up every unknown word in the dictionary, they are using a top-down approach, whereas the opposite strategy would be an example of bottom-up processing. Comprehension is often described as the interaction of both bottom-up and top-down processes.

6. Séguinot (1989) observes the same behavior in a case study of one professional translator.

7. Schemata also contain knowledge of textual features, text types, genres, parallel texts; that is, they are not exclusively limited to content or domain knowledge.

8. The fact that many recent approaches to language teaching, e.g., Communicative Language Teaching, make extensive use of the results of reading and psycholinguistics research may make instruction easier for the translation teacher by familiarizing many students with these processes in their language courses.

9. The sequence just proposed is similar to the one suggested for teaching reading comprehension in language classes.

10. For more sample activities, see Colina (2003).

References

Anderson, R. C., and Pearson, P. D. 1984. "A schema-theoretic view of basic processes in reading comprehension." In *Handbook of Reading Research*, P. D. Pearson (ed), 255–292. New York: Longman.

Bachman, L. F. 1990. *Fundamental Considerations in Language Testing.* Oxford: Oxford U. P.

Bell, R. T. 1991. *Translation and Translating.* London and New York: Longman.

Bransford, J. D. 1979. *Human Cognition: Learning, Understanding and Remembering.* Belmont, CA: Wadsworth.

Cao, D. 1996. "A model of translation proficiency." *Target* 8 (2): 325–340.

Colina, S. 1997. "Contrastive rhetoric and text-typological conventions in translation teaching." *Target* 9 (2): 353–371.

Colina, S. 1999. "Transfer and unwarranted transcoding in the acquisition of translational competence: An empirical investigation." In *Translation and the (Re)location of Meaning. Selected Papers of the CETRA Research Seminars in Translation Studies*, J. Vandaele (ed), 375–391. Leuven, Belgium: CETRA.

Colina, S. 2003. *Communicative Translation Teaching: From Research to the Classroom.* New York: McGraw Hill.

Fillmore, C. 1976. "Frame semantics and the nature of language." In *Origins and Evolution of Language and Speech*, J. Harnard et. al. (eds), 20–32. New York: Annals of the New York Academy of Sciences.

Fillmore, C. 1977. "Scenes and frames-semantics." In *Linguistic Structure Processing*, A. Zampolli (ed), 55–88. Amsterdam: North Holland.

Guilford, J. P. 1975. "Creativity: A quarter century of progress." In *Perspectives in Creativity*, I. A. Taylor and J. W. Getzels (eds), 37–59. Chicago: Aldine.

Harvey, S., Higgins, I., and Haywood, L. M. 1995. *Thinking Spanish Translation.* New York and London: Routledge.

Harvey, S., Higgins, I., and Haywood, L. M. 1996. *Thinking Spanish Translation. Teachers' Handbook.* New York and London: Routledge.

Hatim, B., and Mason, I. 1997. *The Translator as Communicator.* London and New York: Routledge.

Hönig, H. G. 1988. "Wissen Übersetzer eigentlich, was sie tun?" *Lebende Sprachen* 1: 10–14.

Jääskeläinen, R. 1990. *Features of Successful Translation Processes: A Think-Aloud Protocol Study.* Licentiate Thesis. University of Joensuu, Savonlinna School of Translation Studies.

Jääskeläinen, R. 1993. "Investigating translation strategies." In *Recent Trends in Empirical Translation Research*, S. Tirkkonen-Condit and J. Laffling (eds). *Studies in Languages.* University of Joensuu, Faculty of Arts, 28, Joensuu.

Jääskeläinen, R. 1996. "Hard work will bear beautiful fruit: A comparison of two think-aloud protocol studies." *Meta* 41 (1): 60–74.

Kiraly, D. 1990. "A role for communicative competence and the acquisition-learning distinction in translator training." In *Second Language Acquisition/Foreign Language Learning*, B. Van Patten and J. Lee (eds), 207–215. Bristol, PA and Clevedon, UK: Multilingual Matters.

Kiraly, D. 1995. *Pathways to Translation*. Kent, OH: Kent State University Press.

Königs, F. 1987. "Was beim Übersetzen passiert: Theoretische Aspekte, empirische Befunde und praktische Konsequenzen." *Die Neueren Sprachen* 86 (2): 193–215.

Krings, H. 1986. "Translation problems and translation strategies of advanced German learners of French (L2)." In *Interlingual and Intercultural Communication*, J. House and S. Blum-Kulka (eds), 263–276. Tübingen: Narr.

Krings, H. 1987. "Der Übersetzungprozeß bei Berufsübersetzern — Eine Fallstudie." In *Textlinguistik und Fachsprache. Akten des Internationalen übersetzungswissenschaftlichen AILA-Symposiums Hildesheim*, R. Arnts (ed). Hildesheim: Olms.

Kussmaul, P. 1995. *Training the Translator*. Philadelphia and Amsterdam/Philadelphia: John Benjamins.

Ladmiral, J. R. 1977. "La traduction dans le cadre de l'institution pédagogique." *Die Neueren Sprachen* 76: 489–516.

Laukkanen, J. 1993. *Routine vs. Non-routine Processes in Translation: A Think-Aloud Protocol Study*. Unpublished *pro-gradu* thesis. University of Joensuu, Savonlinna School of Translation Studies.

Lee, J., and Van Patten, B. 1995. *Making Communicative Language Teaching Happen*. New York: McGraw Hill.

Lörscher, W. 1991. *Translation Performance, Translation Process, and Translation Strategies. A Psycholinguistic Investigation*. Tübingen: Narr.

Lörscher, W. 1992. "Process-oriented research into translation and implications for translation teaching." *Traduction, Terminologie, Rédaction (TTR)* 5: 145–161.

Lörscher, W. 1993. "Translation process analysis." In *Translation and Knowledge. Proceedings of the Fourth Scandinavian Symposium on Translation Theory*. Turku, Finland: University of Turku.

Lörscher, W. 1997. "A process-analytical approach to translation and implications for translation teaching." *Ilha do Desterro* 33: 69–85.

Nord, C. 1991. *Text Analysis in Translation*. Amsterdam and Atlanta, Georgia: Rodopi.

Nord, C. 1997. *Translating as a Purposeful Activity: Functionalist Approaches Explained*. Manchester: St. Jerome.

Rumelhart, D. 1977. "Toward an interactive model of reading." In *Attention and Performance 4*, S. Dornic (ed), 573–603. New York: Academic Press.

Rumelhart, D. 1980. "Schemata: The building blocks of cognition." In *Theoretical Issues in Reading Comprehension*. R. Spiro, B.Bruce and W. Brewer (eds), 33–35. Hillsdale, NJ: Lawrence Erlbaum.

Saboia, P. 1990. "Arte del nuevo mundo en Europa." *Americas* 42 (1): 59.

Savignon, S. 1983. *Communicative Competence: Theory and Classroom Practice*. Reading: Addison-Wesley.

Séguinot, C. (ed). 1989. *The Translation Process*. Toronto: H. G. Publications. School of Translation. York University.

Shreve, G. 1997. "Cognition and the evolution of translation competence." In *Cognitive Processes in Translation and Interpreting*, J. Danks, G. M. Shreve, S. B. Fountain, and M. K. McBeath (eds), 120–136. Thousand Oaks, London, and New Delhi: Sage.

Tirkkonen-Condit, S. 1992. "The interaction of world knowledge and linguistic knowledge in the process of translation. A think aloud protocol study." In *Translation and Mean-*

ing. Proceedings of the Lodz Session of the 1990 Maastricht-Lodz Duo Colloquium on Translation and Meaning, B. Lewandowska-Tomaszczyk and M. Thelen (eds), 433–440. Maastricht: Faculty of Translation and Interpreting.

Tirkkonen-Condit, S., and Jääskeläinen, R. 1991. "Automatised processes in professional vs. non-professional translation: A think-aloud protocol study." In *Empirical Research in Translation and Intercultural Studies*, S. Tirkkonen-Condit (ed), 89–109. Tübingen: Gunter Narr.

Tirkkonen-Condit, S., and Laukkanen, J. 1996. "Evaluation: A key towards understanding the affective dimension of translational decisions." *Meta* 41(1): 60–74.

Toury, G. 1986. "Natural translation and the making of the native translator." *TEXTconTEXT* 1: 11–29.

Vienne, J. 1994. "Toward a pedagogy of translation in situation perspectives. "*Studies in Translatology* 2(1): 51–59.

Wilss, W. 1976. "Perspectives and limitations of a didactic framework for the teaching of translation." In *Translation*, RW. Brislin (ed), 117–137. New York: Gardner.

Wilss, W. 1993. "Projekt übersetzungsdidaktische Grundlagenforschung." *Lebende Sprachen* 28 (2): 53–54.

Wilss, W. 1997. "Translator awareness." *Ilha do Desterro* 33: 87–98.

Think-alouds as a pedagogical tool

Judy Wakabayashi

Introduction

The think-aloud method, which involves taping subjects as they verbalize their thoughts while working on a particular task, has often been used by translation researchers in an attempt to gain a better understanding of the cognitive processing that occurs during translation (e.g., the various chapters in Tirkkonen-Condit and Jääskeläinen 2000). I would like to explore the usefulness of bringing this psycholinguistic research tool into the classroom as a device for diagnosing and addressing recurring problems in how students approach the task of translation. Kiraly (1995: 51) has emphasized that "An understanding of what translators actually do mentally when they translate is essential for the development of translation pedagogy." My goal here is to use the insights offered by this research method for the benefit of the teacher and students themselves. As House comments,

> Despite the fact that there remain basically undispelled doubts about the status of introspective data in translation process research, the *pedagogical* potential of this research is considerable [....] The initial interest in investigating translation processes was in fact pedagogical (cf. the majority of the early studies included in House and Blum-Kulka 1986 and in Faerch and Kasper 1987). (House 2000: 152)

In this article, I would like to delve further into this potential, based on think-aloud data collected over the past decade from postgraduate students of Japanese-English translation, all translating into their native language, English. I will also make some recommendations as to how students at this level — and also, perhaps, more experienced translators — might adopt more effective strategies.

The desired outcome of bringing think-alouds into the classroom is to make students aware of their ineffective problem-solving strategies, which is the first step toward overcoming such inefficiencies. The greater awareness resulting from the think-aloud process itself and from the teacher's subsequent feedback will, it is assumed, encourage more informed reflection and hence better translations. Kiraly suggests that through such consciousness-raising "Students will be building a translator's self-concept and the ability to monitor translations" (1995: 113). The benefit to the teacher is that the think-alouds provide insights into problems not always apparent from finished translations, so that these problems can be discussed and addressed.

Nevertheless, the literature attests to various problems with these introspective reports. First, think-alouds might represent an *inaccurate* reflection of the actual translation process. Translators are not necessarily capable of giving an accurate description of what they are doing. Moreover, even though some translators do talk to themselves as they translate and others translate aloud using Dictaphones or voice recognition software, Toury warns that "there is a real possibility that spoken and written translation do not involve the exact same strategies" (1995: 235). Second, it is likely that the very act of verbalizing *interferes* with the translation process. In addition, the translator might feel uncomfortable with the think-aloud process or the presence of the researcher (even if this presence is only in the translator's mind), thereby creating a further layer of interference. Third, think-alouds are an *incomplete* reflection of what is occurring in the translator's mind. It is impossible to verbalize one's thoughts fully, and the translator's motivation, concentration, tolerance of stress, fatigue, the time of day, the difficulty of a particular item, and its position in the text further affect the completeness of the reports. Automated processes in particular are not accessible to introspection, as they involve ingrained, unconscious skills. Yet despite such limitations, think-aloud studies undoubtedly provide a somewhat fuller or at least somewhat different picture of the translation process than traditional text-based approaches, whose sole source of information is the product that is the outcome of these mental processes.

The students participating were all postgraduate students of Japanese-English translation (mostly first-year MA students) at the University of Queensland in Australia. They were given written and oral instructions before the think-aloud sessions, which they conducted in the privacy of their own homes, and they had full access to all their normal resources such as dictionaries and the Internet. They were required to verbalize the entire process through completion of their final version. Because the present exercise had a pedagogical purpose, rather than being intended for research, I did not attempt to transcribe or analyze the tapes fully, simply taking notes on points of particular interest. Inevitably, therefore, the observations are somewhat impressionistic and far from an accurate reflection of the students' overall performance, as they focus mainly on problematic areas or particularly interesting solutions. These notes were subsequently given to the individual students and also discussed in class. The categories described below were not established in advance, but emerged from the data. Many other minor categories and idiosyncratic (student-specific) problems are not discussed here.

Initial approach to the text

The students' initial approach to the source text revealed various inefficiencies and difficulties in their pre-translation reading. In fact, this was the most problematic and time-consuming phase in the whole process. Two key aspects of this were the handling of unknown words and Chinese characters, the main script used to write the Japanese language. Since the latter aspect is language-specific and not a matter of translation competence per se, it will not be discussed here except to say that poor recognition of Chinese characters and inefficiencies in looking them up accounted for a considerable portion of the tapes and were one of the most striking features of the think-alouds of these particular students. With unknown *words*, two main inefficiencies were evident:

1. Looking up all the unfamiliar words in *advance* without having read the text properly and without understanding the context in which these words appeared. This was largely a waste of time and effort, as the students found it difficult to make an appropriate choice from the various equivalents offered in the dictionary because they had not understood the context. This meant they often had to look up the same word again after having read the text properly.
2. Simply highlighting unfamiliar words and passing over them until *later*. Although skipping lexical items for the time being can be a valid reading strategy (particularly when it is obvious that they are not of central importance), when there are many unfamiliar words, as is typically the case for students, this approach makes it difficult to follow the thrust of the text, rendering the initial reading largely meaningless.

Based on the above, it might seem that the obvious recommendation would be for students to look up any unfamiliar words (or at the very least, any words that seem to be key words) as they come to them and on the basis of their understanding of the text up to that point, rather than before or after reading the text. This would assumedly make the initial reading more meaningful, enable the selection of equivalents based on context, and obviate the need to look up the same word again later. Such an approach does, however, interrupt the reading process. Useful here would be an empirical study comparing the effectiveness of different approaches to the timing of looking up unfamiliar words. It is possible, however, that no general conclusions can be drawn, as this might be a translator-specific matter. At the very least, though, on the basis of what emerges from the think-alouds, teachers can encourage students to experiment with different approaches to looking up unknown vocabulary.

The students typically read through the entire assigned passage before starting to translate. It was, however, rare for them to read beyond the assigned portion, despite having been repeatedly told of the importance of overall context. For most students, the reading process presented such difficulties in terms of unknown vocabulary and Chinese characters that the initial reading had little to do with apprehending or internalizing the meaning. The result was that, after reading through the text, the students often commented, for example, that "I didn't really understand anything there," so they had to read the text again. It is undoubtedly beneficial to read the whole text through before translating it *if* one is capable of grasping the overall meaning at first reading, but at least in the case of the Japanese language, even postgraduate students are often not yet at this level of understanding. For them, it would seem to be more efficient just to read any headings first and then to translate each sentence in turn, without wasting time on reading that is not accompanied by comprehension. This flies in the face of the oft-heard and commendable recommendation that translators should work at the level of the text rather than at lower levels, but for students who still face many linguistic difficulties, this sentence-level approach would ensure that they have a reasonable understanding of what they have read so far and would help guide the selection of subsequent equivalents. Once the 'building blocks' are in place, the text can then be considered as a whole, particularly in terms of cohesion and coherence.

Unfamiliar words and dictionary use

Some students used various 'codes' (e.g., underlining, highlighting, circling) to indicate unfamiliar or problematic words or phrases. There was, however, no direct evidence in the tapes that this was of practical use. Many students are also in the habit of making a list of unfamiliar words, presumably with the aim of facilitating vocabulary revision at a later stage. Although this is admirable, students should be encouraged to do this on the computer rather than on paper, as computerized glossaries make for later ease of use, and glossary compilation and terminology management are important skills for translators today.

One difficulty for students is not knowing when to trust their guesses or proposed equivalents. They often inferred the meaning accurately or came up with quite acceptable equivalents, but lacked the confidence to adopt these without verifying them in a dictionary or with a native speaker of the source language. The confidence to trust one's intuitions is probably something that comes only with experience and cannot be imparted directly, and no doubt it is better to be 'safe than sorry.' Reassuringly, however, the students did generally exhibit an ability to recognize when a word was important in a particular text, even if they did not understand its meaning.

Below are some of the main problems in dictionary usage revealed by the students' think-alouds.

(a) Use of monolingual SL dictionaries

Translators are often advised to use monolingual source language dictionaries and reference works because they give more accurate and full descriptions than bilingual sources. When students' skills in the source language are still not up to par, however, monolingual source language references often simply compound their confusion. On the other hand, the tapes suggest that students might put monolingual *target* language dictionaries to greater and more effective use, rather than relying solely on bilingual dictionaries.

(b) Over-reliance on dictionaries

The think-alouds revealed students' clear over-reliance on dictionaries instead of using their own heads. They often made little or no effort to infer the meaning from the context, preferring to reach for the dictionary even when they already knew or had correctly surmised the meaning. This is in line with the findings of other studies. For instance, Kovačič notes that the less experienced translators in her study "typically sought help from dictionaries (either traditional or electronic) much sooner than more experienced ones, who first searched in their memory or used deduction" (1997: 234). Immediately resorting to a dictionary tends to narrow the range of possible equivalents down to those listed on the page, bypassing renditions that might be more creative or more appropriate in a particular context. In her study of the use of dictionaries, House hypothesized that "dictionary searches disturb the flow of thought, preventing the strategic generation of near-synonyms and the internal parading of paradigms and repertoires" (2000: 156), and this hypothesis was amply borne out by my students' think-alouds.

(c) *Inefficient use of dictionaries*
Despite their extensive reliance on dictionaries, few of my students read the dictionary entries thoroughly, sometimes overlooking valuable information that would have solved their difficulty. This feature of the think-alouds has led to class discussions on more effective ways of using dictionaries. The students also often ignored or forgot equivalents that they had looked up previously, failing on the second occurrence to make the connection with meanings found earlier. This suggests that the short-term memory span available is limited when the linguistic load is heavy. Some students did, however, exhibit very practical dictionary strategies, such as using markers in the dictionary so that they could later come back to that word easily if necessary.

(d) *Specialized dictionaries*
Students' difficulties in recognizing and understanding specialized terminology highlighted the need to develop an intuition for which words are technical terms, the need to utilize specialized dictionaries appropriately (e.g., paying attention to subject labels), and the general need to do background reading of specialized texts beyond the reading required for particular texts being translated. Some students tended to use specialized dictionaries as a last resort toward the end of the translation process, rather than having them on hand from the outset. There were also basic mistakes such as using general dictionaries instead of specialized dictionaries, or looking up mechanical engineering terms in a medical dictionary.

(e) *Failure to use non-dictionary sources*
Although the students made much use of the Internet for researching the subject matter, they seemed less aware of its value as a means (albeit far from infallible) of verifying English usage. For instance, one student said that both "refugee recognition" (the correct term) and "refugee designation" sounded odd to her, but she made no attempt to check the relative validity of these terms as indicated by their frequency on the Internet. Field-specific language is what translators need, rather than de-contextualized words from the dictionary, and the Internet acts as an invaluable corpus and is generally quicker and easier to access and search than other reference sources.

Comprehension

Patently obvious from the think-alouds was the fact that the main problem, at least with this particular cohort of students, was not a matter of translation at all, but the fact that they are still in the process of mastering the source language. To improve their comprehension, students need to do much more reading in the source language. Since mere reading tends to remain at a rather superficial level, however, it is useful to translate what one reads, as this helps reinforce the acquisition of new vocabulary and pinpoints the source of comprehension difficulties. With this sort of translation practice, the emphasis is not on translation *per se* or on polishing the target text, but simply on understanding the source text more fully.

For these students, both the unit of comprehension and the unit of translation typically lay below the sentence level. It was obvious from the tapes that lexical and grammatical difficulties interfered with the students' ability to chunk their reading in phrase or clause groups so as to grasp the overall structure and thrust of the sentence. The process was very much a bottom-up, rather than a top-down approach to the text. Apart from linguistic comprehension problems, when trying to apprehend the meaning the students often seemed to be working in a vacuum or at the micro-level, without drawing on the broader context. This lack of contextual understanding meant that sometimes they were reluctant to accept the proper explanations even when they found them. The tendency to work on individual sentences (or lower units) in isolation also meant that at times students failed to realize they had used the same word in adjacent sentences. In general, however, they seemed aware of the desirability of avoiding repetition in their English, although they did not always follow up on this verbalized awareness by using a thesaurus when they could not think of a synonym. The think-alouds revealed much less awareness of the desirability of eliminating verbiage. These findings reinforce the importance of emphasizing and demonstrating to students the usefulness of thesauri and the need to tighten up their prose.

One problem specific to Japanese-English translation was the habit of 'translating forward' linearly in the order of the source text words. This meant that students often mistakenly linked the subject or topic of the sentence with the immediately ensuing verb, which often belonged to a subordinate clause rather than the main clause. In translating from Japanese, the main clause often needs to be identified right at the beginning and the rest of the sentence built around it by adding in the subsidiary elements later. The students' difficulties highlight the need to give formal training in old-fashioned parsing techniques, sometimes referred to as 'block analysis.' Students occasionally seemed unaware of even basic and seemingly obvious strategies, such as skipping over phrases in parentheses when reading so as to focus on the main structural and semantic elements, leaving the parenthetical parts for later. The tapes showed that even correct renditions were sometimes based on a fortuitous patching together of the structural elements rather than a sound understanding of how these elements are related.

In a particularly challenging sentence, one student found it helpful to replace the Japanese nouns with English equivalents while retaining the Japanese grammatical structure; this lessens the cognitive burden when simultaneously faced with lexical and grammatical complexities.

Paraphrasing

Paraphrasing is a useful strategy when a translator has diffculty expressing meaning using a single lexical item. One striking feature of the think-alouds, however, was the students' repeated failure to make use of their often-excellent oral paraphrases. They seemed to be unaware that they had just voiced a quite acceptable version or a rendition that could be fashioned into a more concise equivalent, and so these paraphrases often simply disappeared into thin air without being written down. For instance, one student rendered the economic slogan "*Kaikaku nakushite seichō nashi*" (literally, 'no growth without reform') as "No pain, no gain," which is a reasonable rendition, and she then voiced a more literal version, "No development without reform." Regrettably, neither version was written down. Another student had the good habit of 'previewing' each sentence and roughly paraphrasing it to herself before attempting a written translation, but she failed to put these paraphrases to actual use. One student gave the following oral rendition rapidly and fluently: "To those of you involved in the noble cause of protecting the nation's people and keeping the peace of the international community, ..., I express my feelings of respect and gratitude to you." He commented: "I guess that's what it means. That's a crap sentence." This initial quite good rendition was, however, not written down and the translation had to be redone later in writing, resulting in wasted time and effort. One student who paraphrased the meaning as she read through the source text did not start typing until after about 40 minutes, letting all these paraphrases slip beyond reach. She then had to reread each Japanese sentence, wasting more time. At another point she wrote herself an explanatory note, which again could have been used as a basis for the translation of that segment. She specifically asked if using this would be adding too much, and commented that she thought that this is exactly what the text meant and that it would clarify things for the reader, yet she seemed hesitant to use this, perhaps because of a literalist concept of translation.

An alternative explanation might be that students regard paraphrasing as an activity unrelated to translation. A similar observation led Kussmaul to suggest that the traditional view of comprehension and reverbalization as two separate stages should be replaced by "a model that leaves room for overlapping of the phases" (1997: 243). He suggests that in fact the two phases are often identical, and hypothesizes that the failure to use verbalized renditions can be attributed to a lack of self-confidence, "the fact that microstructures become predominant and are no longer related to macrostructures," and the possibility that "maybe they also thought that translating and comprehending were two separate phases" (246). Kussmaul concludes by recommending that teachers "point out that verbalising comprehension can be translation" (247). Teachers can suggest that students try 'telling' the meaning, as if to a friend — i.e., just explaining what the word or sentence means. This helps students break free from the constraints of the source text and think about the meaning at a deeper level. They could be encouraged to write down these initial paraphrases and later, if necessary, to tighten them up into a word or phrase expressing the same meaning — something that is easier to do after distancing oneself from the wording of the source text. It is important for students to listen more carefully to their inner discourse and to use what they come up with, placing greater faith in these provisional renditions rather than discarding or hardly even noticing them.

Students who are good at thinking aloud or interpreting could be encouraged to try voice recognition software. This might also have the benefit of capturing some paraphrases that are often otherwise lost.

Deverbalizing

Related to the question of paraphrasing is that of deverbalizing. One student gave a vivid description of the process of deverbalization, observing that his translation was "too *chokuyaku* [literal], so I need to look at it, understand it, assimilate it, juggle it around, put it in English and spit it out and then be done with it." Another student commented to herself, "Stop looking at the paper.

Think what it's trying to say," while one student explicitly said, "Just think about how we'd normally say it." At one point a student apologetically said, "I'm just doing this from memory here," but reading through each sentence a couple of times until the meaning has been internalized is in fact a very valid way to approach translation, working from memory traces rather than the printed words (although it is always important to double-check against the source text so as to prevent unjustified omissions or changes in meaning). This approach frees translators from the wording of the source text and allows a more natural rendition. In the present study, when sentences were easily understood the students were generally quite good at moving away from the form of the source text to come up with a meaning-based rendition. It was when they had comprehension difficulties that they were forced to rely on a literal rendition and a more communicative approach took a back seat.

In a wonderful illustration of the power of the subconscious and a confirmation of oft-heard translators' anecdotes, one student said, after translating a text that mentioned the birth of Japan's new princess in 2001, that he had dreamed about the emperor and the chrysanthemum (the symbol of the Japanese imperial family) the previous night before completing his initial draft, and how Japanese princesses are "imperial," not "royal," the term he had used until then.

Failure to follow through and to learn from experience

One notable inefficiency in these think-alouds was the students' failure to follow through on problems they had identified and commented on. They often simply continued on to the next phrase, deferring a solution until later. This inevitably involved coming back to the problem, sometimes repeatedly, and having to reacquaint themselves with the surrounding text each time. Where possible, it is more efficient to come up with a rudimentary solution upon first encountering a problem, even if the solution requires subsequent refining. Although making use of the subsequent context is a valid strategy, at least an elementary understanding of a given sentence is necessary before effective use can be made of it. Sometimes students indicated an awareness of where or how to find a solution but could not be bothered to track this down or made comments such as, "That doesn't make sense, but anyway, moving on." The resulting lack of understanding had a cumulative adverse effect on comprehension. If a sentence does not 'make sense,' students should be encouraged to try and *make* sense of it. Teachers need to inculcate high standards of professionalism to overcome such lackadaisical attitudes. A related aspect was that students frequently had difficulty concentrating on one problem or section at a time. They tended to jump around considerably rather than solving the problem at hand.

Encountering a term or problem once is not always sufficient to learn from the experience. For instance, one student said he thought a particular term had appeared in the previous week's translation passage, but still he was unable to recall its pronunciation or meaning. Elsewhere, the same student looked up an unknown word and saw that he had already underlined it in his dictionary on a previous occasion. Such memory lapses also applied to the shorter timeframe of working within the same text. One student started her think-aloud by reading about a particular term on a class handout and actually told herself to take note of this, but when she came to that term in the title of the text she had already forgotten about it. Students need to develop strategies for remembering what they have already encountered. One approach is the rather mechanistic but effective procedure of using a newly encountered term three times that same day in one's conversations, which is a technique used also for moving vocabulary from passive to active vocabulary status. The tapes did, however, contain some evidence of learning from one's mistakes — for example, one student highlighted a number because he had made a number error the previous week.

Research

Despite having been told repeatedly of the importance of checking the official English version of proper names in the source text, the students frequently guessed at possible renditions of Japanese organizations and laws, often not even mentioning the need to check for an official version. Even when research into proper names or other aspects of the text was carried out, the strategies adopted were sometimes very inefficient. Students often skimmed the reference material without fully absorbing it. Translators need to be *careful* readers and to cultivate their linguistic antennae so that they notice possible equivalents when reading background materials in the target language. In a financial text on derivatives, several students came across the term 'underlying assets' but failed to realize that this was the very term they were seeking, because they had not fully understood the English explanation they were reading.

Some students spent far too much time perusing articles on the Internet. One devoted about 90 minutes to terms in the title alone, before moving on to the first sentence of the text. Elsewhere, she found the term she was seeking ('institutional investors'), but went on to read lengthy explanations of what it meant. Although such diligence is laudable, usually it is more efficient to find a brief but to-the-point definition or explanation and then get something down as a draft translation, doing further targeted research later if necessary. Reading 'around' the topic is something that should be done at other times for general improvement of one's knowledge, not in the midst of a translation. Students need to learn to *get in, get what they need, and get out*. It is also important not to become overly dependent on external resources at the expense of relying on one's own knowledge or common sense.

Most of the students left any necessary research until after producing their first draft. One student, however, did some research using databases right at the beginning. Perhaps because of the knowledge gained, her translation went smoothly — although it is difficult to separate this variable from others. Certainly it is important to grasp any *key* concepts from the outset, doing quick research on the topic if necessary. Doing *extensive* background reading before tackling a text could, however, be counter-productive if one researches 'up the wrong tree' based on a cursory examination of the source text. I would suggest that it is generally more beneficial to postpone research (as did the majority of students in this study) until one has a clearer idea of what needs to be found, otherwise much time can be wasted on researching the subject in an overly broad and imprecise manner. Focusing the research more narrowly requires first gaining some understanding of the passage by doing a preliminary draft.

Use of informants

Occasionally the students asked Japanese informants for help, but not always in an effective way. Some sought help without first even checking a dictionary, though it is clearly preferable to use informants as a last resort, otherwise their goodwill is likely to be exhausted quickly. Moreover, having a good knowledge of the text before asking questions allows the students to assess the reliability of the answers received. Sometimes students asked their questions in Japanese, but their language skills were not always good enough to phrase the question in sufficiently precise terms. In such cases, if the informant understands English well it might be advisable to ask the question in English to ensure that the intended meaning has been expressed clearly. Sometimes the students failed to explain the context when asking their question or did not give the informant a proper chance to read the surrounding text, and at times they cut off informants when they were in the middle of an explanation. Students need to be cautioned that it is important to pay attention to what the informant has to say, without trying to formulate their own ideas at the same time.

Some students used native speakers of the target language, English, to obtain feedback on proposed equivalents or on whether the draft translation read smoothly. One student had her father check the draft, but he simply said it was fine, although in fact it contained many awkward expressions. This highlights the desirability of choosing informants who are sensitive to language and constructively critical, and of alerting them to particular aspects to which they should pay attention. One student asked her roommate for comments on grammar, punctuation, and any awkward or unnatural constructions, but one of the suggestions she received and implemented actually *introduced* an error, so students need to be cautioned not to accept informants' suggestions uncritically. They should also be made aware of the importance of thanking the informant properly, even if it is a fellow student, so as to ensure that help will be forthcoming again in the future — some of the tapes revealed very cursory words of thanks.

Checking strategies

Some students were not in the habit of checking their draft against the source text after each sentence, resulting in minor errors and unjustified omissions. Leaving the accuracy check until the stage of polishing the whole draft not only requires reacquainting oneself with the source text but also means that the accuracy check 'competes' with the polishing of the target text to the possible detriment of both processes. It is more effective to do the accuracy check immediately after drafting each sentence, while the source text is still fresh in the mind. Later, at the revision stage, it is only necessary to refer to the source text if there are particular problems. Leaving intensive polishing of the language of the translation until later, when the source text is less vivid in the mind, provides the necessary distance from the source text and allows the translation to be examined as a text in its own right.

There were two trends evident in relation to the time spent on polishing the translations. Some students tended to spend too long on this phase, with one student devoting more than half of the total time to honing her initial draft, which was already reasonably usable. Although refining the draft is of course desirable, it is also important to be efficient and decisive, without spending excessive time evaluating each sentence. One way of doing this is to correct other people's work, where it is easier to be objective as there is no emotional investment in the text. These skills can then be transferred to revision of one's own translations.

The opposite trend, evident among some of the students, was a rather lax attitude toward revising the draft. Some quickly gave up the effort, despite admitting openly that they did not understand parts of the source text. Nor did they seem troubled by the fact that the English did not read well in places. Moreover, once a draft version had been written down, there was often a tendency not to revise it much, and there was far less concern for style than was evident in the think-alouds of the professional translators (see below).

The students' reading of their draft translations often seemed to lack a clear purpose and led to very few changes. Brian Mossop's *Editing and Revising for Translators* (2001) contains recommendations on various parameters that can usefully be addressed in successive 'sweeps' through the draft. For novice translators in particular, this targeted approach might help focus attention on specific issues. At a more advanced stage, they might be ready to adopt what is probably the more common approach among experienced translators — i.e., focusing more or less simultaneously on all of the parameters within each sentence, re-reading the sentence several times until satisfied with it, and then reading the whole text as a cohesive piece at a later stage, checking for inter-sentence connections. The students in the present study made few attempts to consider wholesale restructuring or significantly different forms of expression during the polishing stage. Encouraging them to be more open to rewriting their translations quite radically might produce more natural renditions less constrained by the wording of the source text.

One of the texts translated in this study was a speech, where it is important for translators to check that the level of orality is appropriate. One student made frequent comments about the speakability of the translation, demonstrating an awareness of this aspect. Although particularly vital with speeches, an aware-ness of how a translation sounds is important with other text-types as well. Some students, however, read through their draft translations very rapidly without really 'hearing' it. It is advisable to slow down the (silent or audible) reading of the translation, monitoring it for readability and 'listenability.' This also helps students avoid the common pitfall of reading what they *expect* to see, not what is actually on the page. Using text-to-voice software also helps trans-lators hear their rendition in a more objective manner.

On the whole, the think-alouds contained virtually no comments about punctuation, although punctuation errors are present in nearly every transla-tion submitted by students. This suggests the need to place (even) more emphasis on training students to be aware of punctuation and to institute systematic punctuation checks, perhaps in a separate 'sweep' that focuses solely on this aspect.

Computer use

It came as something of a shock to me to realize that some students turned on the computer only after compiling a word list, giving an oral rendition that vanished without a trace, or writing out a handwritten version. One student did not start typing at all until after completing a handwritten draft *and* the first revision. Although there is nothing inherently wrong with this, it adds an extra layer of work; moreover, a handwritten draft is more difficult to consider objectively than a text on the screen. The fact that the computer was not turned on also meant that students could not use the Internet as they proceeded through the text. Another disconcerting aspect was that some students did not *save* their text for a long time (not until the end of tape 1 in the case of one student), thereby risking the loss of all their work. It seems that teachers cannot take such things for granted, and need to specifically tell students to use a computer from the outset and to save their work regularly, even after every sentence.

Response to the think-aloud experiment

On completion of the taping and before the class session, the students are required to fill out a questionnaire about the think-aloud process — i.e., whether it brought to their attention any problems and strategies of which they were previously unaware. The purpose is to further focus their thoughts on how they go about translating, and their answers serve as a basis for class discussion, again with the goal of reinforcing students' awareness of their own approach to translation and of any problems or inefficiencies that need to be addressed. The questionnaires also provide an indication as to whether think-alouds are a beneficial exercise from the students' perspective. Not unexpectedly, students typically comment that thinking aloud interfered with their thought processes, but some also say they find it useful or even "fun." Comments from the students in one recent class, for example, indicated that the exercise highlighted "just how confused my process is," how problems in looking up unknown characters and words greatly slowed down the translation process, how the frequent lack of an explicit subject in Japanese caused difficulty, how problems in understanding the source language constitute "about half" of the difficulties, and how it is important to read the source text at a deeper level. These particular comments are not necessarily representative, but it is noteworthy that they focus predominantly on the linguistic aspects of translation and suggest little evidence of having acquired new strategies or having learned how to overcome problems. This is, however, only to be expected, as the bulk of the learning occurs during the subsequent class discussion and reflection rather than during the think-aloud task itself, whose challenging nature precludes directing attention to explicit reflection on the task in which the student is engaged. To the extent that these *post hoc* comments indicate an enhanced attentiveness on the part of students to the *sources* of their difficulties, it can be said that the think-aloud exercise is useful in raising students' awareness of how they go about the task of translating, which is surely the first step toward making their approach more effective. As Kiraly suggests, participating in a think-aloud exercise and analyzing the results afterwards "would encourage students to think of translation in terms of process as well as result" (1995: 113).

Alternative pedagogical approaches

In the week after the students have completed the think-aloud exercise and the implications have been discussed in class, I often give them the opportunity to listen to a think-aloud recorded by a professional translator, sometimes using the same text the students had translated. Chesterman has suggested that "if non-professionals know what professionals do, they can learn to imitate them and (in theory) hence improve the quality of their own work" (1997: 138). Although it has not been proven that observing how professional translators work results in transferable knowledge, it is probably safe to assume that 'eavesdropping' on a professional translator can be of interest and value to novice translators — not least of all because it demonstrates that professionals face many of the same difficulties as the students themselves, albeit to a lesser degree. When I play the professionals' tapes, I have the students listen actively by jotting down their observations — e.g., what impressed them or what strategies they might be able to emulate. Almost invariably, the students comment on how the professionals think much more deeply about the meaning 'between the lines' and how they draw on other parts of the text and their extralinguistic knowledge to make sense of particular passages. Other features that students note include how the professionals are much better at freeing themselves from the original wording so as to express the meaning in natural English and how they are more conscious of the settings of the source and target texts. Although I make a point of specifying the translation 'brief' (i.e., an indication of the target audience and the use to which the translation will be put) when assigning homework, students' think-alouds generally showed little indication of consideration of this brief, as their attention was focused on the linguistic aspects rather than on the end use of the translation. This was in marked contrast to the think-alouds of the professional translators.

As a variant on the above approach, I recently decided to have my class watch and listen as I myself thought aloud while translating a text I had not seen before, with the translation being projected onto a large screen at the front of the class. This decision was partly prompted by a comment from a graduate student who told me that throughout her undergraduate Bachelor of Science in Translation degree she never once saw an instructor translate in front of the class. Even if this is not particularly useful in strictly pedagogical terms, it does satisfy students' curiosity to see how their teacher translates an extended piece rather than isolated phrases or sentences. Providing a model of 'how to translate' is not the purpose here, and it is important not to present the teacher's approach as 'the' way to go about the task of translation — just as teachers need to be careful not to criticize students simply for approaching the task differently. I asked my students to jot down their observations while watching me (mainly to ensure that they were watching actively rather than letting their minds drift) and also had them fill out a questionnaire afterwards. The responses are shown below. (Since this program was newly established in 2002, the class was small, consisting of only four students — two native speakers of English [A and B] and two native speakers of Japanese [C and D].)

1. Did watching someone else translate make you more aware of how **you** translate, what you know and do not know? Please describe.

Student A: I received a lot of useful information from watching you, but after the first half hour or so, I had a hard time paying attention. Maybe a shorter passage would be better. One thing that struck me in particular is at how many different levels you revise when you translate. Usually I only do one main revision.

Student B: Yes! I realized that the same problems occurred (i.e.: bad spelling, missing prepositions, strange word choice at first, doing *chokuyaku* [literal translation] before smooth English. Also, had the same feeling of getting sick of a sentence and moving on, coming back to it later.

Student C: It was very useful to see how a professional translator actually translate [sic] Japanese text into English. I was very surprised to know that I take almost the same approach when I translate except for revising draft. I always revise after I finished rough translation, but I learned it is better to revise after every sentence. Also it made me think how I can polish my translated English so that it will sound more like English.

Student D (the following is my translation of her comments written in Japanese): I learned to do just a rough translation of the title and headings and then come back and fix them up after translating the text. I feel that in my case I'm too caught up in the words and spend more time than necessary on translating that part.

I was struck by how once the "contents" of the Japanese had been accurately conveyed you did not do a lot of to-ing and fro-ing between the Japanese and English, instead concentrating on the flow and expression in English. I feel that I'm nowhere capable of this yet. I'm so busy worrying about whether the Japanese parts and words are right that I neglect the overall flow of the text and whether it all makes sense.

I feel that my way of looking up vocabulary and other things is unsystematic. For instance, I feel that when there's a word I don't know I try one method and if that's no good I try another, all without keeping the source properly in mind.

When I set it aside for a while before revising it, there are lots of things to revise. That's okay, but then when I leave it for even longer I want to revise it even further, and in the long run it's often the case that it would have been better if I hadn't revised it at all. I'd like to know where the problem lies here.

With your approach you did not seem to be marking up the Japanese text at all. How do you make sure you haven't omitted anything? In my case I add a mark to words and parts that I haven't yet translated, but even so I still forget to translate some parts. Do you have any good methods how to avoid this?

I thought it was really good how you more or less polished each paragraph as you went.

I realize I must make continual efforts to improve my English.

2.   Did you pick up any useful techniques? Please describe.

Student A: I liked your word index [my personal computer glossary]. Seeing how that worked was interesting. The problem is, though, I only noticed techniques you already are teaching us, such as block analysis.

Student B: Block analysis. Skipping around text until you have a good grasp on the meaning. Revising after a paragraph. Cutting apart sentences that are too long in Japanese. Also, how to set apart set phrases to help you figure out the meaning of the sentences. Compiling a glossary for translation. Re-reading Japanese after composing an English sentence.

Student C: Save after every sentence. Use bold for the words that needs [sic] to be reconsidered.

Student D: [See her comments above.]

3.   Do you think you might change your approach to translating as a result of this exercise? If so, in what way?

Student A: I actually have been trying to emulate that style (from our practice session too), which you use, but since we have such different problems (i.e. I can't understand everything easily), it is too hard for me to use right now. I have to have a good grasp on what is being said before I can translate.

Student B: Yep. Just relax and translate and not get frustrated at what I don't know, but find effective ways to look up *kanji* [Chinese characters], vocab or research subjects. Also, compile a terminology database.

Student C: To be honest, I don't really know what my approach to translating is, but I would like to know if there is any better approach to translating.

Student D: [See her comments above.]

4.   Any other comments.

Student A: [No response.]

Student B: It is interesting to see how grammar/structure will always slow down translation, but when you know vocab and *kanji*, it cuts time in half.

Student C: I feel keenly my lack of knowledge about Japanese and also common sense.

Student D: [See her comments above.]

Another variation I use is to have the students work as a group to produce a translation projected onto the screen at the front of the class, discussing their rationale and decision-making as they go. Here students are learning from their peers rather than from more experienced professionals, but each year they comment that they learn a great deal from this exercise. Having students do pair work on a translation in class seems to be another effective method of stimulating their creativity and encouraging them to stretch the boundaries more than when working individually. During pair work, the students brainstorm extensively, jotting down phrases almost at random as they come to mind, and bouncing ideas off each other. Afterwards they usually comment that this is a very useful exercise, but as with the group translation not much can be achieved in terms of text length within the given time.

Conclusion

The problems evident from students' tapes suggest that more emphasis needs to be placed on actually *teaching* effective cognitive strategies and strategies for tackling texts. We cannot assume that students naturally or automatically adopt the strategies that seem obvious to more experienced translators. The class discussion following the think-aloud exercise is one useful means toward this end. (It is also important, however, to recognize that some students are already using generally sound *strategies*, even though linguistic difficulties might detract from the quality of their translated texts.)

When choosing passages for use in think-aloud exercises, it might be beneficial at different times to select texts that present a challenge mainly in one particular area, so that it is easier to focus on how students handle that specific aspect. For instance, sometimes a text presenting comprehension problems could be used, while at other times one that is more demanding in the formulation stage might be chosen, as this is likely to produce more interesting and useful data about *transfer* problems. Alternatively, a specialized text might be chosen so as to focus on research and terminological strategies or the students' use of extralinguistic knowledge. Admittedly, however, it is difficult to separate out the variables in this manner.

Because think-alouds usually produce lengthy tapes, it is important to consider practical issues such as the teacher's workload. The use of relatively short passages (e.g., no more than three paragraphs) is recommended so as to lighten the burden on both student and teacher. Listening to and commenting on tapes (even without transcribing them) is a very time-consuming task, so rather than have every student do a think-aloud in the same week, it would be less taxing to do this exercise on a rotating basis, one student at a time. I have not yet tried this approach, which would raise further questions about the best way to give feedback. Another approach adopted by one teacher I know is to have students transcribe each other's work. Not only does this alleviate the teacher's workload, but in her opinion it is also a useful exercise for the transcribers as they listen to their peers' tapes. Because a large proportion of students' tapes is devoted to purely linguistic problems rather than to translation problems *per se*, it might be more productive to limit this exercise to classes where the students are largely beyond the stage of linguistic problems and are focusing mainly on genuine translation problems. That would probably yield more useful results and would also perhaps be less time-consuming for the instructor. Another avenue to explore is the use of Translog[1] or other software that tracks keystrokes as a means of monitoring the translation process as it evolves.

Diaries are another instrument for gaining some insights into students' thinking, although they do not represent the process as fully or objectively as tapes or computer logging. My students are required to submit a commentary with every homework passage, detailing their comprehension and reformulation problems and the rationale behind any particularly noteworthy decisions or renditions. This encourages them to reflect upon the task of translation, assess the acceptability of different solutions, and assume responsibility for their decisions. It also helps the teacher differentiate between linguistic and translation errors — a difference that is not always apparent from the text itself.

One of the outcomes of think-aloud exercises is that they indicate just how long students are spending on the different phases of the translation process (e.g., reading the source text, doing research, preparing the draft, revising). Given the great time investment required to produce this information, however, a less time-consuming alternative is simply to require students to append to their translations a chart showing roughly how much time was spent on each activity. If this chart is presented in a standard format and filled out each week, it becomes a useful resource indicating to both student and teacher where difficulties and inefficiencies lie, as suggested by the amount of time spent on that particular activity. (Obviously, the difficulty of the texts translated is a variable here.)

Kovačič notes that think-aloud research on translation increasingly highlights the "great diversity in the behaviour of the experimental subjects" (2000: 100). It is admittedly difficult — not to mention problematic — to generalize from the sample of problems encountered by the students in this study and to extrapolate this to professional translators. Nevertheless, some of the problems are, I believe, shared by both groups, albeit to different degrees.[2] Unfortunately, the attempt to distill general problems from the mass of details on the tapes accumulated over the past decade means that I have ended up with just that — generalizations. Moreover, Kiraly warns that "we cannot assume that strategies effective for one translator will be generally suitable for all translators" (1995: 113). Yet if participating in think-aloud exercises can reveal new insights to students or teachers about how the students go about the translation process then they will have served a valuable pedagogical purpose.

Notes

1. See Hansen, G. (ed.). 1999. *Probing the Process: Methods and Results.* Copenhagen: Samfundsliteratur. Translog is available directly from Arnt Jakobsen, email elc@post9.tele.dk.

2. Kiraly (1995, 90) concluded from his study of the think-alouds produced by translation students and professional translators that "there do not appear to be major differences between the way translations were processed or in the quality of the translations produced by these two groups." Although the quality of the output of the students in my study was generally not yet, in my view, akin to that of professional translators of Japanese, Kiraly's findings about the similarities in the translation process of the two groups are of interest. Whether these similarities in process exist only when the quality is also comparable between the two groups is a topic meriting further research.

References

Chesterman, A. 1997. *Memes of Translation: The Spread of Ideas in Translation Theory.* Amsterdam/Philadelphia: John Benjamins.

House, J. 2000. "Consciousness and the strategic use of aids in translation." In *Tapping and Mapping the Processes of Translation and Interpreting,* S. Tirkkonen-Condit and R. Jääskeläinen (eds), 149–162. Amsterdam/Philadelphia: John Benjamins.

Kiraly, D. C. 1995. *Pathways to Translation: Pedagogy and Process.* Kent, Ohio: Kent State University Press.

Kovačič, I. 1997. "A thinking-aloud experiment in subtitling." In *Translation as Intercultural Communication,* M. Snell-Hornby, Z. Jettmarova, K. Kaindl (eds), 229–238. Amsterdam/Philadelphia: John Benjamins.

Kovačič, I. 2000. "Thinking-aloud protocol — interview — text analysis." In *Tapping and Mapping the Processes of Translation and Interpreting,* S. Tirkkonen-Condit and R. Jääskeläinen (eds), 97–109. Amsterdam/Philadelphia: John Benjamins.

Kussmaul, P. 1997. "Comprehension processes and translation. A think-aloud protocol (TAP) study." In *Translation as Intercultural Communication,* M. Snell-Hornby, Z. Jettmarova, K. Kaindl (eds), 239–248. Amsterdam/Philadelphia: John Benjamins.

Mossop, B. 2001. *Editing and Revising for Translators.* Manchester: St. Jerome.

Tirkkonen-Condit, S., and R. Jääskeläinen (eds). 2000. *Tapping and Mapping the Processes of Translation and Interpreting.* Amsterdam/Philadelphia: John Benjamins.

Toury, G. 1995. *Descriptive Translation Studies and Beyond.* Amsterdam/Philadelphia: John Benjamins.

Teaching translation as a form of writing

Improving translator self-concept

Alexander Gross

As former chair of the American Translators Association Public Relations Committee, I have long been concerned by the overall perception of translators in our society. Altering that perception, however, requires concerted effort in a number of areas. Professional organizations must strive to educate the general public, while ensuring that translators themselves have a healthy self-image is a central problem in translation pedagogy (Kiraly 2000), and one that I have tried to address as a teacher in the New York University Translation Studies Program (under the School of Continuing and Professional Studies).

All too often, one encounters a built-in self-deprecation about translation, even among its most fervent advocates, almost a form of professional inferiority complex. After all, translation is not "real writing." Since it largely derives from another text, it can only be a less than perfect version, almost as flawed as that dated artifact, the carbon copy. It is sometimes conceded that translations of literary or stage works demand a higher level of creativity, but even these may be dismissed by some as flawed or second-hand renderings of allegedly superior originals. And when we come to technical, commercial, and scientific texts — comprising some ninety percent of all translation work — many observers find it hard to imagine that any creative effort may be required at all.

The problem is a central one, for, as Ros Schwartz put it, "the status of translators is closely bound up with how they see themselves" (Durban et al. 2003). She goes on to argue that, "we [translators] have to see ourselves not as the humble scribe or slave who does what they are told, but as writers who take a text and make it our own and do what needs to be done" (ibid.).

In this article, I provide, first, an overview of historical attitudes toward translation and translators, and then suggest how such attitudes can be countered by teaching translation as a form of target language (TL) writing, a view supported negatively by the fact that "the majority of English mother-tongue applicants for translation posts in the European Commission fail *because of the poor quality of their English*" (McCluskey 1987: 17, quoted in Hervey and Higgins 1992: 18).

The view of translation as derivative and uncreative has been voiced repeatedly by authors, critics, and — sadly enough — translators themselves. Indeed, a recent *ATA Chronicle* piece cites a critic who referred to translators as "that problematic necessity," though as we shall soon see, this is a relatively kind assessment (Russell-Bitting 2001: 31). In many different ages and cultures, one may encounter even more emphatic slights and slurs. These range from the nearly folkloric "something has been lost in the translation" to the endlessly repeated *traduttore traditore*[1] or perhaps the famous observation by Cervantes:

> ...translating from one language into another...is like gazing at a Flemish tapestry with the wrong side out: even though the figures are visible, they are full of threads that obscure the view and are not bright and smooth as when seen from the other side. (1949: 923)

Or even Wilhelm Von Humboldt's almost despairing assessment that "all translating seems to me simply an attempt to accomplish an impossible task" (cited in Morgan 1959). Or the nineteenth century French critic Edmond Scherer's condescending aspersion: "Translation always resembles a tiring Chinese puzzle: you can be sure ahead of time that the solutions will leave something to be desired" (Scherer 1878–1886, V: 333). Or the truly religious zealotry of a historian and classicist writing in 1916:"...translation is sin... meddling with inspiration, blasphemy against the Holy Ghost" (Showerman 1916: 100).

As we shall soon see, such righteous fervor about translation may not be entirely accidental. Even George Steiner, surely one of translation's warmest advocates, has observed, "The perennial question whether translation is, in fact, possible is rooted in ancient religious and psychological doubts on whether there ought to be any passage from one tongue to another" (1975: 239).

This view, which goes beyond translation and encompasses all of language, is both echoed and confirmed by the statement by Japanese linguist Takao Suzuki intended as a criticism of his own people: "There is here in our country a general feeling that it is not natural for foreigners to understand Japanese" (Miller 1977: 83).

At the very least, even when such outright challenges are absent, one may still detect among some translators a certain defeatism, starting as early as Roger Bacon in 1268: "But it is impossible that the peculiar quality of one language should be preserved in another...therefore an excellent piece of work in one language cannot be translated into another as regards the peculiar quality that it possessed in the former" (1928: 75).

Even earlier, in 330 C. E., the Hellenistic scholar and mystic Iamblichus of Chalcis, who was attempting to translate the sacred works of Egypt into Greek, observed: "Terms when translated do not always preserve the same meaning; and every nation has certain idioms impossible to express intelligently to others. You may possibly translate them, but they no longer preserve the same force" (1989: 129).

And yet at the same time — amid these claims that the movement of meaning between foreign languages is difficult, impossible, or even sacrilegious — almost no one doubts that translation is necessary and, at least to some extent, feasible. When so many misgivings are raised about an almost every-day occurrence, we are surely faced with a remarkable anomaly — and one that requires detailed explanation.

Despite the almost unending sea of doubt, self-deprecation, and even despair surrounding translation, such an approach is largely mistaken. The ancient Greek (and even Latin) words for interpreters are so broad in their meanings as to include the concepts of mediator, deal-maker, and even marriage-broker. Today's interpreters — particularly those who must meet the demanding needs of conference, courtroom, or hospital interpreting — are also obliged to play many roles.

From the smallest families and clans of the past to today's mammoth nation states, at every stage of this process translators and interpreters are likely to have played a crucial role in negotiating the finer points of verbal agreements and later in creating the fine print of written ones. Today we differentiate between vast numbers of language-related professions and activities: writing, editing, translating, interpreting, teaching any and all of the preceding skills, clarifying religious or legal texts, language training for singers and actors, and of course the far more recent activities of advertising and public relations. Yet all of them can be seen as outgrowths of the work performed by the earliest interpreters, arguably the first humans charged with defining and explaining the distinctions between various forms of language. Their role may even be par-tially commemorated by the popular usage of the word "translate," which itself could be "translated" as 'to explain,' 'to summarize,' 'to clarify.'

Far from being an ancillary activity, and far from being a second-hand copy of anything, translation — or a process remarkably close to it — can be shown to lie at the very center of all communication and may in fact have served as its exemplar and model throughout the entire epoch when language evolved, however long that period may have lasted. And far from being an object worthy of blame, we may find that the true source for our doubts about translation is ultimately based in our own fears about language and its relationship to the world around us. It can be quite clearly demonstrated that there is nothing wrong with translation that is not also wrong with language itself. Expressed a bit differently, the processes of translation merely replicate and recapitulate processes inherent in the nature of language.

Such seemingly reckless assertions as these can be both justified and grounded by the description of a very simple experiment, as expressed here just slightly more than a *Gedankenexperiment*, but one nonetheless quite likely to work out in reality much as outlined here. Its foreseeable results are likely to be confirmed by the experience and common sense of most readers, while the task itself may also serve as a useful exercise for beginning translation students — and as a revealing one even for more advanced practitioners — as it lies at the very center of what the process of translating truly entails.

Our experiment begins with the assumption that a group of highly trained journalists has gathered in a room and is seated around a table. These journalists, all roughly of the same age, are seasoned and respected members of their profession. Moreover, they have all studied at the same school of journalism and received their training under the very same professors. It might therefore be assumed that they not only spring from a common background but that they also share overall outlooks and attitudes towards writing and editing to an uncommon extent.

These journalists are now presented with a paragraph written in their native language, along with blank sheets of paper, and are prompted to compose a paraphrase of this passage. Since paraphrasing is a common journalistic exercise and bears a close resemblance to work they routinely perform each day, namely editing, they all immediately set to work, and each one creates his or her own paraphrase of the very same text.

It would be theoretically possible to assume, given the nearly identical background of the participants, that their paraphrases would turn out to be remarkably similar, differing only in a few slight touches. But I do not believe for an instant that this would prove to be the case, nor do I anticipate that any reader sophisticated about the nature of language will draw such a conclusion. If, in fact, we now collect these paraphrases — five or ten or however many there may be — and read each of them aloud to our circle of journalists, I believe we will be amazed by how many different approaches have suddenly sprung from the same original passage. And if this is our result among this remarkably homogeneous group of journalists, it will surely take place to an even greater extent among writers or journalists coming from more diverse backgrounds. And if we now choose to substitute translation students for journalists and ask them to translate rather than to paraphrase a brief passage, I do not believe that any reader will doubt that something remarkably similar will now take place, on this occasion involving two languages rather than a single one.

I also fearlessly predict that the various individual differences of style and wording we discover, whether among the journalists or the translators, will fall into two general categories. The first of these, by far the greatest number, will consist of slight liberties each of the journalists has taken with the original text in creating his or her paraphrase. In fact, as the various versions are read aloud, our participants may even begin to disagree with each other whether or not a specific word or phrase is an adequate equivalent for the word or phrase in the original. It is likely that most of their discussion will be devoted to such minor disagreement, most often friendly and collegial in tone.

The task of creating an ideal text — as neutral in tone as possible while still perfectly representing the original — is one that journalists face each day. It is for this reason that reporters at major publications may, where necessary, rewrite, reedit, and/or "re-tweak" each other's work, always in the hope of approaching ultimate perfection, much as the lonely translator — or the translation editor — must do in creating a final draft.

But there is also almost certain to be a second category of divergence present in the journalists' work, one which will provoke somewhat more heated discussion. It may well be discovered that in at least a few instances one or another of these professional writers has committed an outright *error* of paraphrase, has in fact actually overlooked the meaning of a word or phrase in the original text and replaced it with what can only be described as an incorrect solution.

At this point the purpose of the experiment will have certainly become clear to readers. What we have just discovered while using a single language is so remarkably close to what can happen while translating between a pair of languages as to be for all practical purposes indistinguishable. We all know perfectly well that a group of translators sitting around the same table and presented with a paragraph to translate into a second language would surely go through a remarkably similar process. And once their translations were collected and read aloud, these writers would certainly also embark on a similar series of discussions and disagreements.

In other words, the idiosyncrasies of trained writers are indistinguishable from those of trained translators, and vice versa. Whereas society at large tends to accept such variations by journalists, that same society tends to focus on them if translators have been the perpetrators, even to suppose that something in the process has gone seriously awry. Indeed, this plethora of individual variations has not escaped the attention of machine translation specialists, who have in some cases chosen to view them as evidence that human translation is unreliable and must one day be replaced by the trustworthy logic of computer programming.

At this point, a closer look at this experiment can be helpful in providing a few practical examples of what might take place. And since machine translation has been mentioned, it may also be useful to glance at the problems programmers might face in an attempt to improve on the work of human translators. The following sentence, taken at random from a text, will play the role of our paragraph to be paraphrased:

> In April, 1800, the position of city A had under these rapidly developed circumstances become so dangerous for foreigners that it was deemed advisable to dispatch a relieving force from the port city of B.

Now let's see what a paraphrase of this sentence might look like if we change as many of the original words as we possibly can:

> By the early spring of 1800, because of these swiftly unfolding occurrences, the situation in the city A had grown so perilous for outsiders that it was considered prudent to send assisting troops from the coastal town of B.

We can see immediately that the paraphrase has become longer than the original passage (a common outcome in many translations from English as well), but other differences are also obvious. While the paraphrase conveys the essential meaning of the original, a number of questionable changes have been made, though perhaps only one could be characterized as an outright error. This comes at the very beginning, for by changing "In April, 1800" to "By the early spring of 1800," a certain degree of precision has clearly been lost. Other possible solutions might be "During the fourth month of 1800" or "As April of 1800 began" or "March was barely over when...," but all of these are overly elaborate and/or add something not present in the original. The original text does not claim that this situation arose "early in April" or "during" April, merely "in April." On the other hand, the wording of the source text does not provide us with sufficient information about the exact time to proclaim any of these variants as being devastatingly wrong. Perhaps a useful rule of thumb in a manual for paraphrasing would be never to change the names of months or days, though there might be instances, as with all rules of thumb, where this too might work less than perfectly.

A similar problem crops up at the very end of the sentence when "the port of B" is rendered as "the coastal town of B." Unlike the month of April, there is no way we can avoid using the name of the town. Even though it would be technically accurate to call it "B, the port city of A," this involves inserting a geography lesson into the paraphrase where none occurs in the original. In any case, a "coastal town" is not necessarily a "port city," nor would calling it "the seaside town" or "the embarkation point" help us very much. "Harbor town" might be even less correct, as a harbor town is not necessarily a port — the word "harbor" describes mere topography (ships may occasionally enter a harbor, but no docking system may be present), while the word "port" describes a function and often the presence of complex machinery.

Readers are free to examine the many differences between these two sentences at their leisure and are equally free to decide if they can arrive at any truly preferable solutions. These are likely to be few and far between, even though perfectly valid objections can be directed towards every single element of this paraphrase. "To send assisting troops" is not the same thing as "to dispatch a relieving force," nor can "it was considered prudent" be accepted as a perfect equivalent for "it was deemed advisable."

This intricate conversion has taken place entirely in English, a language which we like to believe enjoys an uncommonly rich vocabulary. Yet no end of legitimate questions can be raised about the overall process of paraphrasing, much as they have been raised about the process of translation. In fact, the very level of disagreement likely to arise among readers of this brief passage serves to prove the point being made — that writing and editing in a single language is no more precise or secure than translating between two languages.

Though some readers may disagree, there is probably no major error as such in this paraphrase, as much as it leaves to be desired. Such an error might have occurred if one of the journalists had substituted "Europeans" or "Westerners" for "foreigners," since during this historical episode Americans were also included. Another error might have arisen if the phrase "it was deemed advisable" had been rendered as "it was judged urgent," since this would introduce a true difference in meaning. It may well be that our languages — all languages — provide us with far less "wiggle room" than we are accustomed to believe. While we are capable of saying almost the same thing in many different ways, not all the synonyms in Roget's Thesaurus will unfailingly enable us to convey exactly the same information in all instances — not to mention expressive or emotional meaning. Our synonyms may often not be as fully synonymous as we tend to believe.

Although we have been working within a single language, the similarities with translating between two languages are obvious. Clearly no two "natural" languages have ever been constructed — whether in their vocabulary or their syntax — so as to be fully synonymous with each other, which of course explains many of the problems involved in translation, even before cultural factors enter the picture. None of this of course exonerates the translator from attempting to choose the best possible translation for every word in a text, any more than it excuses journalists from seeking out the very best choice among competing synonyms. This can sometimes be an excruciatingly difficult task, and the words of Martin Luther still ring true today: "And it's often happened to us that we've searched and asked for fourteen days, even for three or four weeks, after a single word, and in all that time we haven't found it" (1530/1951: 15).

I believe these observations may also call to mind Umberto Eco's distinction between intralingual and interlingual translation, as first voiced by Jakobson (himself deeply influenced by Peirce). The former refers to the "rewording" of texts within a single language, the task assigned to our group of journalists. The latter term embraces what Eco calls "translation proper," the skill we seek to impart to our students. Once again following Jakobson, Eco expands this domain to further include what he terms "intersemiotic" translation, or "transmutation," the conversion of a work into a completely new medium, i.e., a novel into a film or a symphony into a ballet (Eco 2001). Since my work experiences include translator/dramaturg and adapting non-stage works for the theatre, Eco's reflections strike me as correct.

Here again, we can perhaps begin to discern the morass of difficulties lying in wait for computerized solutions to these problems. Only three years ago, on an Internet newsgroup for advanced computer programmers, I discovered a message from a member asking where he could find a "paraphrasing program." This programmer clearly assumed that such a program must exist and that his colleagues would be able to provide information about it. Although this was an extremely active newsgroup and had many knowledgeable members, his query never received an answer. The reason here, as I have verified by subsequent research, is that no one has ever succeeded in creating a paraphrasing program that truly works for all texts (as is the case for machine translation as well).

When I later raised this issue on a different newsgroup, this one populated by computational linguists, I was told that such a paraphrasing program was "trivial" in nature and could not be easier to construct — an argument one may still sometimes hear voiced about machine translation. Using a few examples from the preceding experiment, it can be demonstrated why this argument is likely to prove untrue. While the steps in writing such a program may each be "trivial," many unforeseen problems lie in wait. It would only be necessary to take each of the above alterations between the two sentences and turn them into computer commands, which might convert into readable "pseudocode" as follows:

if find string "position" then substitute string "situation"
if find string "developed" then substitute string "unfolding"
if find string "relieving" then substitute string "assisting"
etc.

The problem with such a program is that it would wreak absolute havoc with the very next text it might try to paraphrase, so that "a man of position" would become "a man of situation," "he developed a rash" would become "he unfolding a rash," and "for relieving diarrhea" would become "for assisting diarrhea."

And here, too, certain similarities with "machine translation" begin to emerge all too recognizably. Once again, some authorities in this field still dismiss such difficulties as "trivial" in nature, certain to be overcome by more advanced methods of syntactic analysis. But as we have seen, no two trained journalists are likely to agree on how to paraphrase a given sentence, so it becomes a truly challenging task to grasp how a machine will ever achieve such precision where human beings have failed to do so. Since we have seen our carefully selected journalists disagree on many details even where a single language is involved, it is scarcely surprising that translators would do so between two languages. Not even the English word "good" and its supposed French counterpart "bon," as I have observed elsewhere, cover precisely the same semantic and connotational territory in their respective languages (Gross 1993: 251–253, figs. 3A, 3B, 3C).

Is it possible to state the precise reason for these variances within a single language? Regarding paraphrase, one may readily point out that even within the same language — and even among professionals trained in a single language specialty — every single human being nonetheless speaks a slightly separate and different idiolect. At one point or another, each of us simply differs with some, with many, or in a few cases with most of our peers about the precise range of meaning of a specific word.

By drawing attention to the similarities between the work of journalists and that of translators, we, as translator trainers, can present translation as a form of target language writing, relating it to larger issues of communicative competence. In doing so, I believe we can begin to positively affect translator self-concept from a student's first day in the classroom.

Notes

(Where not otherwise stated, translations are by the author.)

1. This famous epigram about translation apparently arose as a criticism of Anníbal Caro's sixteenth century translation of Virgil's Aeneid into Italian. The author is grateful to Maria Galetta of the Italian Cultural Institute for this information.

References

Bacon, R. 1928. *The Opus Majus of Roger Bacon.* Translated by R. B. Burke. Philadelphia: University of Pennsylvania Press.

Brower, R. A. 1959. *On Translation.* Cambridge (USA): Harvard University Press.

Cervantes, M. de. 1949. *The Ingenious Gentleman Don Quixote de la Mancha.* Translated by S. Putnam. New York: Viking Press.

de Waal, F. 1997. *Bonobo: The Forgotten Ape.* Photographs by F. Lanting. Berkeley: University of California Press.

Donato, R. 1994. "Collective scaffolding in second language learning." In *Vygotskian Approaches to Second Language Research,* J. P. Lantolf and G. Appel (eds), 33–56. Norwood, NJ: Ablex.

Durban, C. et al. 2003. "Translator training & the real world: Concrete suggestions for bridging the gap." *Translation Journal* 7 (1): <http://www.accurapid.com/journal/23roundtableb.htm> accessed on February 3, 2003.

Eco, U. 2001. *Experiences in Translation.* Toronto: University of Toronto Press.

Griffen, D. R. 1984. *Animal Thinking.* Cambridge (USA): Harvard University Press.

Griffen, D. R. 1992. *Animal Minds.* Chicago: University of Chicago Press.

Gross, A. 1993. "Selected elements from a theory of fractal linguistics." In *Scientific and Technical Translation, American Translators Association Scholarly Monograph Series, Vol. VI,* S. E. and L. D. Wright (eds), 235–263. Amsterdam/Philadelphia: John Benjamins.

Gross, A. 2000. "Hermes — God of translators and interpreters." Paper presented at the NYU "Translation2000" Conference *(Global Links, Linguistic Ties: Forging a Future for Translation and Interpreting).*

Hervey, S., and Higgins, I. 1992. *Thinking Translation: A Course in Translation Method: French to English.* London & New York: Routledge.

Humboldt, A. von. 1796. *Letter to A. W. v. Schlegel, July 23.* Cited by Morgan 1959, 275.

Iamblichus of Chalcis. 1989 (Ca. 330 C. E.). *On the Mysteries.* Translations by T. Taylor and A. Wilder. Hastings, England: Chthonius Books.

Kiraly, D. C. 1995. *Pathways to Translation: Pedagogy and Process.* Kent, Ohio: Kent State University Press.

Kiraly, D. C. 2000. *A Social Constructivist Approach to Translator Education: Empowerment from Theory to Practice.* Manchester, UK & Northampton, MA: St. Jerome.

Luther, M. 1530/1951. *Sendbrief vom Dolmetschen.* Herausgegeben von K. Bischoff. Halle: Max Niemeyer Verlag.

Lantolf, J., and Appel, G. 1994. "Theoretical framework: An introduction to Vygotskian approaches to second language research." In *Vygotskian Approaches to Second Language Research*, J. P. Lantolf and G. Appel (eds), 1–32. Norwood, NJ: Ablex.

McCluskey, B. 1987. "The chinks in the armour: Problems encountered by language graduates entering a large translation department." In *Translation in the Modern Languages Degree*, H. Keith and I. Mason (eds). London: Information on Language Teaching and Research.

Miller, R. A. 1977. *The Japanese Language in Contemporary Japan: Some Sociolinguistic Observations*. Washington: American Enterprise Institute.

Morgan, B. Q. 1959. Bibliography chapter in Brower 1959.

Page, G. 1999. *Inside the Animal Mind*. New York: Broadway Books.

Russell-Bitting, S. A. 2001. "Eliot Weinberger on translation, 'That problematic necessity.'" *ATA Chronicle:* XXX 2: 31–32, 65.

Scherer, E. 1878–1886. *Études sur la littérature contemporaine*, ten volumes. Paris: Calmann-Lévy.

Showerman, G. 1916. "The way of the translator." *Unpopular Review* 5: 84–100.

Steiner, G. 1975. *After Babel: Aspects of Language and Translation*. Oxford: Oxford University Press.

Vinay, J.-P., and Darbelnet, J. 1958. *Stylistique comparée du français et de l'anglais; méthode de traduction*. Paris: Didier.

Welty, J. C., and Baptista, L. 1988. *The Life of Birds*. Fort Worth: Saunders College and Harcourt Brace Jovanovich.

2. Translation as product

Learning through portfolios in the translation classroom

Julie E. Johnson

Introduction

Portfolios burst onto the academic scene (primarily at the secondary level) about a decade ago as part of the authentic assessment movement (Herman et al. 1996: 27). They have become *de rigueur* in many writing and language arts classrooms across the United States, and are also showing up in many other disciplines where critical thinking is central.

Portfolios that are intended primarily as a summative assessment tool typically consist of a selection of student work aimed at demonstrating accomplishments, progress, and/or readiness to meet future challenges. Some portfolios include cover statements presenting why each piece was included or what it shows. Learning-focused, or formative, portfolios often include reflective statements by the student (goals, progress, strategies, frustrations), as well. Such statements can serve a number of different purposes, one of the most important being reflective learning.

Reflective learning occurs when students gain and reinforce their own insights by reflecting on their own work. In a profession like translation, this is key. According to Dewey, the student

> "has to *see* on his own behalf and in his own way the relations between means and methods employed and results achieved. Nobody else can see for him, and he can't see just by being 'told,' although the right kind of telling may guide his seeing and thus help him to see what he needs to see." (1974: 151)

Because of their focus on process as well as product, portfolios make an ideal tool for fostering and assessing student learning in the translation classroom, particularly the kind of on-going *reflective* learning required of a professional translator.

This article discusses the advantages of portfolios in translator education, presents the specific purposes, content, assessment, and impact of portfolios as used in translation courses in the Graduate School of Translation and Interpretation (GSTI) at the Monterey Institute of International Studies, and proposes design considerations for translation educators wishing to implement a similar approach.

Advantages of portfolios

A portfolio approach to both summative and formative assessment can support a "social constructivist approach to translator education." In his book by this title, Don Kiraly (2000) argues that the goal of translation programs is not merely to help students develop technical skill, but to transform them into competent translators. Describing how this is achieved, he states:

> If we see translator competence as a creative, largely intuitive, socially-constructed, and multi-faceted complex of skills and abilities, then the primary goals of translator education will include raising students' awareness of the factors involved in translation, helping them develop their own translator's self-concept, and assisting in the collaborative construction of individually tailored tools that will allow every student to function within the language mediation community upon graduation. (Kiraly 2000: 49)

A number of points in this summary paragraph merit highlighting. First, note the absence here of any reference to domains of knowledge or specific skills that must be "taught." Translation is not a mechanistic process, the translator being a kind of language-manipulation machine that spits out product according to a defined set of rules. It involves a whole complex of skills and abilities, and a good dose of intuition — which is developed. Translation quality is a function of translator competence in a holistic sense that involves the translator as a person.

Take, for example, an apprentice translator we'll call Bob. Bob has a wonderful knack for expressing French statements in natural, idiomatic English. Unlike many novice translators, he doesn't get hamstrung by the grammatical form and syntax of the source language. But every one of his translations contains instances of this very idiomatic English significantly diverging from the message conveyed in the French. Why? By Bob's own admission, he has a short attention span. He works fast and furiously in short spurts, then loses all interest, eager to move on. Consequently, he simply runs with whatever idea he first formulated upon reading the French. He rarely pauses to reconsider whether his initial understanding makes sense in context, only sporadically bothers to double-check lexical meaning in a dictionary or other resource, and almost never goes back to edit and revise beyond an electronic spell check and cursory read through.

While Bob recognizes this about himself (the most important step) and knows what he could do to ensure that his translations more accurately reflect the message of the source text, he usually can't be bothered. His engines are revving too fast. This is not about linguistic or translation ability in a technical sense. It's about Bob. He is not likely to become a reliable, competent translator until he resolves to harness and focus his restless energy, and discovers for himself how to use it to advantage.

Self-confidence is another extra-linguistic factor that often emerges as a prerequisite to translator competence. Apprentice translators make astounding leaps in translation quality and professional readiness once they gain enough confidence to stand on their own authority. This mental/emotional shift manifests itself in tangible breakthroughs that leave professors thinking, "Wow! What happened?"

How then, do student translators learn to tame their own demons? How do they develop self-confidence? Not in a vacuum. Not through mere practice and correction. This kind of personal evolution happens through interaction, dialogue, and collaboration. It is socially constructed. Only as students articulate their reasoning for others does it concretely enter their own consciousness and become a foothold they can confidently re-utilize to navigate similar territory and rise to new challenges. Only as they consider the multiple perspectives elicited through dialogue do individual and collective insights emerge. In Kathleen Blake Yancey's words:

> We learn to reflect as we learn to talk in the company of others . . . it is in seeing something from divergent perspectives that we see it fully. Along the way, we check and confirm as we seek to reach goals that we have set for ourselves. Reflection becomes a habit, one that transforms. (1996: 90)

Take for example, the small but significant transformations that occurred through a collaborative project in the first-semester Basic Translation Exercises course. When presented with the opportunity, the eight students in the class collectively agreed to undertake as their last project for the semester the translation of a 2600-word French business article for posting on the English version of a consulting-firm website. The content of the article (the notion of *emergence* as applied to the phenomenon of the Silicon Valley) was beyond the abilities of any one of the students individually and would be a challenge for a professional translator. But these students had worked together enough to know that they were up to the task collectively, under guidance. After previewing the text, identifying all unfamiliar concepts and references (e.g., Heisenberg, Prigogine, complexity sciences, catastrophe theory, fractals), and dividing the preliminary research among themselves, they each translated a section of the article and brought it through several revisions based on numerous discussions and proposed edits by fellow classmates and myself as the professor. They then merged their work into a single document and began the work of smoothing for style and consistency.

One student, Roxanne Elliott, wrote:

> The "Manageur ou Emergeur" translation was definitely my favorite out of all of the translations we have done. I really needed to fully understand the meaning of the text before I could translate the first word, which was a challenge but a pleasure. . . [I] was an important influence in my group. I was reading the translations of three other people, all of whom had translated the words without truly understanding the underlying concepts. By saying that, I do not intend to say that I am a genius or anything, just that perhaps my background and interests are conducive to my grasping of Baudry's ideas with facility. I spent time explaining the ideas to my classmates, which in the end helped them to produce a good translation. (2000)

Elliott's statement offers a glimpse into the substantive peer-to-peer learning that was transpiring with no teacher intervention, the collective benefit of multiple perspectives, and the students' mutual support, respect and reliance on one another. It also shows Elliott's growing awareness of and confidence in her own abilities.

Without such dynamic interaction, students tend to repeat past strategies, banging their heads against the same unyielding walls. Going solo — trying on their own to satisfy some elusive standard they assume to exist based on everything they're told they've done right or wrong — they may progress by sheer force of will, honest self-examination, and keen observation . . . but ploddingly so. Interaction, dialogue, and collaboration accelerate and enrich the process, which becomes stimulating and engaging — perhaps the most important carry-overs into professional life. Furthermore, it is only through interaction with peers and members of the professional community that students develop a sense of belonging and legitimacy within that community. This is how they develop the nucleus of a professional network and the self-assurance they will need to land a job or attract clients.

From this social-constructivist perspective, Kiraly identifies three goals of translator education:

– Raise students' awareness of the factors involved in translation,
– Help them develop their own self-concept as a translator, and
– Assist in the collaborative construction of individually tailored tools that will allow [them] to function within the language mediation community upon graduation (ibid.: 49).

If these are the goals of translator education, then they must also be the goals and whole thrust of the assessment method used. Otherwise, both students and teachers may be left with a sense of incongruity. On the one hand, classes are dynamic workshops in which everyone's insights, questions, contributions, and strokes of brilliance are relied upon and collectively appreciated; on the other, each piece of student work is autocratically assigned a definitive grade by the teacher.

Pedagogically, one might aim to raise students' awareness of factors involved in translation, inspire reflection on the translation process, help them develop the practices and instincts of a seasoned translator, improve the quality of their translations, and initiate them into the community of translators. But if any of this is accomplished, it is typically through class discussions, collaborative activities, detailed written feedback, process modeling, and one-on-one conversations — not through assessment. Assessment tends to be incidental to, if not at cross-purposes with, the intended learning.

Many teachers of translation and other applied disciplines assume that teaching in an academic institution means they have no choice but to dutifully assess their students according to the traditional paradigm. In translation programs, this means assigning a series of translations and exams, grading them all oneself, and calculating the average at the end of the semester. But there remains a nagging awareness that such practices are incongruous with efforts to empower students and help them become competent, autonomous translators able to succeed professionally. To compensate, teachers who recognize the social constructivist nature of translator education innovate around the edges. They may introduce collaborative work, peer editing, real projects for real clients, reflective self-assessment statements, and student-selected specialization projects. They may also conduct "toolbox" workshops that guide students through a critical analysis of their own ingenious solutions and chronic difficulties to heighten their awareness and enable them to identify and internalize strategies to the point that they become reflexive, intuitive. But typically the basic assessment framework remains unchanged.

I myself operated in this fashion for many years — until I learned of the portfolio approach successfully instituted in the teacher training masters program for Teachers of English to Speakers of Other Languages (MA-TESOL) at my own institution.

Under the guidance of professors Jean Turner and Peter Shaw, MA-TESOL students benefited immensely from developing portfolios at the course level. Then, in 1993, the graduation requirement of a final 3-hour closed-book written comprehensive examination and 15-page position paper were replaced (primarily in response to student dissatisfaction with the existing mechanism) with a student program-portfolio "intended to reflect the accumulated work and learning achieved during the course of study." (Leng et al.: 4)

Based on the MA-TESOL experience, a similar approach has been piloted in translation courses within the Graduate School of Translation and Interpretation (GSTI) to bring assessment practices into line with a social constructivist teaching philosophy, provide students with a more coherent academic experience, and transform the very mechanism of assessment into an "integral part of the teaching/learning dialogue" (Kiraly 2000: 140) and a springboard for successful transition into professional life. Through this pilot, it has become apparent that assessment does not have to be endured as a necessary academic evil, but that it can provide a positive framework enhancing the coherence, meaning, and value of efforts by both faculty and students — at last partners in this endeavor.

Several types of portfolios have been piloted in GSTI. This article describes the "course portfolio" and the "professional portfolio" as a basis for further discussion and as examples of the range of forms portfolios can take in the translation context.

The course portfolio

The course portfolio is limited in scope to a single course and aimed at providing a framework for learning and assessment over an entire semester. It is what Herman et al. call a "working" portfolio (1996: 34), in that it contains all of the work performed in the context of the course. The pedagogical purposes in assigning the portfolio are (1) to support student reflection and the development of professional discretion (the ability to think like a translator to solve unique, complex problems), (2) to enable the students to experience the satisfaction of bringing their work to completion, i.e. up to publishable quality, (3) to provide students with a framework for organizing their work and documenting their progress, and (4) to provide faculty and the students with a basis for measuring progress, readiness for subsequent courses, and the effectiveness of teaching.

The portfolio guidelines provided to first-semester students are shown in Figure 1.

Course Portfolio Guidelines

Basic Translation Exercises

Purpose
The purposes of the portfolio for this class are:
- To help you glean as much learning as possible from the work you are doing this semester.
- To serve as a significant basis of assessment (40%) for this course.
- To assemble model translations and related material for future reference.

Contents

Midterm and end-of-semester self-review
Based on a review of all of your work to date, write a statement (approx. 2-5 pp.) discussing the following:
- How your knowledge and translation skills have evolved. Please provide concrete examples from your work.
- What you got out of the various assignments.
- What you need to work on.
- Any concerns you have.
- How you are feeling about translation as a profession; how this has evolved; directions you want to pursue.

Work product
A) All write-ups on readings.
B) All translation assignments with source text (marked assignment originally submitted/peer edited and all revisions, in reverse chronological order).
C) All timed translations (revisions optional).
D) Other projects that have been key to your learning this semester.
E) Useful ancillary material you gathered or developed in conjunction with the above (terminology, parallel texts, resources).

Assessment
The portfolio will be assessed on the following criteria:
- Average of original grades on translations (= baseline grade).
- Learning achieved as evidenced by your self-reviews and revised translations.
- Completeness.
- Professional presentation (organized, nicely formatted, polished).
The last three criteria will not lower but may significantly improve your baseline grade.

Figure 1. The portfolio guidelines provided to first-semester students

Teachers who have worked significantly with portfolios and authentic assessment will surely see much here to criticize: the students have been *told* what to include, not asked to *select* specific pieces based on teacher-defined or student-defined criteria; the basic coursework consists of *assignments* rather than projects undertaken by choice; assessment is still largely based on discrete grades and on only two perspectives — that of the student and that of the teacher. Indeed, each of these "problems" indicates a new direction to be considered and explored.

Yet the course portfolio already presents a number of advantages over traditional assessment in translator training:

Revision

The whole focus of this portfolio, and the corresponding course, is on revision, shifting value from the grades earned on weekly assignments to all that can be learned from grappling with one's own honest assessment and feedback from teachers, peers, and others. It is one thing to acknowledge, "Oh yeah, what I wrote in English doesn't really capture the idea in the French" or "I see now how that heavy string of nouns obscures the point." It is quite another to go back and concretely grapple with the problem, to find a solution. This is where the real learning takes place, where seeing becomes knowing. But students are not inclined to go back and seriously revise unless significant assessment value is placed on that process. As one student, Julia Noguchi, put it: "Although it is tempting, and even a habit in most classes, to just put a difficult assignment aside after receiving a grade on it, I found that reworking these translations made a huge difference in how much I got out of them."

Practically speaking, the students are encouraged to undertake revisions shortly after discussion and feedback so they can resubmit them and/or have them reviewed by peers or others one or more times until completely satisfied.

Process-oriented

The portfolio thus engages the students in this learning-through-revision process by placing value not just on the product of their initial efforts, but on what happens to their work and to themselves as translators as they see those products evolve to publication quality. What naturally emerges over the course of the semester is an appreciation of the fact that everyone's abilities, the teacher's included, are a work in progress, and that the whole value of a translation class lies in the heightened competence everyone achieves through the contribution of each person's talents, knowledge, and perspectives.

Grounded reflection

Much is to be said for reflective statements in general. They enable the writer to self-observe and hence to self-mentor. However, reflection is all the more fruitful when grounded in a given problem. "Knowing and learning — and therefore reflection — occur within the context of a problem" (Yancey 1996: 90). In translation, the problem may be a particular text or a recurring strategy, technique, tendency, or difficulty encountered in a series of translations.

It is in this regard that portfolios differ from journals. Like the course portfolio, journals usually focus on a student's insights and experience with respect to a class and its coursework. Yet the reflection and the work itself exist in parallel, side by side, like the two tracks of a railroad that one "sees" converging on the horizon. The reflection may carry over into the work, but tangible bridge-building between the two is often left to chance and the student's own initiative. In portfolios, the two are intimately intertwined, presented as an integrated whole in a single physical "container," typically a binder. The reflective statement directly introduces and discusses the works presented, and these works, along with all drafts, provide the raw material on which the insights and conclusions in the reflective statements are based.

Value-creation and meaning-making

Despite good intentions, we all know what typically happens to coursework after a course has ended: it remains stuffed in a folder, never to be touched again until summarily tossed five years later when rediscovered by chance in a dusty cardboard box in the garage. Just as the value of a new car drops precipitously the moment it is driven off the dealer's lot, so coursework tends to lose any future usefulness the moment the last class session has adjourned.

In contrast, the portfolio requires that students organize and present their materials and work as *part of the course itself.* After each course and upon graduation, portfolio students thus have all significant artifacts of their prior academic endeavors neatly organized and presented such that they can be relocated easily and used for various future purposes. Students typically present their portfolio in a labeled binder with tab dividers, and each piece is showcased in a plastic sheet protector whose upper left edge opens for easy removal and re-insertion of the document. The very presentation says, "What you are about to read is both impressive and important."

These details of presentation may seem mundane, but have immense psychological impact analogous to the effect on an artist of seeing his canvases framed, displayed, and lighted just so on a gallery wall and contextualized by a biography, his own accompanying commentary, and critics' reviews.

The acts of compiling, reflecting on, and presenting a body of work lead to an expanded view and give new meaning to each element within that continuum.

Student voice

The portfolio is introduced by the student's own experience, self-assessment, and reflective discussion of the work presented. His or her own voice thus becomes a framing factor in assessment of the work and in the focus of future efforts. As Porter and Cleland point out in their book *The Portfolio as a Learning Strategy*: "The answer(s) to the question, 'What needs to be done next?' can only be determined when individual strengths, weaknesses, needs, and questions are brought to the conscious level of both student and teacher" (1995: 45). The reflective nature of the portfolio does just that, the student's own reflections becoming the basis, the starting point, for a written dialogue between teacher and student and potentially with peers and professionals outside the academic program. While the teacher is the one who assesses the course portfolio, that assessment is subsequent to and framed by the student's own self-assessment in the introductory reflective statement. In other words, the teacher has at least begun to share, if not "vacate" judgmental space. As Yancey points out in discussing findings by Hilgers (1986):

> [T]o the extent that teachers evaluated student texts, the students deferred making judgments about their texts themselves, preferring teacher judgment to peer response or self-assessment. It is as though there is only a certain amount of space for judgment; if the teacher takes that space, students can or will not, as authors or as peer respondents. (Yancey 1996: 92)

Aside from assessment, hearing the student's voice is significant in other regards as well. It makes the translator behind the work very evident. Here, we have the translator laying out the thought processes and considerations that went into the translations: why certain suggested edits have been intentionally rejected, what difficulties were encountered, how the translations evolved, and in what ways they manifest the individual translator's talents, insecurities, experimentation, and mental/emotional state when producing and revising them and considering them in hindsight as elements in a body of work. The portfolio itself stands as evidence that all of these factors *do* influence a translation, whether or not the translator is consciously aware of it. It also shows that conscious awareness of these influences translates into greater mastery. Extralinguistic factors of time constraints, mental/emotional state, work environment, etc., cease to be wild cards that can make or break the success of a translation, and instead become explicit parameters of a process that the translator actively controls to achieve an optimum outcome.

Written dialogue

As discussed above, assessment is traditionally one-way. The teacher has the only say. In contrast, the portfolio creates a concrete framework for dialogue back and forth about the student's work, insights, frustrations, and accomplishments.

This physical, written mode of dialogue is qualitatively different from oral discussions in class and one-on-one conferences outside of class. It distills and crystallizes insights that might otherwise remain ephemeral, documents those insights as they apply to the student's own work, and provides a structuring mechanism for their integration.

Completion

Through iterations of feedback and revision, even beginning students are able to produce work that meets professional standards. Rather than ending the semester with a pile of marked-up translation exercises, they have a showcase of publishable-quality translations they have produced — along with the sequence of drafts it took to get there. "It is very satisfying to see a final version along with the revisions and thus, laid out before you, the progress you have made," explained Hilary James upon completing her first semester (2000). This achievement brings a huge sense of accomplishment that directly nourishes the students' self-concept as translators. They more readily see themselves as "legitimate" translators honing their art, not as lowly "wannabe" translators.

Furthermore, these polished translations become a personal corpus of model translations to which the students can refer when grappling with a text of the same type or on the same subject. In other words, they can begin to refer to their *own* work for reliable guidance and not just to that of outside authorities.

Assessment

In the context of the Basic Translation Exercises course, the portfolio currently accounts for 40% of the course grade. It essentially corresponds to the formative "homework" portion of the grade, the remaining 60% being divided between timed translation exams (50%) and sight translation (10%). In accordance with the overall GSTI curriculum, the exam scores are summative for purposes of entry into subsequent courses and as practice for the GSTI professional exit exams and for employment exams administered by international organizations, government agencies, and some translation companies. Sight translation — reading a newly encountered text aloud in a language other than that in which it is written — is assessed separately given its oral nature.

Students are informed that assessment of the portfolio is based on four criteria:

- Average of grades on original translations (= baseline grade)
- Learning achieved, as evidenced by student statements and revised translations
- Completeness
- Professional presentation

There is no detailed definition of each criterion. There are a number of reasons for this. First, translation grading criteria are provided and discussed separately in accordance with the nature of the various projects. For an insightful discussion of approaches to translation scoring criteria, see Kiraly's chapter on assessment (2000: 140–168). Second, rather than make the students' eyes glaze over with involved written qualifications of each criterion, detailed guidance is provided through a mid-semester portfolio review.

The mid-semester review offers a concrete context for clarifying discussions about the purposes, audience, content, and assessment of the portfolio in direct connection with a "problem," i.e., the time has come to translate the idea of a portfolio into the physical thing. At this point, the portfolio includes a mid-semester self-review and work to date (original translations submitted along with all subsequent revisions, and any other work and materials). It is not graded. But the students do receive detailed feedback under each assessment rubric and are able to compare their various "embodiments" of the portfolio for inspiration. The advantage of this approach to criteria definition — as opposed to a static, written definition that the professor provides in advance in anticipation of needed clarification — is that it uses the students' own work in progress as exemplars, responds to real questions, and incorporates surprise innovations by the students, thus becoming part of a dynamic process.

Impact on classes, teaching, and students

As the preceding discussion makes evident, the portfolio offers many tangible benefits as a course framework, a basis for reflection, a mechanism for dialogue, a measure of progress, an organizational tool, a showcase of student work, and so on. As summarized by Maja Kos, a first-semester student:

> The assignment that has been the most beneficial to me this semester has been putting together the portfolio. It has given me a chance to review all of my work, learn from my mistakes, see my progress and, most importantly, it has given me something to show for all of the work I have done thus far — a collection of finished products. It has given me a sense of satisfaction. (2000)

From a teaching perspective, the most profound impact of the portfolio is a psychological one. As the focal point of the course, the portfolio sets a tone. It makes clear that students have both the freedom and the responsibility to be the masters of their own learning; it legitimizes them as professional translators whose work merits being showcased; it serves as a constant reminder to faculty as well as to students that the teacher is there to accompany and support them along their own paths, not run them through a particular academic obstacle course. These psychological outcomes may not be tangible in the sense of hard metrics, but they are most definitely palpable. In short, the portfolio lends credibility to teachers' claims of support for socially constructed learning.

The professional portfolio

A persistent problem in the three months or so preceding graduation has been that students lose focus and motivation. What difference is doing one more translation or tracking down one more specialized term going to make in whether they pass their classes and their professional exit exams? Why invest more than the bare minimum? Of more pressing concern is landing a job, deciding where to move, setting up shop as a freelancer and finding clients, being able to start paying off tens of thousands of dollars in student loans, etc. Rather than fight this natural tendency, I decided to work with it full throttle using a "professional" portfolio in the context of the Advanced Translation Seminar class. Figure 2 shows the guidelines provided to students.

This type of portfolio incorporates more of the characteristics typically advocated:

Professional Portfolio Guidelines

Advanced Translation Seminar

Purpose
The portfolio for this class is a "professional portfolio," meaning that it is not designed so much to deepen learning as it is to compile the sample work and business tools you will likely need as you embark upon your career.

Format
Generally a binder, but well-organized portfolios presented as websites, on other electronic media, or in hybrid form are welcome. Use the medium or media that you feel will best serve your practical needs in the future.

Contents

I. Cover statement

In your cover statement, please cover the following points:

- The nature of translation (and potentially interpretation) work you are pursuing (in-house, freelance, where, subject areas . . .), and your vision of what you would like to be doing in 3 years.
- What skills, knowledge and know-how you've developed that will enable you to be successful in your chosen path.
- How those skills, knowledge and know-how are reflected in the format and content you have selected for your portfolio. Discuss why you included each piece that you did and what it shows.

Figure 2. Part 1 of professional portfolio guidelines

Selection

Within the guidelines provided, the contents of the professional portfolio are left entirely to the discretion of the student according to his or her personal goals. Those goals must be articulated, and each piece presented in light of them.

As I now teach it, the Advanced Translation Seminar consists principally of translation and peer editing of projects of the students' own choosing, ideally "authentic" remunerated or *pro bono* projects for real clients. These translations can, but do not have to be, among the translations included in the professional portfolio. The main criteria for inclusion are relevance to and evidence of competence in the type of work the student is aiming to secure professionally.

II. Work product
A) A selection of 5 to 8 perfectly polished original translations along with a clean, legible copy of the source text.
B) If applicable, terminology or other types of work related to your objectives.
C) Your own business development research and tools.

For future freelancers, these might include, for example:

- a business card,
- letterhead,
- a c.v.,
- an invoice form,
- a model contract,
- a translator's affidavit,
- application for a fictitious business name,
- sample Schedule C and other tax information,
- a system for tracking business income and expense,
- a system of contact management and job tracking,
- an inventory of potential sources of work (on-line and other) along with any action you've taken with regard to specific ones,
- steps toward or evidence of membership in professional organizations and securing various credentials (e.g., State Department, ATA accreditation, U.N., E.U., OAS, AIIC, World Bank).

If you are seeking in-house employment:

- job leads,
- applications,
- c.v.,
- cover letter(s),
- research into and action toward obtaining any residency, work-permit and tax-related papers you will need if seeking employment abroad.

Assessment

The portfolio will be assessed on the following criteria:

- To what extent would your statement and sample work convince an employer/client to hire or contract with you for a job.
- To what extent do your business development research and tools show that you are ready for business and/or well positioned to land an in-house job in your desired location and to start working there.

Figure 2. Part 2 of professional portfolio guidelines

Audience and assessment

Like the course portfolio, the professional portfolio represents only a portion of the course grade. The intended audience for the introductory statement and work product elements of the portfolio consists of potential employers and/or clients. In reality, the audience is essentially the course professor. This discrepancy has led to some confusion, with students personally addressing the professor in the familiar form of a letter as they might for a course portfolio focused on learning. For the portfolio to be a means by which students refashion and present themselves as fully autonomous professional translators, such traces of "studenthood" must be dropped. Such reframing is easily achieved through a mid-semester portfolio review. Another more fundamental remedy would be to have the audience for all or part of the portfolio include real outside reviewers from the student's targeted segment of the translation industry, much along the lines practiced by Kiraly (2000: 140–163).

Impact on classes, teaching, students

The main impact of the professional portfolio is that it has brought coursework and assessment in the Advanced Translation Seminar into congruity with the students' true needs and interests at this point in their transition from academic to professional life. The portfolio makes that transition *the very focus* of the course, not something that is hoped will, with luck, happen subsequently. The course thus does not *compete* with the students' personal post-graduation agendas, but explicitly supports and furthers them.

The professional portfolio enables the students to walk away with a concrete showcase of their work and a personally developed kit of business development tools to jump-start their careers. It also has significant psychological impact. By affirming each individual as an autonomous, uniquely skilled practitioner on a unique professional path, the portfolio helps build the confidence and wherewithal it takes to actually move down that road.

Design considerations

In their myriad forms, portfolios offer a concrete framework for fundamentally shifting the basis of classroom instruction and student assessment away from discretely graded assignments to students' own appreciation — in dialogue with teachers and peers — of their evolving body of work and development as "reflective practitioners" (Schön 1987). But what type of portfolio is appropriate for a given context and purpose? How does one go about defining what it will and will not include and how it will be assessed?

A helpful guide in this regard is an article by J. Herman, M. Gearheart, and P. Aschbacher entitled "Portfolios for Classroom Assessment: Design and Implementation Issues" (1996). The authors begin by cautioning that

> [B]ecause portfolios contain the products of classroom instruction, by defini-
> tion, they should be integrated with it, not an intrusive add-on. In contrast to
> the focus of traditional testing on discrete skills, well-designed portfolios contain
> student work reflecting students' accomplishments toward significant curricu-
> lum goals, particularly those that require complex thinking and the use of mul-
> tiple resources. (27)

First, the portfolio should "serve a clearly specified assessment purpose" (ibid.: 28). Portfolios have many possible purposes. Those cited by Herman et al. include:

- Accountability; evaluating program or curriculum effectiveness
- Evaluating individual student progress; grading; certifying student accomplishment
- Diagnosing students' needs; informing classroom instructional planning;
  improving instructional effectiveness
- Encouraging teacher efficacy; encouraging reflective practice at the school
  and classroom levels; supporting teachers' professional development
- Encouraging student efficacy; promoting student self-assessment; motivat-
  ing student performance. (ibid.: 29)

In most cases, portfolios serve multiple purposes, and those purposes can come into conflict. Herman et al. thus recommend setting priorities: What are the most important aims of the assessment — the purposes that absolutely need to be achieved? Which are of secondary importance, and may be phased in after critical priorities have been met? (ibid.: 30).

In sum: keep it simple. Complex hybrid portfolios at the course level are often less effective than portfolios with a singular primary purpose. Straight-forward portfolio purposes make for clear goals and expectations, which in turn facilitate assessment and enable students to focus on the tasks at hand rather than waste time and energy feeling overwhelmed or confused. Less is more, especially in early experimental phases when both students and teacher(s) are just beginning to work with portfolios.

The next step is to determine priority goals for student performance. "Portfolios focus classroom attention on and communicate about what students should be learning and what curriculum outcomes are most valued. [. . .] What should students know and be able to do?" (ibid.: 31). More specifically, consider:

1. What concepts and principles central to a working knowledge of this discipline do I want my students to understand and be able to apply?
2. What are the important dispositions and social skills that I want my students to develop?
3. What reflective and analytic strategies do I want my students to develop? (Herman et al. 2000: 32)

In the context of a translation course, concepts and principles might include: translating meaning versus translating words, text type, distance from source text, register. Desired dispositions and social skills could be: spirit of teamwork, process skills that facilitate collaboration, appreciating one's individual strengths, having confidence in one's abilities. Strategies might include: reflecting on the translation process used, evaluating its effectiveness, deriving one's own plans for how it can be improved.

Other questions adapted from Herman et al. include: should it be a showcase portfolio (i.e., contain best pieces only), or should it be a working portfolio (i.e., contain all work)? Should students include their work from all of their courses or just one class? Should they write a letter of introduction to their portfolio? Should it contain only final versions of work, or also notes, drafts, and other evidence of the processes students used when producing the work?

The answers to these questions naturally point to what the portfolio should include. When it comes to identifying specific tasks, one might ask, "What can I have my students do to show how well they have achieved a particular outcome or goal?" (ibid.: 33).

Finally, scoring criteria must be defined and communicated. "The structure and content of scoring need to reflect the purpose of the portfolio assessment, and criteria need to be focused on aspects of student performance which are consonant with those purposes" (ibid.: 36). Most fundamentally, is the assessment to be summative or formative, focused on accomplishment or progress? The translation course portfolio described focuses on both, but emphasizes the latter. The professional portfolio focuses squarely on accomplishment and professional initiative.

Conclusion

A portfolio approach to course design can bring one's teaching and assessment practices into greater congruity. It offers students a more coherent and empowering academic experience through which they can gain the authority, confidence, skills, tools, and sample work products they will need to successfully embark on their careers as autonomous, competent translators.

References

Burch, C. B. 1999. "Inside the portfolio experience: The student's perspective." *English Education* 32 (1): 34–49.

Duffy, M. L., Jones, J., and Thomas, S. 1999. "Using portfolios to foster independent thinking." *Intervention in School and Clinic* 35 (1): 34–37.

Dewey, J. 1974. *John Dewey on Education: Selected Writings*, R. D. Archambault (ed). Chicago: University of Chicago Press.

Elliott, R. 2000. "Basic translation exercises course portfolio." Monterey, CA: Monterey Institute of International Studies. Photocopy.

Grusko, R. 1998. "Realizing the power of reflection." In *Why Am I Doing This? Purposeful Teaching Through Portfolio Assessment*, G. Martin-Kniep (ed), 99–111. Portsmouth, NH: Heineman.

Herman, J., Gearheart, M., and Aschbacher, P. 1996. "Portfolios for classroom assessment: design and implementation issues." In *Writing Portfolios in the Classroom: Policy and Practice, Promise and Peril*, R. Calfee and P. Perfumo (eds), 27–62. Mahwah, NJ: Erlbaum.

Hilgers, T. 1986. "How children change as critical evaluators of writing: Four three-year case studies." *Research in the Teaching of English*, 20: 36–55.

James, H. 2000. "Basic translation exercises course portfolio." Monterey, CA: Monterey Institute of International Studies. Photocopy.

Kiraly, D. 2000. *A Social Constructivist Approach to Translator Education. Empowerment from Theory to Practice*. Manchester, UK: St. Jerome Publishing.

Kos, M. 2000. "Basic translation exercises course portfolio." Monterey, CA: Monterey Institute of International Studies. Photocopy.

Leng, J. 1997. "The multi-faceted professional portfolio." Monterey, CA: Monterey Institute of International Studies. Photocopy.

Leng, J., Shaw, P., and Turner, J. "The triune portfolio: Resolving the tensions among the personal, the academic and the professional." Monterey, CA: Monterey Institute of International Studies. Photocopy.

Porter, C., and Cleland, J. 1995. *The Portfolio as a Learning Strategy*. Portsmouth, NH: Heinemann.

Schön, D. 1987. *Educating the Reflective Practitioner*. San Francisco: Jossey-Bass Publishers.

Shaklee, B.,Barbour, N., Ambrose, R., and Hansford, S. 1997. *Designing and Using Portfolios.* Boston: Allyn & Bacon.

Yancey, K. 1996. "Dialogue, interplay, and discovery: Mapping the role and the rhetoric of reflection in portfolio assessment." In *Writing Portfolios in the Classroom: Policy, Practice, Promise and Peril.* R. Calfee and P. Perfumo (eds), 83–102. Mahwah, NJ: Lawrence Erlbaum Associates.

Assessing assessment

Translator training evaluation and the needs of industry quality assessment

Fanny Arango-Keeth and Geoffrey S. Koby

For the last two decades, translation scholars have been working to develop the various fields involved in translation studies: theory, practice, pedagogy, and evaluation (or quality assessment). Of these four fields, however, translation evaluation has remained the least developed, and for many scholars it is still perceived as a "probabilistic endeavor," one in which subjectivity constitutes the most salient criterion. This subjectivity complicates the question of "measuring" or "judging" translation by introducing 'highly variable notions' "that frequently are not expressed overtly" (Maier 2000: 137). Another factor that can affect objectivity when judging translation evaluation is related to the many different purposes that a given translation may serve and the different contexts in which translation can occur. In this regard, Susanne Lauscher reminds us of a number of different purposes that an evaluator may have in mind when assessing the quality of a translation:

> The judgment itself fulfills a purpose. It may serve to examine a translator's qualification for a particular translation job, to assess whether he or she has satisfied the requirements for a specific translation task, to inform a translation student about his or her progress, to inform the reader about the quality of the translation of a new work of fiction, etc. [...]. A judgment is also oriented towards a prospective addressee. It will look different depending on whether it targets professional translators, the audience of the target text, clients or translation students [...]. (Lauscher 2000: 163)

Recognizing the need to analyze the notions and variables that surface in the process of judging the quality of translations, scholars in the field as well as translator trainers began to focus on setting standard procedures to evaluate translations, procedures which would result in the creation of translation quality assessment instruments that encompass what Lauscher calls the "complexity of the translation process" (164).

Despite this growing preoccupation, translation scholars, translation agencies and professional accreditation organizations have yet to collaborate in setting these evaluation standards. Lauscher argues that any scholarly effort to theorize about translation and to create evaluation procedures that meet didactic purposes must also be informed by the professional world of translation in order to represent more universal and realistic evaluation standards:

> At the same time, those involved in translation practice, i.e., people who need and are involved in the production of translations, could become more aware of their respective roles and responsibilities in the translation and evaluation processes. Translation quality assessment and the judgment of translations are matters of communication, co-operation and consent. (164)

In addition, Gerard McAlester recommends that a consensus for evaluating translation adequacy should arise by first setting basic standards for professional accreditation that reflect professional needs and standards, and then applying these standards when training translators in an academic setting:

> In short, what is called for is a set of international standards of translation adequacy. This could well be done under the auspices of an international organization such as FIT (*Fédération Internationale de Traducteurs*) and transmitted down through national affiliates. A profession should be able to define its own standards of competence. It would be a suitable project for the new millennium. (2000: 240)

In order to help bridge the gap between the evaluation standards and procedures used in academic settings and the quality assessment standards and procedures used in the translation industry, we conducted a Survey of Translation Quality Assessment (see Appendix A). This survey was designed to allow us: (1) to identify and characterize the translation evaluation procedures and guidelines used in academic programs and the quality assessment procedures and guidelines used in the translation industry; (2) to compare and contrast these procedures and guidelines; and (3) to propose adjustments in the areas of assessment that reflect McAlester's ideal of consensus. The survey was sent electronically to academic and non-academic translation professionals in North America.[1] Although our analysis of the results of the survey will be essentially descriptive, we propose to demonstrate which evaluation variables may represent obstacles to consensus-building with regard to translation quality standards.

Prior to conducting the actual survey, we identified three theoretical considerations that have been extensively addressed by translation scholars when describing the confusion that exists today regarding the evaluation or assessment of translations. By taking these ideas into consideration, we hoped to ensure that the survey would encompass a measurable body of information addressing issues underlying potential consensus. The three considerations were: (1) lack of a standardized terminology for evaluating translations; (2) existence of a variety of assessment procedures resulting from different theoretical approaches to translation; and (3) lack of a consensus regarding what translation competence involves. The first consideration is addressed in items 5 and 6 of the survey, the second in item 7 and the third in item 5.

The first consideration we have identified in the survey is related to the interchangeable use of the terms "evaluation" and "assessment." In a special issue of *The Translator* entitled *Evaluation and Translation*, Maier asserts that determining the value of a translation is considered by some as *evaluation* and by others as *assessment*. She points out that these two terms can sometimes be considered synonymous: "[s]ome refer to this determination as *evaluation*, others use *assessment*; and many, if not most, use the two interchangeably, often without indications that they consider the terms synonymous" (137). Nevertheless, some efforts have been made to clarify this terminology and to identify and define different types of translation quality assessment procedures. In this light, Paul Kussmaul describes two types of evaluation protocols in translation: product-oriented error analysis and quality assessment (1995: 5). The first type corresponds to the process of evaluating a translation for didactic purposes and the second to verifying the suitability of a translation as a product to be submitted to a client. We propose to use Kussmaul's terminology in our descriptive analysis of the survey results each time the terms "evaluation" and "assessment" are used in items 6 and 7.

Louise Brunette has also addressed this problem in her article "Towards a Terminology of Translation Quality Assessment." Observing both academic translation programs and the translation industry, she identifies the types of evaluation procedures used in the two settings and distinguishes five assessment procedures: (1) didactic revision — conducted by translation trainers, focusing on the formative or summative evaluation of translated texts; (2) translation quality assessment — conducted by translation managers, concentrating on the quality of a translated text for productivity purposes; (3) quality control — conducted by revisers in order to assure that the translated text complies with linguistic and pragmatic standards; (4) pragmatic revision — conducted by revisors who compare source and target texts in order to improve translation performance; and (5) fresh look — conducted by persons fulfilling the role of the first reader who read the target text as an independent unit and verify that it is coherent and cohesive (2000: 173). We have employed both Kussmaul's and Brunette's terminology in order to identify the lack of agreement in the use of evaluation terminology and to identify the different evaluation and assessment procedures used.

A second consideration related to the translation theories from which these procedures are derived further complicates the standardization of evaluation procedures. This consideration is discussed at length by Juliane House when she traces the five different theoretical approaches used by translation trainers and scholars to create evaluation criteria. Her classification of evaluation approaches ranges from the identification of anecdotal and subjective models to her highly sophisticated "functional-pragmatic model for translation quality assessment" (1999: 199).[2] When comparing and contrasting the evaluation and assessment criteria used by the participants in our survey to formal evaluation procedures, we will keep this terminology in mind so as to determine with more precision which translation theory or theories (if any) informed the evaluators' frame of reference.

Our third consideration is related to the way translation evaluators define translation competence. Translation scholars believe that the variety of criteria used to conceptualize "translation competence"[3] and the lack of a consensus as to what skills are necessary in order to be able to produce a competent and reliable translation significantly impact the selection of criteria in the creation of translation evaluation instruments.

For some of these scholars, translation competence is primarily conceived as a linguistic competence, as is the case with Jean Delisle et al. in *Translation Terminology*. According to these authors, translation ability consists, for the most part, in the translator's capacity to successfully manipulate source and target languages (1999: 152).[4] For other scholars, translation competence involves other sub-competences in addition to the linguistic one. Beverly Adab considers five competences that should be addressed when evaluating translations for training purposes: (1) language accuracy, (2) accuracy of message, (3) assumed knowledge and needs of target reader in both SL and TL, (4) any intertextual references contained in the ST, and (5) acceptability/readability (2000: 225).

Moreover, scholars constituting the membership of PACTE[5] define translation competence as "the underlying system of knowledge and skills needed to be able to translate" (Orozco 2000: 199). Mariana Orozco, a member of this research group, describes the sub-competences of this "underlying system." The first one is transfer competence, which is divided into four subcomponents: comprehension competence, deverbalization competence, re-expression competence, and competence in carrying out the translation project. In addition, she proposes five other components of "translation competence surrounding the transfer competence": (1) communicative competence in two languages, (2) extralinguistic competence, (3) instrumental-professional competence, (4) psycho-physiological competence, and (5) strategic competence (200–01).[6]

All the components and sub-components of translation competence and transfer competence characterized by Orozco can be equated to the various roles we asked the surveyed population to identify: quality assurance manager, project manager, translator, editor, proofreader, editor/revisor. Thus, by recognizing these roles and by analyzing the combinations in which they can occur, we are able to compare and contrast academic versus non-academic ideas of what constitutes translation competence.

Survey description and analysis

In Appendix A, we include the survey we used in order to meet the objectives mentioned in the introduction to this study. The survey consists of a questionnaire that is divided into three sections. The first section comprises items 1 through 3; it provides information about the surveyed population's professional profile. The second section includes two structured questions (items 4 and 5), where the fifty-two individuals responding to the survey were asked to identify the type of translation organization or organizations they belong to (translation agency, academic institution) and also to indicate the role or roles they fulfill in these organizations: quality managers, project managers, translators, editors/revisors, proofreaders, and professors/teachers. Section three presents two unstructured questions. In item 6, the individuals surveyed were required first to indicate whether they use a formal translation quality evaluation procedure and then to briefly describe it. In item 7, the survey participants were asked to indicate whether they use any formal evaluation guidelines or a grading scale for rating translation quality. If the answer was affirmative, they were prompted to describe the guidelines or scales they use.

A total of 873 questionnaires were sent by e-mail to a broad range of translation professors, teachers, agencies, and translation professionals in North America; approximately 100 professors representing about 50 institutions, 325 translation agencies, and 440 translation professionals listed in the American Translators Association database as possessing a doctoral degree were identified and sent materials. Fifty two individuals returned their questionnaires, a return of just under 6%.[7] (Many other professionals responded that they had never evaluated translations and thus their answers would not apply to our survey). From this population, we have established that 42% (15 individuals) work in academic organizations and 58% in non-academic orga-nizations (37 individuals working in translation agencies and freelancing).

When asked about the type of translation programs offered by their insti-tutions, 26% of the academic population responded that their institutions grant both translation degrees and certificates; 23% answered that their institu-tions offer both a translation certificate and translation courses; 23 % replied that their institutions offer translation courses; 18% indicated that their insti-tutions grant translation degrees; 5% stated that their institutions offer a translation certificate; and the final 5% stated that there were no offerings of translation courses at their institutions (Chart 1).

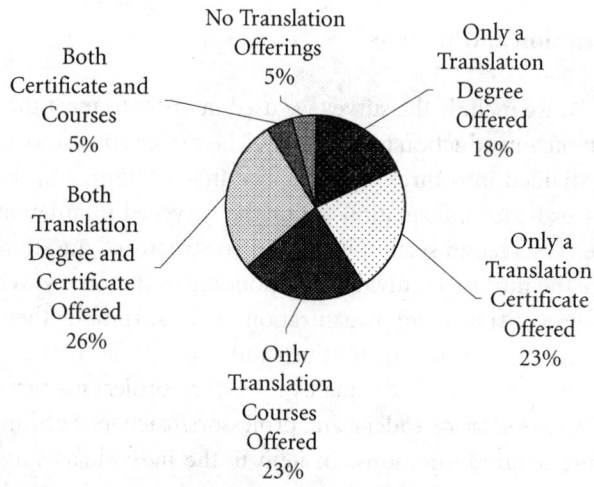

Chart 1. Types of academic programs

Regarding the types of roles that the 52 participants of the survey fulfill within the academic or professional spheres of translation, most of them fulfill at least two different roles simultaneously (See Table 1).

These results seem to indicate that 65% (34 individuals) of the total of the surveyed population fulfill two or more roles in the translation industry. They also suggest that there are eight individuals who work in both academic and professional translation environments.

As mentioned before, the two most relevant items in the survey which contained the information for this study were the open questions, 6 and 7.

Table 1. Types of Roles in Translation Evaluation

Role	Percentage
One role: Translation professor or teacher	27
Five roles: Quality Assurance manager, project manager, translator, editor/revisor, proofreader	12
Three roles: Translator, editor/revisor, proofreader	8
No roles checked	8
One role: Project manager	6
One role: Quality Assurance manager	6
All six roles	4
Two roles: Project manager, translator	4
Four roles: Translator, editor/revisor, proofreader, professor/teacher	4
Five roles: Quality Assurance manager, translator, editor/revisor, proofreader, professor/teacher	2
Four roles: Project manager, translator, editor/revisor, and proofreader	2
Four roles: Translator, editor/revisor, proofreader, professor/teacher	2
Four roles: Project manager, translator, editor/revisor, proofreader	2
Four roles: Quality Assurance manager, project manager, translator, editor/revisor	2
Two roles: Translator, editor/revisor	2
Three roles: Translator, editor/revisor, professor/teacher	2
Three roles: Quality Assurance manager, project manager, editor/revisor	2
Three roles: Quality Assurance manager, translator, editor/revisor	2

Fifteen individuals who identified themselves as translator trainers in academic settings replied to question 6. When asked to describe the procedure, two individuals did not reply, one indicated not understanding "what was [meant] by formal procedure;" one indicated a lack of awareness about the existence of a formal procedure at his/her institution; five answered that they mark major and minor errors (three made a reference to the error marking guidelines of the American Translators Association used as the basis for their evaluation system); 5 explained that the evaluation system used at their institutions depended on each individual instructor; and 1 indicated that "obvious checks for accuracy" were run. Among this population, those who provided a description of the evaluation procedure made no distinction between formative and summative evaluation, as defined by Brunette when she addresses "didactic revision" as a procedure to measure translation students' progress.

Based on these results, it seems that the underlying assumption for the academic population in this survey was to equate quality assurance with summative evaluation. The common denominator in their answers was to describe an "error marking protocol"[8] for assessing translations. Variables ranged from the use of objective categories such as "zero default linguistic product" to subjective appraisals such as "[m]y students and published translators considered me thorough."

On the other hand, the 22 survey participants who work in the translation industry replied that they use a formal procedure to assess translation quality. The majority of these participants agree on the existence of a protocol with four variables that are intended to assure translation quality: (1) selecting the translator, (2) editing, (3) proofreading, and (4) quality assurance. Five of these translation professionals described a protocol that maintains client-specific glossaries which are shared with translators and editors in order to guarantee terminological consistency.[9]

In general, the agencies represented by these participants favor employing translators with academic degrees, with professional accreditation, and with three and a half years of professional experience. They also prefer up-to-date computer equipment, which corresponds to the instrumental-professional competence proposed by Orozco in her description of translation competence. In fact, newly employed translators are tested with small projects and veteran translators and editors evaluate the "new translators' mastery of the subject matter, as well as the grammar, mechanics, accuracy, and style of their translation." Standards of professionalism related to the translators' interpersonal behavior — not their translation competence — are also preferred in the case of both freelance and in-house translators.

The editing process described by the surveyed population consists of verifying the translation's "completeness, consistency, grammatical accuracy," an area of translation evaluation that corresponds to the "quality control" area discussed by Brunette in the introductory section of this study. An electronic spelling check is also conducted as part of proofreading, after which the objective is to verify the target text's integrity, which in turn corresponds to the "fresh look" procedure also identified by Brunette.

Although the majority of the professional participants surveyed specified the formal procedures used in translation evaluation, one subject did not reply and another replied that in his/her agency they did not use any formal procedure.

In the academic/agency population, five individuals answered question 6. Two indicated that they do not follow a formal procedure and three of them replied that (1) the procedure varies by language, and (2) translations are checked by editors for accuracy and should meet the stylistic standards of the target language. One of the individuals in this group recognized that there is a subjective component when stylistically assessing translation quality.

No significant variations from the results stated above for the professionals in the translation industry were found in the freelancers and other groups. It is interesting to note that in one case in the freelancer group, one individual equated "quality assurance" with "editing."

It seems apparent that all the groups converge in perceiving the process of assessing translation quality as product-oriented,[10] a process that is then developed into an error-marking rating protocol, as will be observed in the analysis of question 7. This type of protocol parallels the second procedure studied by Brunette, classified as "translation quality assessment." Furthermore, the term "translation quality assurance" seems to be a term exclusively used by translators in the industry.[11]

When answering the open-ended question 7, 15 individuals from the academic group replied that they employ formal grading guidelines, 4 answered that they did not, and 1 responded that the guidelines were the same as the ones described in question 6.

In the case of the first 15 participants, the quality assessment instruments they use were mainly grading scales constructed around the "major and minor error" guidelines of the American Translators Association, the "Framework for Standardized Error Marking." These scales were, for the most part, based upon the number of errors in the translation (i.e., 3 minor errors and 1 major error or 0 minor errors and 2 major errors), which was then translated into a letter grade scale (i.e., 3 minor errors and 1 major error or 0 minor errors and 2 major errors = A). Besides the use of the "major error" and "minor error" labels, the assessment terms used to identify the error type varied from individual to individual. Nevertheless, most of these respondents take into account the following "translation assessment" or "translators' performance" areas when assessing translation projects and assignments: (1) comprehension of the source text, (2) grammatical appropriateness of the target text, (3) terminology, (4)coherence and cohesion, and (5) style.

One scholar within this group made a clear distinction among major errors (−3 to −5 points), significant errors (−2) and minor errors (−1). This scholar also included bonus marks in her grading scale to reward meritorious translation solutions.

Twenty-four professional translation agencies replied to this question. Fourteen professionals from these agencies stated that they follow formal assessment guidelines, which they refer to as a "checklist." Eight indicated that they do not use guidelines, one stated that she/he follows the ATA error marking framework, and one individual did not reply to the question.

The types of guidelines and/or checklists used vary from agency to agency as observed in the reports of the fourteen individuals that work for translation agencies. Some of them described extremely detailed guidelines that to a certain degree resemble the evaluation scales used by translator trainers in academic settings (i.e., ranging from major errors such as mistranslations, unnecessary additions, or global errors to minor errors such as format, spacing and typos).

One agency within this group indicated that their guidelines are based on the SAE J2450 metric.[12] This choice reflects an effort to standardize assessment criteria. Another agency included the in-house translation quality guidelines in the measures their project managers use to assure an error-free translation. In this particular case, what we found innovative about these guidelines was that they seemed to employ a two-way evaluation procedure. First, the editors use a checklist of questions on a rating scale from 1 to 10 to assess the quality of translations. Then the translators review the changes the editors made to their translations and are allowed to accept or reject these changes and actually "rate the editor's work on the same scale of 1 to 10."[13]

A third case is that of an agency that described its grading scale as addressing the issues that are traditionally used when rating translations, such as accuracy, grammar, word usage, and flow. In this case, however, their translation assessment procedure also includes a variable that is not focused on the evaluation of a given translation as a product but rather on the interpersonal relationships and skills of a given translator: "how easy the translator is to work with and if he or she is open to feedback." This variable goes beyond performance and represents an attitudinal assessment.

In the academic/agency group composed of 5 individuals, two indicated that they use the general error marking guidelines employed by the ATA, aiming at establishing the final quality of a translation project as a product. Two participants in this group replied that neither a grading scale nor an assessment instrument was used and one stated that "translation quality is much enhanced by hiring translators who have advanced degrees in the subject matter of the translation in question." This agency also included the category "translator's computer skills" as part of their assessment guidelines.

Finally, in the categories of academic/freelancer, agency/freelancer, freelancer, and other (8), no assessment scales were described.

It seems that some respondents found questions 6 and 7 to overlap. For all groups, numerical guidelines for rating translations should help translators in academic and non-academic settings detect major and minor errors.

Concluding remarks

When reviewing early approaches to translation quality assessment, we find that scholars such as Günther Kandler in 1963 emphasize the importance of stating the purpose of a given translation in order to assess its quality: "we should not forget that quality cannot possibly be assessed apart from the purpose of the translation" (295). Indeed, the purpose of translating in the academic and professional settings is different. The results of our study seem to confirm that in the case of academic settings, one of our initial theoretical considerations, about the existence of limited applied studies that address quality assessment, proved to be accurate. As Farzaneh Farahzad points out, the number of academic translation programs has increased; however, reliable assessment procedures and guidelines have yet to be developed (1992: 271). Indeed, the survey results for the academic group seem to show that no distinction between formative and summative evaluations within the wider spectrum of what we will call "didactic revision" has been made. At the same time, the academic community still needs to reach a consensus in terms of the evaluation instruments and rating scales they use. We would suggest that given the development of corpora-based translation instruction, new protocols for assessing translations can be established quickly, once the academic community realizes the importance of consensus. For example, Andrew Chesterman and Emma Wagner propose a protocol based on corpora:

> More recently, however, the availability of big computer corpora has led to an interest in what have been called **covert** or **distribution** or **quantitative** errors (see Kenny 1999; Laviosa-Braithwaite 1998). These are things like using a given word or structure much more often, or less often, than it would be used by native speakers writing a text of a similar sort on the same kind of subject. Scholars compare translations with such **parallel texts** in order to discover what marks translations as translations, if anything. Are there too many adjectives? Is the average sentence length too long? What about the distribution of finite verbs? (2001: 29)

In the case of non-academic settings, it is important to point out that the translation industry has contributed significantly to the effort to standardize translation quality assessment protocols. To illustrate the industry's preoccupation, Siu Ling Koo and Harold Kinds comment that "[w]hat is needed is a rigorous yet real-world approach, one that can be used easily, reliably, and consistently, often under intense time pressure" (2000: 147). In this same study, they call our attention to the case of an international localization agency in which the quality assurance model adopted helps develop a standard understanding of quality among translators, editors, revisors, and quality control managers in order to be able to assess translation quality using the same parameters:

> L&L, a Netherlands-based translation and localization services provider, has applied the Quality Assurance Model of the Localisation Industry Standards Association (LISA), and a translation sampling method developed for use with it. The tools used to grade both translators and translations have led to a more explicit, objective, and uniform understanding of quality among translators and reviewers. (147)

If we now turn our attention to the control of subjectivity when assessing translation errors, we find our survey confirms the idea that all groups are aware of this limitation and agree to the fact that subjectivity cannot be totally controlled. However, following Rick Woyde (2001), we suggest that a consensus about measuring "key translation qualities" should be achieved. Nevertheless, according to the survey results, translation agencies have been and are instrumental in creating, monitoring, analyzing and improving procedures to assure a common understanding of the type of translation error encountered in a translation project. For example, returning to the case of L&L observed by Koo and Kinds, the aim of the agency is to reduce subjective judgment since it "renders a sampling method of little use or difficult to implement" (151). The protocol followed to distinguish between a critical error or a major and a minor error is to identify critical errors in the process of evaluating the source text, which corresponds to what Mercedes Pellet describes as the "pre-translation check."[14]

To summarize, regarding the three variables we initially expected when discussing the aspects that constrain standardization of translation assessment tools, our survey confirms that they do affect the creation of assessment procedures and rating protocols. There is a need to standardize assessment terminology in order to reach a common understanding of quality standards demanded in academic and professional settings. Our survey has led us to believe that the first step in resolving this problem would be to create a committee with individuals from accreditation organizations and from academic and professional settings to propose general translation assessment terminology guidelines to ensure a uniform understanding of what it entails.

Regarding the different theories underlying the creation of assessment guidelines and translation quality rating protocols, the answers provided in items 6 and 7 revealed that an eclectic range of theoretical approaches are used, testifying to the complexity of the translation process. Most of the guidelines were based on a multilevel model of source and target text analysis that comprised models derived from language disciplines such as pragmatics, semiotics, semantics, linguistics, and stylistics.

When assessing the third variable, the lack of definition of what constitutes translation, we also observed that all respondents approached the assessment of a given translation according to their conceptualization of what constitutes translation competence. There is a recently developed body of research related to translation competence that can be used and applied to reach a common definition of translation competence, which goes beyond "transfer competence." As suggested by Orozco, other competences such as instrumental-professional competence, strategic competence, etc., surrounding transfer competence should also be considered when discussing the scope of translators' professional profiles.

Lauscher asserts that "translation quality assessment and the judgment of translations are matters of communication, co-operation and consent" (164). We recommend that professional organizations participate in an effort to create reliable translation quality assessment instruments that would go beyond error-marking protocols towards a more comprehensive approach, considering the complexity of what translation is. Concerted efforts should then be made by individuals representing accreditation organizations, academic institutions, and translation agencies to develop common assessment procedures and guidelines, which would then be adapted according to the "purpose of translation" in each of the settings.

Notes

1. Professional accreditation organizations were not included in this survey because our intent was to focus on actual practice in academic institutions and in the marketplace.

2. The five approaches that House distinguishes are: (a) the anecdotal and subjective in which the focus is the faithfulness to the original text; (b) the neo-hermeneutic approach (Stolze 1992); (c) the response-oriented, psycholinguistic approaches based on the dynamic equivalence principle developed by Eugene Nida; (d) the text-based analysis approaches proposed by Katarina Reiss and Hans J. Vermeer, focused on the *skopos* theory or the translation purpose; and (e) the functional-pragmatic model for translation quality assessment, a model which basically considers linguistic-situational particularities between source and target texts. (199)

3. "Although many authors talk of translation competence [...], few authors define the specific skills that constitute this competence" (House 1999: 199).

4. Delisle et al. define linguistic competence as "[t]he translator's ability to manipulate language by first comprehending and then reformulating the sense of the source text" (152).

In a note that accompanies this definition, the authors describe the scope of this competence:

> A translator's linguistic competence involves mastering at least three skills: the disassociation of the languages, the application of translation procedures, and writing the target text. This process takes place on three levels: the interpretation of the text, adherence to writing conventions, and the maintenance of textual coherence. (152)

5. PACTE is a research group from the Universitat Autònoma de Barcelona. They conduct empirical research on translation competence and evaluation.

6. Orozco defines "strategic competence" as "[a]ll the individual procedures, conscious and unconscious, verbal and non-verbal, used to solve the problems found during the translation process" (201).

7. Because the translation industry relies on e-mail, we considered the use of e-mail to be a valid method of reaching the target population. Schonlau et al. note that "for open-ended questions, the literature shows that e-mail responses are either longer than or the same length as mail responses" (2002: 31). Response rates to e-mail surveys range from 6% to 68% depending on the population surveyed (see Table A.4 in Schonlau 2002: 90). However, since our survey addressed as complete a group of the target populations as we could identify, we consider the response rate to be at least reasonably indicative of industry or academic practice.

8. When error marking, the basic distinction was made between major errors (mistranslations, missing text, major grammatical problems) and minor errors (poor word choice, poor sentence structure, translationese).

9. To assure terminological consistency, most of the agencies noted that they work with the final client in advance to approve the specialized glossaries.

10. Two limiting factors were detected in our survey. The first was that frequently no distinction was made between formative and summative evaluation procedures when assessing translation quality in academic settings. The second was not making a distinction between graduate and undergraduate levels when carrying out "didactic revisions."

11. As defined by international translation agencies: "quality assurance (QA) [refers to] checks based on sampling and quality control (QC) [...] entails a 100-percent review" (Koo and Kinds 2000: 148).

12. In 1997, the Society of Automotive Engineers created the J2450 Task Force on a Quality Metric for Language Translation of Service Information in order to avoid the subjectivity of quality measurement on language translation in the automotive industry (Woyde 2001).

13. The only limitation observed in the description of this procedure is that when making reference to their translation staff, the individuals were identified as linguists and not as translators.

14. Pellet indicates that in the case of M2 Limited, the "pre-translation check" is conducted by the in-house translation staff and includes: (1) identifying the purpose of the translated text, (2) defining the client, (3) standardizing the specialized terminology, (4) identifying questions for the client, and, (5) determining the needs of the end user (2001: 12).

References

Adab, B. 2000. "Evaluating translation competence." In *Developing Translation Competence,* C. Schaffner and B. Adab (eds), 215–228. Amsterdam/Philadelphia: John Benjamins.

Brunette, L. 2000. "Towards a terminology of translation quality assessment." *Evaluation and Translation.* Special issue of *The Translator,* C. Maier (ed), 6.2: 169–182.

Chesterman, A., and Wagner, E. 2001. *Can Theory Help Translators? A Dialogue Between the Ivory Tower and the Wordface.* Manchester, UK/Northampton, MA: St. Jerome.

Delisle, J., Lee-Jahnke, H., and Cormier, M. C. (eds). 1999. *Terminologie de la traduction/ Translation Terminology/Terminologia de la traduccion/Terminologie der Ubersetzung.* FIT Monograph Series 1. Amsterdam/Philadelphia: John Benjamins.

Farahzad, F. 1992. "Testing achievement in translation classes" In *Teaching Translation and Interpreting: Training, Talent and Experience.* Papers from the 1st *Language International* Conference, Elsinore, Denmark, 31 May-2 June 1991. C. Dollerup and A. Loddegaard (eds), 271–278. (Copenhagen Studies in Translation). Amsterdam/Philadelphia: John Benjamins.

House, J. 1998. "Quality of translation." In *Encyclopedia of Translation Studies,* M. Baker and K. Malmkjær (eds), 197–200. London/New York: Routledge.

Kandler, G. 1963. "On the problem of quality in translation: Basic considerations." In *Quality in Translation: Proceedings of the IIIrd Congress of the International Federation of Translators (FIT), Bad Godesberg, 1959,* E. Cary and R. W. Jumpelt (eds), 291–298. New York: Pergamon Press.

Koo, S. L., and Kinds, H. 2000. "A quality-assurance model for language projects." In *Translating into Success: Cutting-Edge Strategies for Going Multilingual in a Global Age.* American Translators Association Series 11. R. C. Sprung and S. Jaroniec (eds), 147–157. Amsterdam/Philadelphia: John Benjamins.

Kussmaul, P. 1995. *Training the Translator.* Amsterdam/Philadelphia: John Benjamins.

Lauscher, S. 2000. "Translation quality assessment. Where can theory and practice meet?" *Evaluation and Translation.* Special issue of *The Translator,* C. Maier (ed), 6.2: 149–168.

Maier, C. 2000. "Introduction." *Evaluation and Translation.* Special Issue of *The Translator,* C. Maier (ed), 6.2: 137–148.

McAlester, G. 2000. "The evaluation of translation into a foreign language." In *Developing Translation Competence*, C. Schaffner and B. Adab (eds), 229–241. Amsterdam/Philadelphia: John Benjamins.

Orozco, M. 2000. "Building a measuring instrument of the acquisition of translation competence in trainee translators." In *Developing Translation Competence*, C. Schaffner and B. Adab (eds), 199–214. Amsterdam/Philadelphia: John Benjamins.

Pellet, M. M. 2001. "Translation quality is the difference between 'March Madness' and the craziness of March." *ATA Chronicle* 30 (5): 11–13.

Schonlau, M., Fricker, Jr., R. D., and Elliott, M. N. 2002. *Conducting Research Surveys via E-mail and the Web.* Santa Monica, CA: RAND.

Woyde, R. 2001. "Introduction to the SAE J2450 Translation Quality Metric." *Language International* 13 (2): 37–39.

Appendix A — Survey of translation quality assessment

Kent State University
Institute for Applied Linguistics
Survey of Translation Quality Evaluation
Dr. Geoffrey S. Koby & Dr. Fanny Arango-Keeth

December 31, 2001
Dear Translation Colleague:

As part of an article we are writing for the next ATA scholarly research volume, we are researching the different ways in which translation quality is evaluated by academic institutions and by translation agencies. For this purpose, we have designed the following brief preliminary survey that we would like to ask you to fill out (please type in the boxes). Please return it to gkoby@kent.edu as soon as possible. Individual responses will of course be kept confidential. Thank you in advance for your time!

1. Name and address of organization:

2. Contact person:

3. Contact e-mail and phone:

4. Type of organization (mark as applicable):

(a) Translation agency
a. _____   Multiple languages
b. _____   Single language

Annual volume (words or pages):

(b) Academic institution
a. _____   Offers degree in translation
b. _____   Offers certificate in translation
c. _____   Offers only courses in translation (no degree or certificate)
d. _____   No translation offerings

Number of students in translation studies:

5. Your role:
(a) _____   Quality assurance manager
(b) _____   Project manager
(c) _____   Translator
(d) _____   Editor/revisor
(e) _____   Proofreader
(f) _____   Professor/translation teacher

6. Is there a formal procedure in place for evaluating translation quality? If so, what is the procedure? Does it vary by language or individually?

7. Do you have formal guidelines or a grading scale for rating translation quality? If so, please describe them. (If there are printed guidelines, we would appreciate receiving a copy of them.)
Thank you!

Appendix B — Data

Data Table 1. Types of programs

Academic Programs:		
Only a Translation Degree Offered		4
Only a Translation Certificate Offered		5
Only Translation Courses Offered		5
Translation Degree, Certificate and Courses Offered		0
Both Translation Degree and Certificate Offered		6
Both Translation Degree and Courses Offered		0
Both Certificate and Courses		1
No Translation Offerings		1
	Total	22
No Academic Program:		
	Total	30

Data Table 2. Types of translation roles played by respondents

QA Manager	19
Project Manager	19
Translator	24
Editor/revisor	24
Proofreader	19
Professor/teacher	24

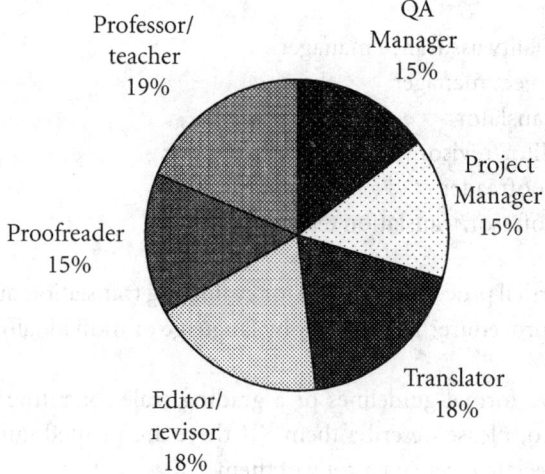

Data Chart 1. Types of roles played

Data Table 3. Program Procedures

Using Formal Procedures	12
Not Using Formal Procedures	40
Total	52

Teaching text revision in a multilingual environment

Jonathan T. Hine Jr.

Introduction

In Spring 2001, a multilingual course dedicated entirely to issues of text revision was taught at James Madison University, a class that may be unique among North American translator education programs. This article documents the class and shares findings, lessons, and ideas that readers may adapt to their own programs. It frames the emotional and historical evolution of this course and defines terms, then reviews the state of text revision instruction, particularly in North America, and lays out what we discovered was and was not being done at the time when we set up this course. The description of the course focuses on the structure of the curriculum and what actually happened.

Because discussion leading to the improvement of other translator education programs is crucial to the success of this article, a section devoted to recommendations lists areas where we discovered a need for more research and exchange of experiences in setting up and teaching a course in multilingual text revision.

Background

In the fall of 2000, preparations were well underway to hire instructors and organize classes for the Spring 2001 semester at James Madison University (JMU) in Harrisonburg, Virginia. Located about halfway down the length of the scenic Shenandoah Valley of Virginia, JMU has enjoyed steady growth for most of its 92-year history. Best known possibly for its Education and Business Schools and its Institute for Applied Science and Technology, JMU is a medium-sized public university that seeks to excel in niches that other schools have overlooked. For example, in 1998, the Department of Foreign Languages and Literatures (FL&L) decided to set up a program to teach technical translation and hired Christophe Réthoré of the University of Montréal as the first Director of the Technical Translation Program. A program in technical translation was a natural complement to the growing program in technical communication in the Institute for Technical and Scientific Communication (ITSC), which shared Keezel Hall with the FL&L Department.

The Technical Translation Program was in its second full year of operation. It offered a minor in Technical Translation (18 credits) that attracted students in a wide range of majors from outside the department, including Business, Technical Writing, Education and Psychology. Although only half the students in the program were majoring in languages, all had to pass prerequisites for bilingual competence either through course work or examination. The program also attracted graduate students, working translators, and career-changers who returned to school to earn a Certificate in Technical Translation.

Christophe Réthoré studied the curricula used in Canada and France in designing the curriculum for the program at JMU. The basic sequence resembled the curricula at the University of Montréal, McGill University, and the University of Québéc at Trois Rivières. He had adapted it to the student body of a Virginia school whose graduates would almost all work in the private sector in a country with no official languages.

The courses required for the Technical Translation minor included TR300 Introduction to Translation, TR400 Text Revision, TR495/496 Internship or Freelance Work, two specialized courses (e.g., Technical Translation or Computer Tools) and two courses from a list designed to help the students acquire subject matter expertise, deepen their knowledge of their source language(s) or hone their target language writing skills.

By November, the director of the program had obtained commitments from instructors for the Introduction to Translation (TR300) and the Technical Translation (TR331) classes for French and Spanish.[1] In mid-December, the Program Director asked me to take on TR 400 (French>English) if enough students enrolled. I met with the outgoing instructor and the teacher of TR400 (Spanish>English) to prepare the syllabus and lesson plans for TR400 (French>English).

The requirement for TR400 was creating a special problem for a small number of students who had completed TR300, the introductory course and were taking their specialized translation courses. They needed TR400 to complete the minor. However, only French>English and Spanish>English had enough students to assemble a minimum section for a class. Four students were working in other language pairs: English>Russian, English>German, German>English and Italian>English. They were assigned to independent study with one of the language faculty. However, it became evident that this would not work for several reasons. First, the material in text revision lent itself to the format for classroom teaching. Second, the individual faculty members were not ready to prepare a study plan for their students. Finally, there was no curriculum for them to follow and no textbooks or booklist they could give their students.

I was assigned an independent student of Italian. This third-year student was already taking Technical Translation as an independent study with the Italian teacher. Meanwhile, a similar situation was unfolding with a Russian student and a German student in the new Bachelor of Interdisciplinary Sciences (BIS) program at JMU. The second week of the semester, I met with the Director to discuss what could be done about these three students. I had already prepared Italian>English examples for individual meetings. However, we were going to need to craft some arrangement with the German and Russian instructors. Both students had room in their schedules to join the French students at the normal meeting time for the class.

The Director asked to add an American fourth-year student working from German into English. The following week I continued the semester with what amounted to two sections of TR400. Two students met with me in the morning during office hours. The other six met in the afternoon in the classroom. Both groups received the same material, but the smaller group in the morning session did not need as much time to cover it.

Thus was born the multilingual text revision course at JMU.

Definitions

Text revision as used in this article is a cognate taken from the French *révision*. While "revision" in English usually implies modification of the text, *révision* denotes a series of specific activities performed on a written text, by the author/translator or a second person. These activities include reviewing ("to review" = *réviser*), editing, proofreading, quality control, and content verification. The *réviseur* may or may not modify the text.

Webster's New International Dictionary defines revision thus:

> 1. a. the act of revising: reexamination or careful reading over for correction or improvement. b. something made by revising: a revised form or version. (Gove 1971: 1944)

Contrast this with *révision,* in *Le Petit Robert*:

> 1. Action de réviser (un texte, un énoncé); modification (de règles juridiques) pour les mettre en harmonie avec les circonstances ... 2. Amélioration (d'un texte) par

des corrections … (-> correction, réécriture). 3. Mise à jour par un nouvel examen … 4. Examen par lequel on vérifie qu'une chose est bien dans l'état où elle doit être. -> vérification…. (Robert 1993: 1978)

French definitions 2 and 3 roughly match the English understanding of "revision." French definition 1 would also allow the English sense of "revision"; however, in English one rarely uses "revision" this way. "Updating," "harmonization," "amendment," and "alignment" would be more common. However, French definition 4 refers to verification against standards that is absent in the English.

Juan Sager focuses on revision as "a process of control of document production for accuracy, completeness, stylistic appropriateness, etc., and the necessary modifications of the translation product" (1994: 238). He locates this definition within the larger concept of text modification, which includes correction, editing, and derivation, which capture all four definitions of *révision* as quoted above (1994: 104–108).

Daniel Gile defines revision as reversal of direction in articulating his sequential model for translation. He calls revision "the inspection and correction of a translation by a reviser after the translator has completed the task" (1995: 111). In this article and in other contexts, translators may perform "revision" on their own work during the reformulation task and final proofreading. However, unless qualified as "self-revision," etc., the term usually evokes the image of an external reviser.

Brian Mossop visualized editing and revising as overlapping circles. Technical editing and text revision as taught in the JMU course have a particularly large area of overlap: checking language, style issues, judging suitability for the target reader or client, etc. On the other hand, revisers and editors each attend to activities that are irrelevant to the other. For example, revisers look for mistranslations, while editors often coordinate the details of document production (2001: iii).

The word "revision" is rarely used for *révision* in the United States, where the terms "editing" or "reviewing" capture most of the activity in *révision*. However, in the translation world, the idea of revision incorporates all that *révision* implies for monolingual editing in French, plus checking the target text against the source text, for accuracy, style and register.

Monolingual editing for the purposes of this article means editing a text in one language only. In a translation environment, this is usually the target text without the source text being available. The early lessons in monolingual editing in a text revision course resemble technical editing in one language. However, there are considerations that distinguish monolingual editing from technical editing without a translation component.

A considerable amount of revision work occurs while reading the target text without the source text. An essential skill in text revision is to recognize errors and distinguish three types: poor writing, non-native writing, and poor translation. This skill goes beyond the material in ordinary technical editing.

Monolingual editing of a translated text is an important precursor to bilingual editing. Detecting errors that cannot be fixed without recourse to the source document requires an understanding of the translation process. The ability to detect errors of this kind during a first reading of the target text can make the text reviser more efficient overall. Research is ongoing to determine just how effective monolingual editing of translations can be without the source text.

Bilingual editing as used here means text revision of a translated document, by comparing the source and target texts. A definition of bilingual editing could include a review of a target text for translation errors immediately before comparing it to the source. I have chosen to draw the line between the presence or absence of two physical texts, reflecting the way the course was organized.

A review of text revision instruction today

The danger of using a translation that has not been reviewed by a second qualified person is well understood among experienced language industry professionals. That qualified person should ideally be "a second translator whose language of habitual use is the target language" (Newmark 1991: 38). The fact that the United Nations subjects 80% of its massive translation workload to second revisers highlights the importance that knowledgeable consumers of translation services place on revision (Horguelin and Brunette 1998: 10). Translators need training in revision, both to review their own work, and to perform the revision function for others.

The teaching of text revision as a separate course reflects an understanding of revision as an activity distinct from translation and performed by individuals other than the translator. In North America and Europe, we see this in two visible arenas: the practice of translation in Canada as opposed to elsewhere, and the use of revision in Canadian and international hierarchies.

Canada has a well-established national language industry, flowing from the need to translate enormous amounts of material into the two official languages of the country. In this industry, the role of the reviser appears reasonably well defined. A cadre of translators and former translators work as full-time revisers in both the public and private sectors. Universities and other translation schools in Canada train revisers with dedicated courses in text revision that cover not only text editing but also expose the students to possible careers in revision (Horguelin and Brunette 1998: 75–87).[2]

A curious application of revision occurs in human resources management in Canada and in international organizations, where the translation staffs are large and sufficiently entrenched to develop bureaucracies. In the United Nations, for example, translators are hired and promoted through increasing levels of responsibility that include the revision of more junior translators' work. The ultimate promotion is to be designated as "self-revising," which sounds ominous on the surface. This arrangement flows from the need to perform triage on a massive number of translation documents. "Self-revising" translators would not self-revise a controversial treaty, for example, but would move through more routine documents alone. Conceptually, part of their greater responsibility lies in being trusted to identify documents that should be reviewed (United Nations 2002).

In the United States, where the language mediation industry is less mature, the task of revision is less structured. It may be performed by in-house translators or project managers, or by freelance translators hired for the occasion. Rarely does one encounter a full-time, in-house reviser. Outside the United Nations, there appears to be no identifiable career for revisers in the United States, unless an individual trained as a translator happens to specialize in revision as a freelancer. Revision may be included in the job description of a variety of workers in the language industry, but it is almost always included with (and often subordinate to) the other elements of the job description.

Revision appears as a separate course in the translation curricula of only two translation schools in the United States. The University of Puerto Rico offers three semester-long courses in revision, and JMU offers a single course, Text Revision (Park 1998).

Techniques for revising one's own work may appear in textbooks or in course materials. However, with few exceptions, most books not otherwise cited may make a case for the importance of checking one's own work, but do not provide specific guidance for doing so, e.g., proofreading techniques, style guides or even references to technical editing books or other resources. Delisle provides exercises for the apprentice translator and cites the Horguelin textbook of 1978 for detailed instruction on professional revision (Delisle 1980: 226–234). Dollerup and Loddegaard published some of Mossop's original work on teaching revision (Dollerup and Loddegaard 1992: 79–90).

Newmark provides advice only for self-revision and a list of tips for taking examinations (1988: 36, 221–223).

Possibly the only book in English completely devoted to the subject of revision is the just-published textbook *Revising and Editing for Translators* by Brian Mossop, which is now used in the JMU text revision course (Mossop 2001). It was not available when the course described below was designed.

Description of the course

In setting up the new TR400 course, the faculty of the JMU program agreed that the Text Revision course should interface with the practical material the students would encounter in their technical translation classes. Also, since most translation and revision work today moves as electronic files, some of the time spent learning proofreading marks could be used to learn computer-assisted editing resources, like the Track Changes features of Microsoft Word®.

During our meetings, we determined that a suitable text and lesson outline for the new TR400 did not exist, but *La Pratique de la révision* (Horguelin and Brunette 1998), which had recently come out in its third edition, came closest to suiting our needs. Canadians Paul Horguelin and Louise Brunette wrote it to support revision classes working from English into French. We could not use it as a textbook, but it would support lesson plans and lecture notes.

La Pratique de la révision is organized around six headings:

1. The idea of revision — definitions and background
2. Methodologies for revision
3. General principles
4. Techniques
5. Human relationships
6. Revision as a profession

Examples and principles from both monolingual and bilingual editing appear throughout the text. Converting the English>French bilingual material to support a French>English class involved finding similar examples in the correct direction or translating the ones in the book. There was plenty of material on file for examples of the points being made in the textbook. However, opening the course to multiple language pairs required us to completely rearrange the outline of the French>English course.

The curriculum overhaul was not as complex as first expected. In essence, the material to be covered fell into two groups. The first half of the semester

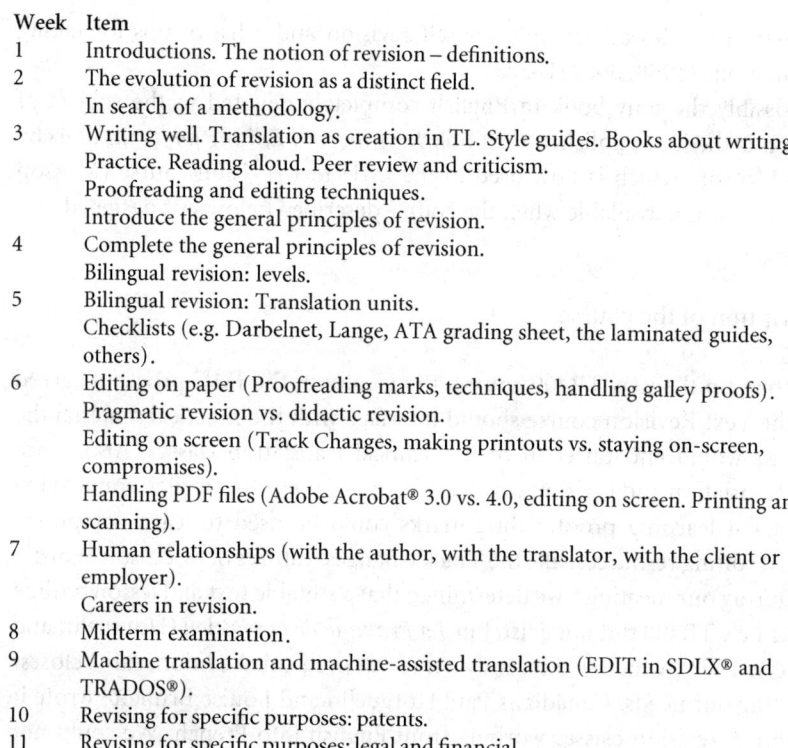

Week	Item
1	Introductions. The notion of revision – definitions.
2	The evolution of revision as a distinct field.
	In search of a methodology.
3	Writing well. Translation as creation in TL. Style guides. Books about writing.
	Practice. Reading aloud. Peer review and criticism.
	Proofreading and editing techniques.
	Introduce the general principles of revision.
4	Complete the general principles of revision.
	Bilingual revision: levels.
5	Bilingual revision: Translation units.
	Checklists (e.g. Darbelnet, Lange, ATA grading sheet, the laminated guides, others).
6	Editing on paper (Proofreading marks, techniques, handling galley proofs).
	Pragmatic revision vs. didactic revision.
	Editing on screen (Track Changes, making printouts vs. staying on-screen, compromises).
	Handling PDF files (Adobe Acrobat® 3.0 vs. 4.0, editing on screen. Printing and scanning).
7	Human relationships (with the author, with the translator, with the client or employer).
	Careers in revision.
8	Midterm examination.
9	Machine translation and machine-assisted translation (EDIT in SDLX® and TRADOS®).
10	Revising for specific purposes: patents.
11	Revising for specific purposes: legal and financial.
12	Revising for specific purposes: medical.
13	Final summary and exam preparation.
14	Final examination.
15	Critique exam. Course Evaluation.

Figure 1. Syllabus for a text revision course

included all six elements of *La Pratique de la révision*. The second half was devoted to bilingual revision, concentrating on a different technical area each week. Figure 1 shows the outline of the course.

Homework consisted of five revision assignments. The first three, during the first half of the semester, were in English. After Spring Break, there were two split assignments (for the different language pairs). Ten days before the class in which we would discuss the assignments, the students received them attached to an e-mail with instructions. The students returned them the same way, saving the assignments to a particular file name to facilitate tracking. Assignments were due two days before the lesson, so that we could discuss each one fully in class.

The instructions accompanying each assignment reminded the students how to format the filenames, and to turn **on** the Track Changes and Comments features of their word processors. These features allowed us to mark up the files visibly and made it possible to provide individual feedback through e-mail, supplementing the general discussion in class (see Appendix).

Only one assignment was not handled entirely by computer. Part of Assignment #3 dealt with proofreading marks. The students submitted that on a printed-out page of the assigned text.

The classroom instruction owed much to Control Theory and my personal respect for the etymology of the word "educate" (Latin 'to lead out') (Glasser 1986). We sat together in a square with one end open for the projection equipment. The assignment became the centerpiece of discussion, with the instructor serving as facilitator. The lesson plan included points to be made. I asked questions if the discussion did not move naturally toward these points. In practice, the class typically covered more than was scheduled, and "facilitating" came quite naturally out of the discussion.

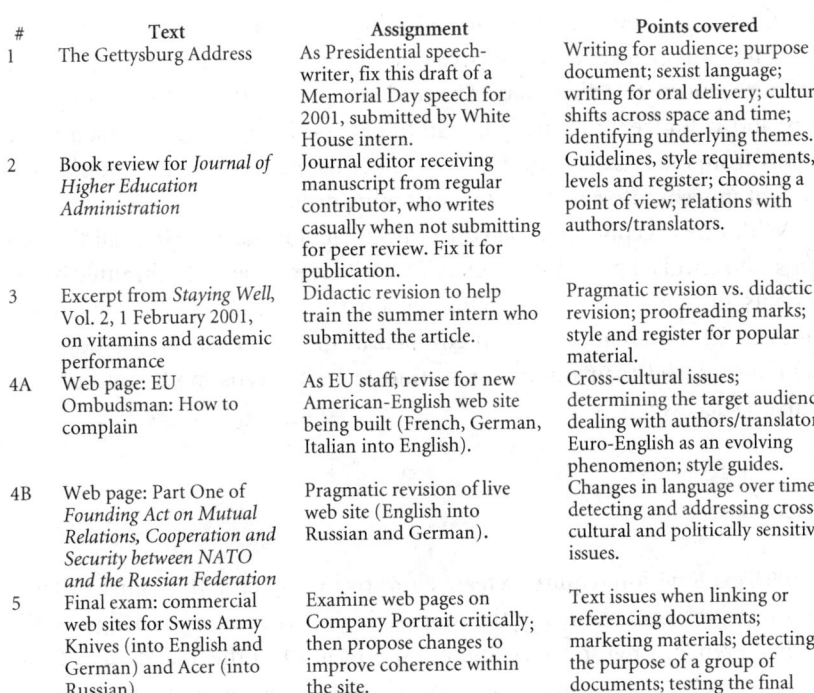

#	Text	Assignment	Points covered
1	The Gettysburg Address	As Presidential speechwriter, fix this draft of a Memorial Day speech for 2001, submitted by White House intern.	Writing for audience; purpose of document; sexist language; writing for oral delivery; cultural shifts across space and time; identifying underlying themes.
2	Book review for *Journal of Higher Education Administration*	Journal editor receiving manuscript from regular contributor, who writes casually when not submitting for peer review. Fix it for publication.	Guidelines, style requirements, levels and register; choosing a point of view; relations with authors/translators.
3	Excerpt from *Staying Well*, Vol. 2, 1 February 2001, on vitamins and academic performance	Didactic revision to help train the summer intern who submitted the article.	Pragmatic revision vs. didactic revision; proofreading marks; style and register for popular material.
4A	Web page: EU Ombudsman: How to complain	As EU staff, revise for new American-English web site being built (French, German, Italian into English).	Cross-cultural issues; determining the target audience; dealing with authors/translators; Euro-English as an evolving phenomenon; style guides.
4B	Web page: Part One of *Founding Act on Mutual Relations, Cooperation and Security between NATO and the Russian Federation*	Pragmatic revision of live web site (English into Russian and German).	Changes in language over time; detecting and addressing cross-cultural and politically sensitive issues.
5	Final exam: commercial web sites for Swiss Army Knives (into English and German) and Acer (into Russian)	Examine web pages on Company Portrait critically; then propose changes to improve coherence within the site.	Text issues when linking or referencing documents; marketing materials; detecting the purpose of a group of documents; testing the final product.

Figure 2. Outline of assignments

The outline of the assignments (Figure 2) combined with the syllabus, indicates how the subject matter flowed during the course.

In-class exercises supplemented the homework discussions. These exercises included all the material on language for specific purposes (LSP) to guide the discussions on such issues as revising patents, medical texts, and financial/legal documents. They also included exercises on style and register, and proofreading marks. After each exercise, we projected the texts onto a screen and discussed them in the same way that we handled the homework.

The midterm examination was administered in class. It covered the principles of monolingual editing and proofreading marks. The final exam consisted of a take-home portion and a paper test for those items that still required paper: didactic and pragmatic revision using proofreader's marks, LSP, and a word-matching quiz. The students submitted their take-home portions no later than the day of the paper test. I graded everything together, after the discussion period.

The midterm examination included a word-matching exercise from an editing textbook, *Stet! Tricks of the Trade for Writers and Editors* (Boston 1986). During the discussion period in the following class, I circled some words which were often misspelled or misused that a good editor should be able to recognize without recourse to a dictionary. The students enjoyed the drill and the discussion, and volunteered to bring in additional vocabulary exercises each week, mainly from old issues of *Reader's Digest*. For the final exam, the material they brought in went into another word-matching drill.

With one exception unrelated to the curriculum or the class, all the students who enrolled passed the course. The private evaluations submitted by the students matched the favorable impression received from them during the semester. The students remained enrolled in the Technical Translation program and earned their minors or certificates. This leads me to consider the course a success.

Discussion

TR400 Text Revision required a team effort by the director, the course instructor, the department chair, and the cooperating instructors. The changes to the original French>English course did not seriously affect the final design. There appeared to be only a limited number of options for offering a multilingual course such as we needed, and only one of them turned out to be feasible.

The protocol for cooperation on evaluating and grading assignments outside the languages of the instructor made this course unlike the other courses I encountered during my research on translator education in the United States (Hine 2000). The combination of a cooperative faculty, a computer-literate student population, and the capillary reach of the Internet made this course possible. It could not have been taught the same way just a few years earlier.

Cooperative protocol

More efficient use of faculty was one of the reasons for replacing the French>English course with a multilingual version. Therefore, we created a protocol for involving faculty other than the instructor that specified that they would be called on only for what the instructor could not handle.

The basic outline of the protocol, which could be used as a model for similar text revision courses, looked like this:

1. The instructor locates the assignments. These usually involve no more than two different texts that have already been translated into the languages represented in the class.
2. The instructor shows the two proposed texts to the cooperating teacher to make sure the latter feels comfortable with the register and the subject matter in the texts. They discuss the purposes of the assignment, and they should agree that the proposed texts meet the needs of the class.
3. The instructor distributes the assignment and collects it as an attachment to e-mail. The students send copies to both the instructor and the cooperating teacher.
4. The cooperating teacher reviews the assignment and provides feedback to the instructor. This may include a marked-up copy of the assignment, a grade, a recommended grade, a verbal summary or a written commentary.
5. Meanwhile, the instructor facilitates a discussion of the passages in class. The structure of the class requires all the students to explain the changes required in their text to an audience that includes non-speakers of their language pairs.
6. Grades are not finalized until the end of the semester. The instructor meets with each of the cooperating teachers to compare the tentative grades that each teacher assigned during the semester. The comments or grades from the cooperating teachers serve to adjust the grade given by the instructor based on performance in class. The instructor remains responsible for the final grade assigned.

This protocol worked particularly well for the unique situation of this class and this combination of instructor and cooperating teachers. In drawing it up, we had to be prepared for some variations.

We were dealing with European languages. In this case, the instructor was familiar enough with the Cyrillic alphabet to align Russian passages for assignment texts. If this had not been the case, or if the language pairs had included Asian or African languages, the cooperating teacher(s) might have had to become more involved in text selection. At the very least, the cooperating teacher(s) and the instructor might have had to look at texts together (on the WWW in this case), so that the cooperating teacher could help choose the passages to cut and paste into the assignment. Compared with the time commitment of advising an independent student, this involvement in text selection seemed reasonable.

Discussion in the classroom focused on general issues in text revision, while specific linguistic and cultural issues were secondary. The students took the lead in discussing the results of their work and when this involved presenting material that was unfamiliar to their peers, they were engaged and articulate, as well as patient.

Making this protocol work may depend on the experience of the instructor. Although I did not know all the languages of the class, I was an experienced technical editor and text reviser. Years of monolingual editing of translated material enabled me to detect points that needed amplification in the class discussion. That experience also allowed me to guide the discussion so that I could assess student learning in terms of specific items in the syllabus.

Using web sites for didactic material

Obtaining teaching materials from the Internet is a practice that is not unique to the teaching of technical revision. Indeed, teachers from kindergarten through graduate school are turning to it for material for their classrooms. The challenges of finding suitable texts for a multilingual revision class included the usual ones encountered in looking through paper sources:

1. Selections of appropriate length
2. Selections that contain enough context for the student editor to make choices
3. Selections with errors or departures from guidelines
4. Selections that are accessible to the student, in terms of both subject matter and reading level

5.   Selections that show the translation problems and revision principles be-
     ing taught.

Length was the easiest to determine. A passage of about 200–250 words provided enough context to make choices, but could still be completed in a
reasonable amount of time. The fastest students finished the assignments in an
hour; the slowest worked on them for up to eight hours. The assignments were
intended to stimulate discussion and to motivate individual research.

Not surprisingly, finding passages that provided other desirable characteristics proved more problematic. No one set of texts provided all of them
equally well. This problem, however, is not unique to text selection on the web.
The Internet did facilitate faster searching, so that more texts could be examined, discarded, or downloaded and modified than might have been possible
using paper resources. However, selecting texts covering five different language
pairs did necessitate some additional steps.

An abundance of multilingual web sites included two or three languages,
especially for a course like this one, which dealt only with European languages.
The most common choices for translated web sites appeared to be French,
English, Spanish, and German, in addition to the language of the home page, if
not one of those four. Thus, Italian web sites tended to have three to five
languages, while French and English web sites typically featured only these two
languages plus German.

The more extensive the planetary reach of the home page owner, the more
languages the web site seemed to offer. In general, Asian multinational companies translated their web sites into more languages than European and American ones. Translation and international documentation companies offered the
widest selection of languages, but their texts were limited in scope.

International organizations provided a wealth of material. They typically
translated into the languages of most of their members, even when the organization declared only one or two languages "official." Thus, the European Union
(EU) and its agencies offered many of their pages in seven to eleven languages,
while the North Atlantic Treaty Organization (NATO), which officially operates
only in English and French, provided translations of much of its material into
as many languages as the EU.

Rarely did a web site contain all its material in all the languages needed for
this multilingual course. German or Russian versions were often not provided.
The challenge was to find as few selections as possible to cover all five language
pairs, and then to apply criteria to make sure the different passages tested the
same knowledge and skill factors.

Two different sets of web pages were assigned. The first assignment focused on style and target audience and consisted of pages that had already been extensively edited and published by international bodies. The second added the challenge of going to the web site of a large multinational company, locating the page(s) assigned, and revising the text as needed to meet the apparent goals of the web site itself. This involved assessing the purpose of the web site and the company's style and register before revising the assigned pages for the intended audience.

The first assignment focused on the text itself, and the revision task was straightforward: revise the text for a different readership. The students working into English received a page from the web site of the Ombudsman of the EU, including the English version and the version in their source language. The students translating into English were to revise the English page for a potential "American English" web site. The students working from English received the preamble and first part of the *Founding Act on Mutual Relations, Cooperation and Security between NATO and the Russian Federation*. The students translating from English were to revise the Act for a modern audience.

Both versions of the first assignment tested general language published by a political body. Providing a rationale for revisions during the class discussion was as important as the revisions themselves.

The second assignment made the students integrate everything that went into presenting a text to a readership, in addition to the text itself. The assignment consisted of a web site address (URL) and a set of instructions. The students working into or from EU languages were directed to the web site of the Wenger Company in Switzerland. The Russian student was sent to the Russian homepage of Acer. Both companies are large multinational firms with sophisticated web sites.

The students were asked to determine the style and target readership of the assigned web sites, then revise any one of three different pages on the sites, using their analysis of the site for guidance. They presented their analysis of the site, their revisions to the selected page(s), and a critique of the selected page(s) in terms of presentation and integration into the site.

Using web sites for didactic material raises issues of intellectual property and fair use under the Copyright Protection Act. Because the selections were all shorter than 250 words, were used for teaching, and were marked up by students, their use qualified as fair use in an educational setting. In no case was any downloaded material a significant part of the total document. Also, the first assignment was taken from the public domain, viz., the EU and NATO. The second assignment used material belonging to private parties, but it was not reproduced or re-published, because the students were directed to work with the page(s) as published by the companies involved.

There are some significant advantages to using hypertext markup language (HTML) documents like web pages in a text revision class. They are easy to handle and to return as attachments to e-mail. Modern word processors, like Microsoft Word®, can easily convert the HTML into a formatted document, ready to mark up using the "Track Changes" feature of the word processor. Material can be easily modified for class without retyping the original. No retyping means that texts can be transferred and modified without injecting new errors.

Modern word processors can also compare documents and track versions. The students in this class used "Comments" (also called "Annotations") to explain their revisions. They also appreciated the "real world" lesson of working with the types of documents and materials they may find themselves editing after graduation.

This course also included units on revising texts in specific domains, with examples drawn from patents, medicine, finance, law, and industry. The tendency of specialized communities to use a lingua franca, often English, and not to translate much of their material, made it difficult to locate texts suitable for homework assignments on the Web in all of the language pairs needed. Because the translation of domain-specific texts was covered in TR331, Technical Translation, the text revision course emphasized those aspects of technical translation that related specifically to editors: research methodology and resources for self-study, such as the US Patent Office web site and the cancer research information at Pennsylvania State University and the Mayo Clinic.

Using web sites for didactic material yielded assignments that involved the integrated knowledge and skills of the students. On the other hand, the WWW did not prove useful as a source of material to support individual units of the course, for example, languages for specific purposes (LSP).

Lessons learned and recommendations

This section contains a list of specific insights, as well as recommendations for future text revision courses, which could also be implemented in other technical translation programs.

1. It is possible to teach text revision in non-language-specific courses. This was the most important finding, as published reports of such courses were unavailable at the time the course was first offered.

2. The monolingual portion of the course initially appears to be an abbreviated technical editing sequence, but this is not the case. The emphasis and the examples focused on the challenge of editing translated material, and the monolingual portion of the course gathered in one place the principles and skills that all language pairs share. A technical editing course would be an excellent prerequisite or elective in a technical translation program, however.

3. Using the web for didactic material speeds up the search for texts, allows electronic handling of the assignments, and reduces the "paper overhead" of the class. During this course, we learned that giving the students the URL of the text and a set of instructions reduced overhead even further, in addition to providing the students with the experience of downloading the material. This also allows the course to be adapted to distance learning.

4. The protocol we developed for dealing with languages outside the expertise of the instructor worked, but needed to be refined. The process of arranging cooperation among the faculty will be highly individual at first, as the instructor of the new course negotiates the different skills and schedules of the cooperating teachers. Over time, a department that makes a commitment to teaching multilingual text revision will probably develop a protocol that may be specific to that department. This would allow the department to move towards uniform handling of student assignments.

5. While we did not develop a distance-learning format for this course, analysis of the course at the end of the semester revealed that we had very little left to do to accommodate that format. Using portable document format (PDF) files, scanners and facsimile technology for the proofreading marks and "paper" testing could surmount the only obstacle we had not prepared for in setting up the course. The vocabulary drills, other matching exercises, or multiple-choice tests could be done using on-line testing forms.

6. Mossop's book, *Editing and Revising for Translators* (2001), is perhaps the only textbook in English of the caliber of *Pratique de la révision* (Horguelin and Brunette 1998) suitable for use in a multilingual course. It was intended to be non-language-specific, and is organized in approximately the same way as our course.

7. The original syllabus included exposure to revision using translation tools, such as TRADOS®, SDLX® or Déjà Vu®. However, scheduling problems precluded the hands-on session in Week 9 (Figure 1). In the Technical

Translation program at JMU, all students receive training in translation tools, but a focused look at how these tools can be used specifically for editing would have been useful. In addition to instant access to the terminology and previously translated segments of a project, these tools offer split-screen facility, locked scrolling and a variety of other features that facilitate the work of the editor. This exposure was incorporated in subsequent offerings of the course.

Future research

This section discusses four areas where future research by scholars and graduate students would be most useful, based on what we learned in designing and teaching this particular course.

Defining a place for text revision

Revision courses lack a clear identity and place in the various curricula used to prepare future translators. A 1998 survey of 59 post-secondary translation programs in North America, for example, revealed that only seven contained a course that addressed revision or editing. Three of these were in Canada (of nine reporting), two in Mexico (of four reporting) and two (of 48 reporting) in the United States. The University of Puerto Rico was the only one in the United States offering two full semesters plus a semester-long workshop (*taller*) in *Redacción*. While some schools have initiated programs since 1998 (e.g., JMU), it is safe to say that in the United States the teaching of revision takes place for the most part in the context of other courses (Park 1993/1988).

Some research in the fields of translation studies and technical communications appears to touch on revision, but only peripherally. For example, there has been a fair amount published on translation quality and on assessment of both classroom translation and the professional translation product, but almost all of this is aimed at evaluation of results. Little is said about how the student or professional achieves these results and nothing is said about how the translator trainer might make use of them pedagogically.

Moreover, revision overlaps with technical editing, although editing in a multilingual environment obviously requires specialized preparation in translation studies, even when editing translated documents without the source text. The Concordia University GREVIS Project is researching monolingual revision of translated documents in Canada, and presented its first results in

Autumn 2002 (Brunette et al. 2002). With the exception of Mossop 2001, there does not appear to be any other published research aimed specifically at text revision or, more importantly, at teaching text revision.

At the same time, translators and translation students need self-revision skills to improve their work and expertise. This is why they learn revision in their practical translation courses. In the absence of research into the pedagogy of revision, who can say if those segments of the translation studies courses are effective? If those who are teaching revision, even as part of a translation course by another name, would write for translation studies and education journals, a substantive discussion on the subject of text revision and its pedagogy could emerge, to the benefit of future teaching.

Evaluation and assessment

Program evaluation of translator education programs is a prerequisite for the development of a mature field of translation studies and translation pedagogy in the United States. Evaluation provides credibility to the discipline and documents the deliberate improvement of individual programs. Assessment of outcomes against objectives provides feedback needed to keep the program or course fresh and growing. Assessment also documents achievement for faculty, administrators, students, and outside sponsors of many types.

The only evaluation included in the TR 400 course was a two-hour de-briefing of the students at the end of the course. Text revision's lack of identity as a subject and the absence of a body of research made articulation of learning objectives problematic. Instructors designing courses in text revision, as with any subject, should include an evaluation plan and articulate their learning objectives and standards for outcome assessment. As more of these courses are published, we can share what works in our institutions and move towards consensus. The emergence of that consensus will facilitate ever more useful evaluation of the revision portion of translator education programs.

Instructor skill set

Research is needed to determine how much and what kind of experience in technical revision is needed to teach a multilingual text revision class. Special subsets of this experience include monolingual editing of translations and multicultural expertise that extends beyond one's own source and target languages. Education and experience in teaching translation or technical editing, as well as training in classroom management and assessment also play an undocumented role in guiding these classes.

Extension beyond European languages

The cultural transfer between European and Asian or African languages may require more course time to support the bilingual component of the course described in this article. Case studies like this one describing the experience of instructors teaching revision in language pairs between different writing systems would be a welcome addition to the discussion.

Conclusion

The multilingual text revision course at JMU during the spring semester of 2001 was a success, based on the continued high performance of the students who took it. We showed that the material could be imparted to the students in a non-language-specific course. This has made it possible to offer text revision, a requirement for the minor/certificate, to all our students without resorting to independent study formats guided by a variety of teachers, with varied results.

The course could have benefited from a decision to create it earlier rather than developing it from an already existing French>English revision course. At the very least, an evaluation plan and an outcome assessment could have been designed into the course. However, the initial syllabus can serve as a solid foundation for more deliberate development of future curricula.

The translation profession in general and translation pedagogy in particular is still finding its voice on the campuses of American institutions of higher education. Text revision as a distinct subject is even farther behind, being a recognized subject at only two American universities. Publication of the experiences of those who are teaching text revision, especially those teaching courses devoted entirely to the subject, would help stimulate the discussion that is essential to the maturing of the translation profession and the coalescing of the academic fields that support it into a recognizable discipline.

Notes

1. The teaching staff included both full-time faculty from the Department of Foreign Languages & Literatures and part-time adjunct faculty recruited among full-time profes-

sionals in the language industry.

2. The seven universities granting degrees in translation are Montréal, Concordia, Québéc-Trois Rivières, McGill, Laval, St. Boniface, and Toronto.

References

Boston, B. O. 1986. *Stet! Tricks of the Trade for Writers and Editors.* Alexandria VA: Editorial Experts Inc.

Brunette, L., Gagnon, C., and Hine, J. T. 8 November 2002. "The GREVIS Project: Not to revise or courting calamity." Translation Research Forum at the 43rd Annual Conference of the American Translators Association. Atlanta, GA: ATA.

Delisle, J. 1980. *L'Analyse du discours comme methode de traduction.* Cahiers de Traductologie, vol. 2. Ottawa: Éditions de l'Université d'Ottawa.

Dollerup, C., and Loddegaard, A., eds. 1992. *Copenhagen Studies in Translation.* Amsterdam/Philadelphia: John Benjamins.

Gile, D. 1995. *Basic Concepts and Models for Interpreter and Translator Training.* Benjamins Translation Library, vol. 8. Amsterdam/Philadelphia: John Benjamins.

Glasser, W. 1986. *Control Theory in the Classroom.* New York: Harper & Row.

Gove, P. B., ed. 1971. *Webster's Third New International Dictionary of the English Language, Unabridged.* Springfield MA: G&C Merriam.

Hine, J. T. 2000. *Translator Education in the United States: A Study of Introductory Translation Classrooms in Three Mid-Atlantic Universities.* Ph.D. Diss., Curry School of Education, University of Virginia.

Horguelin, P. A., and Brunette, L. 1998. *Pratique de la révision.* Montreal: Linguatech.

Mossop, B. 2001. *Revising and Editing for Translators.* Translation Practices Explained, A. Pym (ed). Manchester: St. Jerome Publishing.

Newmark, P. 1988. *A Textbook of Translation.* New York: Prentice-Hall International.

———. 1991. *About Translation.* Multilingual Matters, vol. 74. Clevedon: Multilingual Matters Ltd.

Park, W. M. 1993/1988. *Translator and Interpreter Training in the USA: A Survey,* 2nd edition. Alexandria, VA: American Translators Association.

———. 1998. *Translator and Interpreter Programs in North America: A Survey.* Alexandria, VA: American Translators Association.

Robert, P. 1993. *Le Nouveau petit Robert.* Dictionary. Edited by J. Rey-Debove and A. Rey. Paris: Dictionnaires Le Robert.

Sager, J. C. 1994. *Language Engineering and Translation: Consequences of Automation.* Benjamins Translation Library, vol. 1. Amsterdam/Philadelphia: John Benjamins.

United Nations. 2002, 17 July. Employment opportunities with the United Nations <http://www.un.org/Depts/OHRM/ New York>. Accessed on March 13, 2002.

Appendix

[This excerpt from the first bilingual assignment appears as it was submitted. The assignment was to update the treaty language for a modern audience. The student was a 50-year-old German chemical worker pursuing a Bachelor in Interdisciplinary Studies with a minor in Technical Translation. The class discussion included changes in German, the political sensitivity of word choices and the use of mandated terminology in diplomatic contexts.]

Grundakte
über Gegenseitige Beziehungen, Zusammenarbeit und Sicherheit zwischen der Nordatlantikvertrags-Organisation[1] und der Russischen Föderation[2]
Paris, 27 May 1997[3]

Die Nordatlantikvertrags-Organisation[4]und ihre Mitgliedstaaten einerseits und die Russische Föderation[5] andererseits, im folgenden als NATO und Russland bezeichnet, gestützt auf eine[6] auf höchster politischer Ebene eingegangene dauerhafte politische Verpflichtung, werden gemeinsam im euroatlantischen Raum einen dauerhaften und umfassenden Frieden auf der Grundlage[7] der Prinzipien der Demokratie und der kooperativen Sicherheit schaffen.

Die NATO und Russland betrachten einander nicht als Gegner. Sie verfolgen gemeinsam das Ziel, die Spuren der früheren Konfrontation und Konkurrenz zu beseitigen und das gegenseitige Vertrauen und die Zusammenarbeit zu stärken. Diese Akte bekräftigt die Entschlossenheit der NATO und Russlands,

---

1. Change to North Atlantic Treaty Organization. This organization has been in existence for a long time and is commonly known as NATO among older and younger citizens in Germany.

2. Change to: *den russischen Bundesstaaten* — although *Föderation* is a German word, it is seldom used and *Bundesstaaten* is easier understood.

3. Change date to correct German spelling — *den 27. Mai 1997.*

4. See 1 above.

5. Change to *Bundesstaaten in Russland* to better understand the shortening to *"Russland"* in future text.

6. Change to *unterstützt bei einer.*

7. Change to *den Grundlagen* to reflect plural; there are two *"Prinzipien..."* and *"kooperative Sicherheit".*

ihrer gemeinsamen Verpflichtung[8] zum Bau eines stabilen, friedlichen und ungeteilten, geeinten und freien Europas zum Nutzen aller seiner Völker konkreten[9]Ausdruck zu verleihen. Die Übernahme dieser Verpflichtung auf höchster politischer Ebene stellt den Beginn grundlegend neuer Beziehungen zwischen der NATO und Russland dar. Beide Seiten beabsichtigen, auf der Grundlage gemeinsamen Interesses, der Gegenseitigkeit und der Transparenz[10] eine starke, stabile und dauerhafte Partnerschaft zu entwickeln.

---

8. Change to — *von NATO und Russland um ihre gemeinsamen Verpflichtungen* — to better conform to original text.

9. Take out space, it is one word.

10. Change to *"Offenheit"* — research in several dictionaries identifies *Transparenz* als *"Durchsichtigkeit"* which gives a different meaning to the English word in this context.

Gender, pedagogy, and literary translation

Three workshops and a suggestion

Carol S. Maier

"A lot of education is like teaching marching; I try to make it more like dancing."
Peter Schjeldahl

Introduction

Some of the most challenging issues that arise in the training of literary translators center on the complex role played by a translator's particular set of circumstances and beliefs with respect to both theory and practice. For example, how best to sensitize students to the often subtle presence in translations of class, gender, race, religion, or ethnicity, and to the multiple interrelations between them? How best to prompt students' awareness of their biases and those of other translators? How to explore with them the expressive strategies but also the constraints associated with the individual perspective implied in any approach? How to guide them in the evaluation of theoretical approaches to translation as they form their own approaches?

Although translation theorists and, to a lesser extent, translation practitioners are increasingly addressing these questions,[1] neither their discussions nor those of translator trainers provide much specific guidance in the way of pedagogical methodology. Work such as André Lefevere's *Translating Literature* (1992), Lawrence Venuti's chapter on "The Pedagogy of Literature" (1998: 88–105), and Andrew Chesterman's sections on translation ethics, in particular, values and trust (1997: 172–173), offer comments that might be useful in formulating possible models. Peter Bush's remarks relate to classroom practices, especially those related to the choices that a translator must make "tentatively but with extreme confidence," "the constraints imposed by national frameworks, and traditions," and their bearing on the "qualities" a literary translator needs to possess" (1997: 111). Only in very unusual instances, however, does one find an extended discussion of a proposed pedagogical model that directly addresses the need to make explicit the presence of an instructor's commitment or approach in the preparation and implementation of curricula and syllabi. Rosemary Arrojo's work is an exception. Even in Arrojo's work, however, and despite her rather detailed outline of a possible post-modern "anti-model" (1995: 101–103), the guidelines she describes remain largely at the theoretical level and do not include suggestions for specific teaching strategies or classroom practice.

Given Arrojo's postmodern "critique of all conceptions and systems of thought based on the possibility of universal, essential values and truths which can be known and rationally studied without the interference of the subjective, or the ideological" (1998: 46), it is understandable, even appropriate that she would not propose a rigid pedagogical model. At the same time, however, her "anti-model" is clearly meant to be implemented, or at least essayed in an actual classroom (1999: 276, 1995: 101–103). She offers no suggestions for this implementation, and I cannot help wondering how instructors might actualize it in their dealings with students. Arrojo's own closing remarks in the two articles that refer most precisely to the teaching of translation (1995 and 1999) suggest that she herself may be at a loss for an answer. This may be not only because she considers any model that would dismantle the inevitable "authoritarian homogenization" of all models ultimately impossible to realize (1995: 103). She also finds "utopian" (1995: 103) the goal of transforming "into a clear vision" students' blindness to the inevitable "authoritarian homogenization" operative in traditional notions of translation (1999: 276). Identifying particular techniques or methods is seen to be useless, hypocritical, and self-defeating. Consequently, instructors must work in local, as opposed to universal, contexts and develop strategies appropriate to those specific settings.

Paradoxical? Paralyzing? Yes and no. "Yes," because I find it ironic and discouraging that Arrojo's articles, which in fact do provide practice-oriented remarks about making explicit one's pedagogical allegiances and goals, do not address the active "mechanics" of translator education, of working with students — and of working as a practicing translator. But also "no," for despite finding that absence in Arrojo's articles discouraging, I believe that such an absence can also prove provocative and energizing. Perhaps this is because my goals as an instructor differ somewhat from Arrojo's. I, too, endeavor to prompt students' awareness of the translator's multiple roles, constraints, and responsibilities, and of the unstable nature of all forms of writing. But I am willing to settle for less than "total transformation." In fact, I find Arrojo's suggestion that such a transformation might be the "great revolution that every teaching project should have as its goal" (1995: 103) both contradictory and rather authoritarian. I would prefer instead to think of her general suggestions for "deconstructing" "universal, objective translation rules" as guidelines for devising and articulating strategies that could be used in many different contexts to trouble students, but also to tantalize and challenge them. If the purpose of translation education is to enable students to translate with self-awareness, it is incumbent on instructors to develop paradigmatic but flexible pedagogical strategies that, while created in specific contexts, are not limited to them. But how might instructors create such strategies? How might they involve students as aware participants in practical exercises that train them to work without fear or paralysis in a paradoxical situation that requires them, simultaneously, (1) to question the authority of both a text and their own approach to it, and (2) to attend meticulously to that text, in other words, deliberately to grant it, and perhaps its author, a provisional stability — what might be referred to as a kind of trust?[2]

Those questions had been on my mind for some time when I received invitations to present several workshops on translation pedagogy.[3] One of the workshops was to center on issues of gender, and I decided to focus each of them on the possible role of gender in translator education. My intention was to address gender not only as a discrete issue but also to consider it as an example of possible "essentialism" (to use Arrojo's term [1998]) that, together with a set of multiple translations of two poems, would prompt and sustain discussion about ways in which gender might, and has, figured in the work of various translators. In addition, I wanted to essay the use of multiple versions, which I believed might provide the basis for one possible response to my own questions about the issue of commitment in translation pedagogy and about how to implement Arrojo's call for a translation pedagogy that would encourage students to interrogate, rather than accept immediately, the absolute authority of either texts or rules for working with them.

My thinking on this topic was influenced by several recent pieces related to my topic: "The revision of the traditional gap between theory and practice and the empowerment of translation in postmodern times," Arrojo's essay about post-modern, non-essentialist translation and theory and practice (1998), "Dis-unity and diversity: Feminist approaches to translation studies," an article by Luise von Flotow about the complex, even divisive nature of "feminist" approaches to translation (1998); and "Mi novelista," a short story by Barbara Wilson, a woman translator-turned-novelist who herself becomes the object of translation (1998). I selected those three pieces as background reading that I asked participants to read before the workshops. For the exercise with multiple translations, I chose two poems by Sor Juana Inés de la Cruz, a seventeenth-century Mexican nun whose work has recently been translated by a number of translators, such as Electa Arenal and Amanda Powell, Willis Barnstone, and Margaret Sayers Peden (see Appendix). Since the situations in which I was to present the workshops varied considerably, I hoped that as a group the selections for background readings and the translation examples would enable me to discuss the flexibility and usefulness of multiple translations as a way to enable students to experience for themselves (as opposed to reading about others' experiences) the contextual, contingent nature of a translator's work. In choosing work by a woman writer, I hoped to focus on gender as a way of exploring the influence that a translator's attitudes and beliefs might exert on his or her practice.[4]

Workshops

Workshop One: "Interrogating Gender and/in the Teaching of Translation" Universitat de Vic, Vic (Barcelona) Spain

This workshop comprised two three-hour sessions: "Theory and Practice" and "Instruction." The first was attended by both faculty members and fourth-year undergraduate students. I opened the session with a brief discussion of my interest in exploring pedagogy with respect to such issues as gender, and my hope of discussing this in terms of both theory (what translation can do) and practice (what translation does and should do).[5] Many, although not all, of the faculty members and none of the students had read the three articles beforehand, so I summarized them, gave my reasons for selecting them, and discussed my own work as a "woman-interrogated" translator (see Maier 1998 and 1999). I then asked for audience response to either the articles or my remarks. Comments centered first on von Flotow's article. Participants found her comments accurate, if limited in scope. There was particular interest in her mention of the contribution made by lesbian approaches to translation. This was an area about which several people wanted further information, and we discussed what I consider to be the strong role played by lesbian cultural criticism in the development of current thinking about translation, as opposed to what von Flotow describes as its "still marginal position" (1998: 3). Arrojo's article was considered only briefly. Many of the faculty members present belonged to a discussion group in which they had discussed her ideas at length. In general, they agreed with her arguments for training translators as "self-conscious writers" (1998: 44) who are aware that one cannot grasp the entire "meaning" of a text, much less transport it intact to another context (i.e., that, to at least some extent, all originals could be declared "missing"). Consequently, they endeavor to train their students accordingly. At the same time, however, they explain to students that to work as a practicing translator one must make a commitment to a specific text and, at times, to a specific author. They noted that students almost invariably found disturbing the paradox between commitment and what is implied in the deconstruction Arrojo advocates.

The remaining discussion, somewhat more than half the session, was devoted to Wilson's story, which gave rise to an animated exchange about the many theoretical issues implicitly addressed in it. None of the participants had encountered Wilson's work before, and they all found the story engaging and stimulating. In particular, they spoke about the disputed "original" created by Cassandra Reilly, Wilson's protagonist, linking her implicitly to the issues in Arrojo's article, but commenting on those issues in a more dynamic and immediate way than they had earlier in the session. We also discussed the conflictive, even combative relationship between Cassandra the protagonist and "her" novelist, who is also the self-proclaimed creator of Cassandra — this despite the fact that the two characters enter into a collaboration at the end of the story.

The absence of complicity or solidarity that one might have expected to find between female characters was not mentioned by the participants. Nor did they refer to any of the other ways in which gender might be addressed with respect to the story. Gender, in this instance, was less significant to them than either the arbitrary, indeed unprovable and ultimately contextual nature of authorship and authority in Wilson's story, or the fact that even though a translator is initially a protagonist, that designation eventually shifts to an author, or to the individual who has been able to establish herself as the author.[6]

The second session of the workshop at Vic was devoted to instruction. For this session, I prepared three items as background material: a two-sided sheet with multiple translations of two poems by Sor Juana; a chronology of Sor Juana's life and times; and a bibliography of English-language translations of her work and selected titles related to pedagogy, gender, and translation (see Appendix). Again, the participants had been able to read the material beforehand; again, I gave a brief introductory explanation in which I described my goals for the workshop and my efforts as an instructor to devise teaching strategies that would integrate theory and practice in a way that might enable students, and here I use Peter Schjeldahl's terms, to "dance" with rather than "march" to the ideas of translation scholars such as Arrojo and von Flotow. I also presented my thoughts about the use of multiple versions, explaining that my primary goal was not to determine the quality of the individual versions but to interrogate the notion of a "definitive" translation and the assumed superiority of a work just because it has been published. I explained that, like Rachel du Plessis, I believed that working with several versions of the same text simultaneously can prompt students to identify the challenges a translator would be most likely to encounter.[7] In addition, I commented on my choice of texts, briefly outlining Sor Juana's life and work, focusing in particular on the two poems I had chosen. Since the translation of both poems inevitably raises questions related to gender, I believed that working with versions prepared by a wide variety of translators would occasion discussion about the ways in which a translator's commitment to a specific approach might or might not be evident in his or her work and about whether or not a gender-based approach seemed appropriate in this situation.

My original plans for the workshop had been to convert the discussion into a true workshop session in which participants would talk as a single group or divide into small groups, reading the various translations of Sor Juana's poems and arriving at a consensus about the role gender might have played — or not have played — in the translators' thinking. Since the group was small, however, I decided to open the discussion session by asking the participants to comment on their responses to my introductory remarks, mentioning that I would be grateful for their thoughts about the amount of background material an instructor might best present to students before asking them to work with the translations. This question proved so engrossing to the participants that we discussed it almost exclusively for the rest of the session. Although everyone agreed that the background material students needed would depend on the individual situation, the general consensus was that I had given them too much information. They believed that for students to participate fully in the exercises, they would need to start from whatever was "scratch" for them, after receiving the assignment of preparing themselves to read the translations knowledgeably and/or to translate Sor Juana's poems into English, using whatever guidance they found in the poems themselves. The instructor would stand ready to assist them, perhaps to search with them for material as necessary, should the amount of information available in print and online seem either too small or too overwhelming. The instructor should also be prepared to answer questions and provide further materials when the class met as a whole to discuss the versions. Implicitly, then, considerations of commitment and approach would not be addressed by translators or students who were unfamiliar with the context in which a text was written.

Workshop Two: "Gender and the Pedagogy of Literary Translation" University of East Anglia, Norwich, UK

The second workshop also comprised two sessions, each of which lasted about 90 minutes. The first, sponsored by the British Centre for Literary Translation, formed part of a weekly forum series on literary translation. Presentations are open to the university community and the public. My workshop was attended by a varied audience, which included postgraduate students from a class on literary translation, professional translators from several countries who were working at the Centre as translators-in-residence, members of the faculty at the University of East Anglia, and a few people from the Norwich community. I began the session with an informal lecture, explaining that my interest in exploring commitment, in this case gender, in the context of translation was driven by the need I saw for the development of pedagogical approaches that derived from and integrated theory and practice. Drawing on my presentations and the discussions at Vic, I outlined my concerns and goals and presented a brief introduction to the life and work of Sor Juana. After a short audience discussion, I asked the members of the audience to break into four groups of six or seven, and I assigned one of the two poems on the worksheet to two of the groups, asking participants to read the versions carefully and to discuss as a group the issues they felt might arise as the translators worked with the poems. I did not request specifically that they focus their discussions on the question of gender, because I wanted to see if and how they would find that question pertinent. As the groups engaged in discussion, I moved from one to the other, participating for a short time in each.

After some thirty minutes, the groups were asked to summarize their comments for the audience as a whole. Each group had approached the poems somewhat differently, depending on the backgrounds and interests of the members. All of them felt that the information I had distributed had been appropriate and helpful. In general, their comments focused on the historical periods of both author and translator and its influence on word choice, decisions about language conventions, and formal constraints, especially rhyme. There was also considerable discussion about decisions related to gender. In fact, one of the first things quite a few of the participants noticed about the poems was the absence of conventional titles and Sor Juana's use of descriptive sentences to introduce the poems. The descriptions give no indication of the poet's gender. It would be possible for a translator to avoid a gendered description in English as well, even though the Spanish sentences do not contain an expressed subject (nor do the rules of Spanish grammar require that they do).

Not all of Sor Juana's translators have done this, however. Contrast, for example, Electa Arenal and Amanda Powell's translation of "Arguye de inconsecuentes" as "The poet proves illogical" (1994: 157) with Margaret Sayers Peden's "She proves the inconsistency" (1997: 148) and Alan Trueblood's "She demonstrates the inconsistency" (1988: 111). Such contrasts prompted the participants to consider not only the translation of the titles but also the evident intervention of the translator, whose perspective with respect to gender (as evidenced in even the translation of the introductory sentences) will have clear and far-reaching implications for the translation.

The second workshop at East Anglia was not a formal workshop but a spontaneous session arranged for the following day at the request of some of the participants in the first session. This session was strictly a workshop, in which participants commented on a text that I was currently translating. The group included members of a postgraduate translation class, their instructor, and the translators-in-residence at the British Centre for Literary Translation. I distributed photocopies of several passages and asked the group to comment on whatever aspect of the text they wished, explaining that I had chosen the passages because of the gender-related issues they raised for me.

Although the participants' initial responses addressed those issues, the comments soon focused on the translation of idioms, the use of dialect, and the nature of the narration. The role of gender was mentioned continually throughout the session, but only as it related to individual situations, not as a separate issue.

Workshop Three: "Across the Word: Translating a Mexican Nun" Wagner College, Staten Island, NY

This workshop, like those that preceded it, included two sessions. The first was part of a series of dinner forums for faculty and students from all disciplines. All of the students were undergraduates. Given the fact that most members of the audience had no specialized knowledge about translation, I did not focus my comments directly on translating gender. I did, however, focus on the invariably operative and determinative role of the translator's approach. Although most of the discussion centered on the translation of work by Sor Juana, I began my remarks by reading two dramatically different versions of several verses of the second chapter of Matthew, one from the King James version and one from Clarence L. Jordan's *Cotton Patch Version of Matthew and James* in order to demonstrate the extent to which translations of a single text can vary. The clear, even controversial disparity prompted immediate interest, which made it possible for me to move quickly to the translation of

Sor Juana's poems. I briefly outlined Sor Juana's life, asked the audience to look at the sheet I had distributed, and drew their attention to evidence of the translators' approaches, asking that they notice the particular aspects of the poems and the translation that had interested the groups at Vic and the University of East Anglia. Responses were perceptive, although general, given the nature of the audience; and most of the questions and comments focused on the most salient differences among the versions. Many of those differences gave rise to gender-related issues. For example, there was particular interest in the varied renditions of the word *necios* in the first line of the "Sátira filosófica." That word, which is the second word of the poem and modifies *hombres* (men), appears in the English versions as "foolish," "silly," "misguided," and "stupid." As one would expect, the group's discussion about the translation of *necios* gave rise to comments and questions about the entire poem, especially about gender. In other words, although I had not singled out gender as the focus of my presentation, the question of gender arose spontaneously from a comparison of the multiple versions.

A similar experience occurred the following day when I discussed translation as writing and rewriting in an honors seminar about Latin American literature. Not all of the students were proficient in Spanish, so the class read the works in translation. Although my visit occurred near the end of the semester, translation as such had not been addressed, and the class was conducted in English, as if the fact of translation was not pertinent. I began the class with introductory comments about translation as a form of retelling, using as my example Sor Juana's *Answer* (*Respuesta*), which was one of the first books they had studied. Next, I told them about the three translations of the *Respuesta* that exist in English and distributed copies of two passages from each. (Two of the versions contained both the Spanish and English texts.) One of the Spanish-speaking students was asked to read the first passage in Spanish and then each of the other passages was read aloud and discussed. The students' initial comments focused on word choice, style, and on the presence or absence of notes. The role of the translator's approach and, more specifically, the issue of gender, arose gradually from our discussion about the use of notes. (Two of the versions do include notes, those by Electa Arenal and Amanda Powell, and Margaret Sayers Peden). The notes by Arenal and Powell are more numerous and detailed than those of Peden, and they place a deliberate and explicit emphasis on the role of women in Sor Juan's time and on the possible "feminist" nuances in the *Respuesta*.

The students were intrigued by the differences among the versions and the influence that a translator's reading and intention could have on a text. At no point did I ask them which version they preferred or found "best." When the session ended, however, I did ask them which of the versions they believed would be most appropriate to use in a class such as theirs. Almost unanimously, the students agreed on Margaret Sayers Peden's *Woman of Genius*. Peden's version, they said, has a helpful introduction, with just a few notes, and Sor Juana's position as a woman in seventeenth-century Mexico is adequately discussed. They believed that Arenal and Powell's version might be too narrowly focused on gender and that their annotations might be too detailed for undergraduate students, but they did suggest having it placed on reserve in the library as a supplementary text.

Conclusion

Despite significant differences among the three workshops, my experiences, I believe, make it possible to suggest answers, albeit tentative ones, to my questions (and those raised by Arrojo) concerning the development of flexible pedagogical strategies for training translators to work knowingly with respect to both the trust they invariably place in a text and the limits placed by any and all approaches to translation. One such strategy is the use of multiple versions of the same work. By calling attention to the multiplicity of readings that a text can inspire, multiple versions can give rise to discussions about the commitments that drive those readings and, not incidentally, the aspects of a work that will occasion the greatest challenges to a translator. I would note that, depending on the level of the students and the purpose of the course, readings in theory such as those mentioned above could be used in addition to the multiple versions. With respect to the specific exercises I have described here, I would suggest that at first an instructor make less background information available to students than I did. In fact, I would now be far more likely to follow the method Luis Zukovsky illustrates in *The Test of Poetry* and initially provide only minimal background information, or none. As Zukovsky's book demonstrates, a reader can be prompted to look beyond immediately apparent resemblances and differences and to consider the more complex aspects of a text. When multiple translations of a work are presented without introductory information about either the author or the translator, the reader is drawn into the act of translation itself. The goal is to have the reader dancing rather than marching, motivated not by a belief in an ultimate universal deciphering but by the acceptance of an individual, contextual interpretation.

Notes

1. Concerning theory, I use "increasingly" thinking of the work that has been done since Venuti's groundbreaking article about 'the translator's invisibility' (1986). Concerning practice, see Harvey (1998), Massardier-Kenney (1997), and the work by Arrojo discussed in the present essay.

2. Several references come to mind: Samuel Taylor Coleridge's well-known "willing suspension of disbelief"; the initial trust that fuels Steiner's "hermeneutic motion" (1975: 296–297) and his discussion of reading "as *if*" (1989: 229); and the trust placed in one's memory and imagination without one's "leaning for sentences and authority on anything" (Josipovici 1999: 73). Also pertinent here, although less directly, is Andrew Chesterman's "translational trust," which refers to translation in the context of product and profession (1997: 180–183). In addition, I am thinking of three terms which might also be used to refer to that stability: "power" and the human need for the illusion of it discussed, in a telephone conversation with Maryanne Bertram, with respect to Nietzsche's *Philosophy in the Tragic Age of the Greeks*; Gillian Rose's argument for "attention" rather than "deconstruction" and "acceptance" rather than "mourning" (1999: 42); and the gratitude Underiner describes as "a rigorous mental discipline that will help the contemporary mind overcome its addiction to binaries," recognize the "relationship between giver and receiver," and acknowledge that "in very important ways, we are all beholden to one another" (2000: 1296–1297).

3. For travel support that made the presentation of these workshops possible, I would like to thank the Universitat de Vic, the British Centre for Literary Translation, Wagner College, the Kent State University Teaching Council, and Kent State's Institute for Applied Linguistics. I would also like to thank Martha Tennent, Peter Bush, and Marilyn Kiss for the invitations to present the workshops, and I am grateful to their colleagues and students for their generous comments and hospitality.

4. My thinking here was stimulated by Rachel Du Plessis's provocative use of multiple translations and her comments about the feminine as it passes through the male imagination (1993: 264).

5. I refer here to Toury's definitions (1995: 17–19). They are somewhat simplistic and schematicized, but they also offer guidelines and a definition of theory with respect to its "application."

6. It is interesting to note that the responses to Wilson's story confirm the nature of Cassandra Reilly in the two other novels (*Gaudi Afternoon* and *Troubles in Transylvania*) of which she is the protagonist. In neither of them is her lesbian identity as an individual the determining factor when she works as a translator, which may well be all the time, at least to the extent that her principal identification is that of translator. As she states in *Gaudi Afternoon*, she is neither a woman nor a man, but a "translator" (1990: 74). At the same time, however, Cassandra's identity as a translator and lesbian itself indicates the constant presence (and — perhaps — primary pertinence) of gender. Alice Walker has noted, for example, that feminists and lesbians are constantly "translating the materiality of ... daily experiences into an alien code" (1993: 322). As she explains, however, "materiality does not constitute an 'original,'" since what is at play are language, interpretation, and experience, which implies a task of "double translation, in which there is no original and no target

language" (1993: 324). In other words, in "Mi Novelista" the struggle between translator-author and author-translator is one of power that centers on a specific "original" that never existed and a novel written in Spanish. It is also a power struggle, however, between a dominant language and a weaker one — ironically, but I do not believe coincidentally. In other words, while Spanish is usually the weaker language with respect to English, it is the master language here or, in Parker's terms, the "phallic and patriarchal" one (1993:322), because it is the language of the individual who established herself as the "original" author, a position that automatically grants her superiority and authority, regardless of her language or gender. Thus, Cassandra learns that it is far more difficult than she ever expected for a translator to co-opt language and authorship, and Wilson's reader might be led to reflect on the extent to which an effort such as Cassandra's to co-opt authorship inevitably involves both gender-related concerns and many other factors.

7. Any number of discussions of multiple translations could be used instead of or in addition to the article by du Plessis (for instance, Prins's section on "Afterlife in translation," in "Sappho's broken tongue" [1999: 40-51]). I find du Plessis's essay particularly valuable, though, both because of the way she works with multiple versions and because she does not write as an advocate of her own version (see Gass [1999], for example) or comment negatively on the other translations and their versions (see Weinberger 1987).

References

Arenal, E., and Powell, A. 1994. *The Answer/La Respuesta*. NY: Feminist Press.

Arrojo, R. 1999. "Training the visible translator in the context of anti-essentialism." In *Training Translators and Interpreters: New Directions for the Millennium*. Unpublished papers from the III Jornades de Traducció a Vic, 265–278. Vic, Spain: Universitat de Vic.

Arrojo, R. 1998. "The revision of the traditional gap between theory and practice and the empowerment of translation in postmodern times." *The Translator* 4 (1): 25–48.

Arrojo, R. 1995. "Postmodernism and the teaching of translation." In *Teaching Translation and Interpreting 3: New Horizons: Papers from the Third Language International Conference 1995*, C. Dollerup and V. Appel (eds), 98–103. Amsterdam/Philadelphia: John Benjamins.

Barnstone, W. 1993. *Six Masters of the Sonnet: (Francisco Quevedo, Sor Juana Inés de la Cruz, Antonio Machado, Federico García Lorca, Jorge Luis Borges, Miguel Hernández): Essays and Translations*. Carbondale, IL: Southern Illinois UP.

Bush, P. 1997. "Strawberry flowers in realms of chocolate: The training of literary translators." In *The Changing Scene in World Languages: Issues and Challenges*, M. B. Labrun (ed), 109–117. American Translators Association Scholarly Monograph *Series* IX. Amsterdam/Philadelphia: John Benjamins.

Chesterman, Q. 1997. *Memes of Translation: The Spread of Ideas in Translation Theory*. Amsterdam/Philadelphia: John Benjamins.

Du Plessis, R. B. 1993. "Copying." *Sulfur* 33: 257–292.

Flotow, L. von. 1998. "Dis-unity and diversity: Feminist approaches to translation studies." In *Unity in Diversity? Current Trends in Translation Studies*, L. Bowker et. al. (eds), 3–13. Manchester, UK: St. Jerome.

Gass, W. H. 1999. *Reading Rilke: Reflections on the Problems of Translation*. New York: Knopf.

Harvey, K. 1998. "Translating camp talk: Gay identities and cultural transfer." *The Translator* 4 (2): 295–320.

Josipovoci, G. 1999. *On Trust: Art and the Temptations of Suspicion*. New Haven: Yale UP.

Lefevere, A. 1992. *Translating Literature: Practice and Theory in a Comparative Literature Context*. New York: Modern Language Association of America.

Maier, C. 1998. "Issues in the practice of translating women's fiction." *Bulletin of Hispanic Studies* 3 (1): 95–017.

Maier, C. 1999. "From *Delirio y destino* to *Delirium and Destiny*." In M. Zambrano, *Delirium and Destiny: A Spaniard in her Twenties*. C. Maier (trans), 237–248. Albany: SUNY Press.

Massardier-Kenney, F. 1997. "Towards a redefinition of feminist translation practice." *The Translator* 3 (1): 55–69.

Peden, M. S. 1997. *Poems, Protest, and a Dream: Selected Writings of Sor Juana Inés de la Cruz*. NY: Penguin.

Prins, Y. 1999. *Victorian Sappho*. Princeton: Princeton UP.

Rose, G. 1999. *Paradiso*. London: Menard Press.

Schjeldahl, P. 1998. "The gang theory of art education, or why artists make the worst students." *The Chronicle of Higher Education*. 27 November 1998.

Steiner, G. 1975. *After Babel: Aspects of Language and Translation*. New York: Oxford UP.

Steiner, G. 1989. *Real Presences*. Chicago: University of Chicago Press.

Toury, G. 1995. *Descriptive Translation Studies and Beyond*. Amsterdam/Philadelphia: John Benjamins.

Trueblood, A. S. 1988. *A Sor Juana Anthology*. Cambridge, MA: Harvard UP.

Underiner, T. L. 2000. "Beyond recognition, beholden: Toward a pedagogy of privilege." *Signs* 25: 4. 1293–1298.

Venuti, L. 1986. "The translator's invisibility." *Criticism* 28 (2): 179–212.

Venuti, L. 1998. *The Scandals of Translation: Towards an Ethic of Difference*. New York: Routledge.

Walker, A. 1993. "Under the covers: A synesthesia of desire." In *Sexual Practice/Textual Theory: Lesbian Cultural Criticism*, S. J. Wolfe and J. Penelope (eds), 322–339. Cambridge, MA: Blackwell.

Weinberger, E., and Paz, O. 1987. *Nineteen Ways of Looking at Wang Wei*. Mount Kisko, NY: Moyer Bell.

Wilson, B. 1998. "Mi Novelista." In *"The Death of a Well-Traveled Woman" and Other Stories*, 195–215. Chicago: Third Side Press.

Zukovsky, L. 2000. *A Test of Poetry*. (1948) Hanover, NY: Wesleyan UP.

Appendix

Translation, Gender, Pedagogy, Sor Juana Ines De La Cruz

Selected Bibliography

A. *English-Language Translators of "Hombres Necios . . ." and "A Su Retrato"*

Arenal, E., and A. Powell, eds & trans. 1994. *The Answer/La Respuesta*. NY: Feminist Press.

Barnstone, W. 1993. *Six Masters of the Hispanic Sonnet: (Francisco de Quevedo, Sor Juana Inés de la Cruz, Antonio Machado, Federico García Lorca, Jorge Luis Borges, Miguel Hernández): Essays and Translations*. Carbondale, IL: Southern Illinois UP.

Flores, K. 1986. *The Defiant Muse: Hispanic Feminist Poems from the Middle Ages to the Present*. A. Flores and K. Flores (eds). NY: Feminist Press.

Kittel, M. 1986. In Flores 1986.

Peden, M. S. 1997. *Poems , Protest, and a Dream: Selected Writings of Sor Juana Inés De La Cruz*. NY: Penguin.

Trueblood, A. S. 1988. *A Sor Juana Anthology*. Cambridge, MA: Harvard UP.

Warnke, F. J. 1986. *Three Women Poets (Renaissance And Baroque): Luise Labé, Gaspara Stampa, Sor Juana Inés De La Cruz*. Lewisburg, PA: Bucknell UP.

B. *Additional Translations of Sor Juana's Work*

Arenal and Powell (*La respuesta*).

Barnstone (additional sonnets).

Campion, J. 1983. *El sueño*. Austin, TX: Thorp Springs Press.

Flores (additional poems).

Harss, L. 1986. *Sor Juana's Dream*. NY: Lumen Books.

Pasto, D. 1997. *The House of Trials: A Translation of "Los empeños de una casa" by Sor Juana Inés de la Cruz*. NY: Peter Lang.

Peden (*La respuesta; Primero sueño*; additional poems). Peden's translation of *La respuesta* is also available as *A Woman of Genius: The Intellectual Autobiography of Sor Juana Inés de le Cruz*. 2nd ed. Salisbury, CT: Lime Rock P, 1987

Peters, P., and R. Domeier, O. S. B. 1998. *The Divine Narcissus/El divino Narciso*. Albuquerque: University of New Mexico Press.

Scott, N. M., ed & trans. 1999. *Madres del verbo/Mothers of the Word: Early Spanish American Women Writers: A Bilingual Anthology*. With an introduction by Nina M. Scott. Albuquerque: University of New Mexico Press. ("Letter to R. P. M. Antonio Nuñez," selected poems, including "A su retrato").

Trueblood (additional poems; "La carta de sor Filotela"; La Respuesta; selection from each *Primero sueño* and *El divino narciso*).

Warnke (additional sonnets).

C. *Creative Works Inspired by Sor Juana's Life and Writings*

Ackerman, D. 1988. *Reverse Thunder: A Dramatic Poem*. NY: Lumen Books.

Arenal, E. 1986. "This life within me won't keep still." In *Reinventing the Americas: Comparative Studies of the Literature of the United States and Spanish America*. B. G. Chevigny and G. Laguardia (eds). NY and London: Cambridge UP.

Gómez de Alba, A. 1999. *Sor Juana's Second Dream: A Novel.* Albuquerque: University of New Mexico Press.

Portillo Tremblay, E. 1983. *Sor Juana and Other Plays.* Michigan: Bilingual Press/Editorial Bilingue.

D. Brief Bibliography for Using Translation and/or Multiple Voices in Teaching

Cohen, J. 1988. "Oquendo's 'Rain': A Choral Rendering." *The American Voice* 10 (Spring 1988): 83–113.

Dingwaney, A., and C. Maier. 1996. "Translation as a method for cross-cultural teaching." In *Between Languages and Cultures: Translation and Cross-Cultural Texts,* A. Dinwaney and C. Maier (eds), 303–319. Pittsburgh: University of Pittsburgh Press.

Du Plessis, R. B. 1993. "Copying." *Sulfur* 33: 257–72.

Hass, R. 1999. "Poet's choice." *Book World.* (*The Washington Post*). 26 November 1999.

Peden, M. S. 1989. "Building a translation, the reconstruction business: Poem 145 of Sor Juana Inés de la Cruz." In *The Craft of Translation,* J. Biguenet and R. Schulte (eds), 13–27.

Maier, C. 1994. "Teaching literature through translation: A proposal and three examples." *Translation Review* 46: 10–13.

Walters, D. G. 1998. "Five modes of translation: About Quevedo's 'Miré los muros de la patria mía.'" *Bulletin of Hispanic Studies* 75: 55–67.

Weinberger, E., and O. Paz. 1987. *Nineteen Ways of Looking at Wang Wei.* U. Mount Kisko, NY: Moyer Bell.

E. Gender-Related Criticism about Translation and Sor Juana (A Very Brief Bibliography)

Arenal and Powell.

Arrojo, R. 1994. "Fidelity and the gendered translation." *TTR. Traduction Terminologie Rédaction* 8 (2): 147–64.

Arrojo, R. 1995. "'Feminist' 'orgasmic' theories of translation and their contradictions." *TradTerm* 2: 67–75.

Arrojo, R. 1995. "Postmodernism and the teaching of translation." In *Teaching and Interpreting 3: New Horizons: Papers from the Third Language International Conference,* C. Dollerup and V. Appel (eds), 97–103. Amsterdam/Philadelphia: John Benjamins.

Flotow, L. von. 1998. "Dis-unity and diversity: Feminist aproaches to translation studies." In *Unity in Diversity? Current Trends in Translation Studies,* L. Bowker, M. Cronin, D. Kenny and J. Pearson (eds), 4–13. Manchester, UK: St. Jerome.

Garayta, I. 1998. "Writing and rewriting Sor Juana: A case study in 'feminist' translation." "'Womanhandling' the text: feminism, rewriting, and translation." Ph.D. Dissertation. University of Texas at Austin.

Glantz, M. 1995. *Sor Juana Inés de la Cruz: ¿Hagiografía o autobiografía?.* Mexico: Universidad Nacional Autónoma de Mexico/Grijalbo.

Maier, C. 1995. Review of *The Answer/ La Respuesta* by Sor Juana Inés de la Cruz. Electa Arenal and Amanda Powell (trans). *Comparative Literature* 47 (1): 79–82.

Maier, C. 1998. "Issues in the practice of translating women's fiction." *BHS* 75: 95–107.

Massardier-Kenney, F. 1997. "Towards a redefinition of feminist translation practice." *The Translator* 3 (1): 55–69.

Merrim, S. 1991. *Feminist Perspectives on Sor Juana Inés de la Cruz.* Detroit, MI: Wayne State UP.

Merrim, S. 1999. *Early Modern Women's Writing and Sor Juana Inés de la Cruz.* Nashville, TN: Vanderbilt UP.

After [Isaac] Babel

Teaching communicative competence for translation

Natalia Olshanskaya

The teaching of effective translation methods must, of course, be based on a clear and well-defined notion of what constitutes an adequate translation. One of the most basic requirements for such adequacy is the factual accuracy of the target text. The translator is expected to reproduce the informational content of the original message, and his/her ability to do so depends largely on linguistic skills, knowledge of terminology, and even the appropriate use of dictionaries. However, translation is a much more sophisticated process than the mere 're-coding' of linguistic structures, demanding a high degree of analytical and creative skills. Development of these skills requires a teaching methodology considerably different from those based on traditional language training (Kussmaul 1995; Krings 1986).

Advancements in the field of communication studies over the past several years have led to changes in foreign language pedagogy, making communicative competence a major topic in the literature on foreign language teaching.[1] Translation theory and practice have also benefited from recent developments in communication theory — in particular, the study of functional styles and new approaches to text interpretation — as well as in semantics and comparative linguistics. Consequently, both translators and translator trainers have called for and implemented changes in the professional training of translators and interpreters (Obst 2001).

A "communicative" translation methodology would provide the student with a synthetic strategy for analyzing the meaning of the source text by decoding both its linguistic and non-linguistic clues, based on the understanding that translator competence cannot depend solely on linguistic knowledge, but must include communicative and cultural competence. The translator's ability to reproduce nuances of meaning depends on an ability to interpret a variety of text-forming elements ranging from common rules of logic to graphics accompanying the written text, or body language in oral message delivery. Knowledge of the cultural and historical contexts within which the original text functioned (or functions) is also an essential component of this ability.

Interdisciplinary studies of translation can help to identify stumbling blocks in intercultural communication by analyzing the difference between translations that are culturally adequate and those that are only linguistically accurate, highlighting the difficulties of translating between remote cultures. In this way, translation courses become a key to understanding thought, meaning, and language, and can serve as an important tool in the development of students' written and oral communicative competence.

This article will focus on two interrelated aspects of translation teaching: how to provide students with a basic theoretical understanding of communicative translation strategies, and how to implement this methodology in the classroom.

Translation courses and linguistics

The communicative approach to translation has been largely influenced by various linguistic schools, in particular, structuralism, functionalism, sociolinguistics, and psycholinguistics, that focus on communicative effectiveness and the construction of meaning as central to linguistic analysis. Such approaches to translation stress the function of the text and offer new criteria for evaluating the adequacy of translation. In view of this, providing students with at least a basic understanding of the fundamental concepts of these linguistic schools seems of paramount importance.

Linguists agree that the meaning of a text depends on the semantics of its linguistic elements such as vocabulary and sentence structure and their rearrangement within a particular text, which is manifest in its prosody, intonation, and composition. All of these elements constitute the semantic potentials of the text, which are activated as meaningful by *text function*. The Saussurean postulate of the dual nature of language, which on the one hand is represented in the actual utterance of the speaker (*parole*), and on the other constitutes a socially and culturally shared system of signification (*langue*), plays a key role in understanding the communicative approach to text analysis and in choosing the right strategies for translation.

Concrete utterances as text-forming elements are particularized instances of a complex pre-existing system. This system is comprised of linguistic units of different levels (phonemes, morphemes, words, sentences) that fit into a strict, differential grid recognized and commonly shared by the users of the language. Familiarizing students with this historically created linguistic system has always been the primary goal of traditional methods of second language acquisition, and it has often been extended to translation teaching methodology. This approach narrows the concept of translation to a search for purely linguistic equivalents in the source and target languages and attempts to provide students with a set of ready-made translation recipes.[2] Useful at the beginning level of instruction, this method of teaching translation ignores another important linguistic postulate, according to which specific linguistic rules must be formulated for each stylistic situation defined by its own norms and goals (Jakobson 1923).

Based on Ferdinand de Saussure's theory of language, Roman Jakobson's idea of *functional styles* (or functional dialects) has been most influential in translation theories of the second half of the twentieth century. His view of language as a set of functional styles, each regulated by its own linguistic rules and dependent on the final goal of the text or the utterance, is still regarded as key to achieving adequacy in translation (Hatim 1997; House 1997). According to Jakobson, each text is governed by two sets of rules: the first, more general, is shared by all speakers of a language and is imposed on the text by the internal system of the language (*langue*); the second is determined by the function of a particular text and reflects usage (*parole*), that is, the traditionally accepted stylistic norms according to which text types are organized within a given linguistic system. All texts thus fall into three main groups that correspond to the three main goal-oriented verbal activities — the emotive, the practical, and the poetic.[3]

Jakobson's three *goal-oriented* groups of texts can be related to the oldest classification of rhetorical styles into high, middle, and low, a tradition that has remained popular in twentieth-century studies of rhetoric. For example, in his classification Northrop Frye combines situational factors and language characteristics, assigning the latter a definitely secondary, subordinate role. He distinguishes between "low" style described as "a colloquial or familiar style" "with all its anti-grammatical forms, … its own vocabulary, its own syntax, its own rhythm, its own imagery and humor" (Frye 1963: 41); "middle" style, which is neutral and communicated by articulate persons in a relaxed and informal manner; and "high" style, which is not at all associated with ornate language but is assigned a special ethical role: "Genuine high style is ordinary style, or

even low style in an exceptional situation which gives it exceptional authority... High style in ordinary speech is heard whenever a speaker is honestly
struggling to express what his society, as a society, is trying to be and do" (Frye
1963: 45–46).

User-related studies of text have resulted in other approaches to text
typology, which attempt to classify texts according to the field of discourse —
journalistic, scientific, religious, legal, etc. (Crystal and Davy 1969); according
to the speech situation — formal, informal (Skrebnev 1976); or the combination of various communicative factors — bookish (written) versus colloquial
(oral) — with the field of discourse — academic, official, publicistic, literary
style (Rosental and Telenkova 1976). Despite the unresolved problem of overlap that is obvious in all these text typologies, their importance for translation
teaching cannot be overestimated, since they identify the factors — historical,
regional, cultural, social — that form the *idiolect* of the text, its language
variety. As M. A. K. Halliday has pointed out: "The social functions of language
clearly determine the pattern of language *varieties*, in the sense of what have
been called 'diatypic' varieties, or 'registers'; the register range, or linguistic
repertoire, of a community or of an individual is derived from the range of uses
that language is put to in that particular culture or sub-culture" (1973: 14).

Despite their differences in approach to discourse, all functional studies of
text show that, beyond the lexical and grammatical resources of a language, it is
important to take into account not only the content of an utterance, but also
the circumstances under which the given verbal communication has occurred.
An interest in the study of languages beyond the sentence level has given rise to
discourse-oriented translation studies (Catford 1965). Findings in text linguistics and stylistics have contributed to both the theory and the practice of
translation: "Translating involves much more than finding corresponding
words between two languages. In fact, the words are only minor elements in
the total discourse. In many respects the tone of a passage (that is, the style of
the language) carries far more impact, and often even much more meaning,
than the words themselves" (Nida 1975: 183).

From the point of view of its applicability, the functional approach to texts
opens up a set of operational possibilities for translation. This approach has
had a significant impact on translation theory and practice by encouraging
translators to work with text typologies, to pay attention to the communicative
situation and genre, stylistic reference of vocabulary and syntax, and to analyze
all types of deviations from the linguistic norm. Like any appropriate scientific
methodology, it allows us both to generalize and to individualize the phenomena under study, making it extremely valuable as an organizing principle for

instruction in translation. It also provides connections to other appropriate methods of translation teaching, and gives them new dimensions.

Cross-cultural communication and translation

The attempt to extend the process of translation beyond individual speech acts has shifted the focus of translation courses to cross-cultural communication; speech acts on the level of individual utterances began to be viewed in terms of the way they fit into particular cultures (Bassnett and Lefevere 1990, 1998). Since communication is a social act, translation practice has to determine the circumstances under which the source text has been produced and the factors that may influence the decoding of the message in the target or receiving culture. Developing an awareness of differences in cultural norms and an understanding of the need for cross-cultural adjustments has become an important issue in translation teaching.

The meaning of any text is always deeply embedded in its *context*, a broad notion that includes the physical, psychological, historical, social, and cultural circumstances under which the source text was produced. The success of communication depends on the similarity of text-producing and text-receiving contexts; a communication is considered relevant when the addressee naturally, without any undue effort, decodes the intended meaning of the addresser of the speech act (Sperber and Wilson 1995: 270; Gutt 1998: 43).

The conditions of communicative success are obviously difficult to identify, which means that instruction in translation must devote special attention to all nuances of cross-cultural situations, comparing rules that govern successful performance of various types of communication in different cultures. To what degree should the translator amend the text to comply with the 'rules and regulations' acceptable in the receiving culture? How much background information does the reader need for relevant interpretation? What is the appropriate solution in order to achieve the right balance between 'over-translated' and 'under-translated' utterances? These questions have to be constantly addressed in order to avoid potential miscommunication in translation. Moreover, they will be addressed differently depending upon the type of the source text.

The degree of familiarity in the receiving culture with the specific *social context* in which the source text was produced accounts for the degree of communicative success and programs the acceptance of certain texts by the new cultural community. This is most obvious in the translation of advertisements, which are tailored to target specific social groups and thus have to undergo numerous cultural adjustments when they are adapted to address other groups.

Genre definitions in general, and *literary genre* definitions in particular, are another important factor in programming the interpretation of a text by the receiving culture. By labeling the work as *comedy* or *tragedy*, the author evokes certain expectations in the reader. Genre definitions become codes for interpretation of texts and are often responsible for their misrepresentation in new cultural contexts. For example, Shakespeare's *Troilus and Cressida* or Chekhov's *The Seagull* and *The Cherry Orchard*, labeled as comedies, have often produced false expectations in readers; in particular, the interpretation of *The Cherry Orchard* has often been confined to the most simplistic definition of comedy at the hands of some British and American theater directors.

A shift in *aesthetic standards* from the producing to the receiving culture undoubtedly influences the degree of acceptance of the target text, and can become an insurmountable obstacle for translators. An often-mentioned example is the case of Pushkin's *Eugene Onegin*, whose misrepresentation in translations is mostly associated with differences in the aesthetic norms of English and Russian versification (Nabokov 1955; Scherr 2000). On the other hand, the creative adaptation of Shakespeare's sonnets and Burns' lyrics to Russian poetic standards by Samuel Marshak made these literary works well-known and genuinely popular in Russian culture.

Different text types are based on distinctly varied *norms of structural and linguistic expression*. For example, the intentionally complex syntax of Russian academic papers is simply unacceptable in English academic style, and would require a considerable amount of syntactic simplification to make it readable and coherent for the English reader. In this case, the syntactic complexity of Russian academic prose is a standard stylistic feature, aimed at conveying the image of a learned addresser. It is formed by the cultural tradition of expression for this particular group of texts, and needs to be adjusted to the requirements of the corresponding English text type.

A variety of changes and adjustments must be introduced into the target texts in 'highly regularized' legal documents, such as patents, wills, all sorts of government certificates, and business letters. Russian and English business letters, which differ in the order of elements, their linguistic representation, and punctuation, are a good example of the existing differences in *cross-cultural standardization*. In a Russian business letter, the address starts with the addressee's title and name, followed by the country, the postal code, the city, the street name, the building number; phrases like *To whom it may concern*, or

Attention... are inappropriate; the salutation is followed by an exclamation mark instead of the traditional English colon or comma; each paragraph should be indented, etc. Even the norms of graphic formatting have to be observed in order to create a valid target text, which calls for a thorough knowledge of cross-cultural standards on the part of the translator.

Establishing functional equivalence in *interpersonal communication* is another important factor in achieving adequacy in translation. Cross-cultural differences in expressing sociolinguistic phenomena, such as humor, irony and politeness, have been specifically addressed, and the need for empirical cross-cultural research on norms of linguistic behavior has been stressed in translation studies (Hatim 1998, House 1998).

Politeness in communication, for example, is revealed in the choices of subject matter and its expression in linguistic forms, silences, omissions, taboos, facial expressions and gestures — all elements of social and moral decorum which are relevant in written and oral communication and are thus important for translators and interpreters. Questions about a person's financial standing, considered socially inappropriate in English-speaking countries, are natural in the Russian social context, while a public, explicit discussion of sexual behavior would be avoided by Russians. Similarly taboo for Russians is any indication in discussions between a doctor and a patient that the patient's illness may be terminal. On the other hand, linguistically, the Russian speaker is almost always more forceful and direct, more explicit, than the English speaker. A polite request in Russian can be expressed by an imperative form of the verb combined with a relevant intonation pattern, as in Закройте окно! *(Close the window!)*, while the socially accepted equivalent in English, *Could you please close the window?*, avoids the use of imperatives and is worded in the form of a question. These examples show how potential, implied meanings that are activated and interpreted in one way by the majority of one cultural community might be misinterpreted in another culture, causing serious distortions in translation.

Dealing with language use in natural situations demonstrates that a change in the context can result in a change in the meaning of an utterance. Translation, by definition, leads to a change of context, since it is based on the transposition of the source text into a completely different cultural context. Bridging the cultural gap between the text-producing and text-receiving cultures is the purpose of any successful communication in translation. This process involves a wide range of factors that need to be identified and specifically addressed in a carefully designed course in translation.

Adequacy in translation

Though all translation acts are to a certain extent subjective, based on individual decision-making, they are largely determined by *communicative norms*, that is, previously established prototypes shared by a cultural community. Compliance with these norms determines the adequacy of translation, an important category to be addressed in translation teaching.

Adequacy, as a central concept in translation studies, describes the communicative relevance of the target text in its relationship to the source text and to the new cultural context. It is often referred to as "text-normative equivalence" (Koller 1989: 102), "textual equivalence" (Baker 1992), or "functional equivalence" (Newman 1980), but because of the controversial nature of the term "equivalence," which has been treated too loosely in translation studies,[4] we would suggest a distinction between equivalence and adequacy. *Equivalence* is understood here as a theoretical term describing an ideal relationship between the source and the target texts that can be investigated at the level of similarities in their linguistic expression. *Adequacy* is an empirical category, related to the functional value of the target text, and can be established only after the act of translation has occurred. Non-equivalence at the word or sentence level does not necessarily result in translation inadequacy, since despite lexical and grammatical differences in the source and target languages, "all cognitive experience and its classification is conveyable in any existing language" (Jakobson 1959/1971b: 263).

Each text is represented by various linguistic and non-linguistic elements that are integrated and activated by the text function. Yet in particular text types, some elements enjoy a higher communicative status than others. The progression in meaning, the logic of the utterance, and the coherence of the text depend on the specific combination of these text variables. Consequently, in translation, one distinguishes between invariants and variants: *invariants* are elements that must be rendered in the target text; *variants* are those that can be modified.

It is obvious that variants and invariants differ not only from text to text, but also from one functional style to another. Texts whose primary function is purely informative will be represented by one set of invariants, while for texts with a dominant aesthetic function there will be a different set of invariants. At the initial stage, the mechanism for achieving adequacy in translation lies with the translator's ability to identify variants and invariants.

Connecting theory and practice

In light of what has been said above, it is important to develop a set of exercises that will sensitize students of translation to practical issues of working with texts representing different functional styles. These classroom exercises should be both descriptive and prescriptive, aiming at analysis and synthesis, and can encompass several stages:

1. Analysis of the source text, including:
   a. Study of its genre, composition, vocabulary, and syntax
   b. Identification of its invariants and variants
2. Detailed discussion of functional norms of similar groups of texts in the target culture
3. Assessment of the adequacy of any existing translation(s)
4. Development of translation strategies and recommendations for particular functional styles and genres

Since one of the main goals of this methodology will be not to find equivalents, but to explore the available possibilities, the study of multiple translations of the same literary text is recommended as one of the most fruitful areas of investigation. In the selection of texts, instructors must be guided by the genre, composition, and linguo-stylistic parameters of the source text that can best serve their purposes and demonstrate specific techniques of translation. (Thus, the technique of *compensation* can be illustrated in the analysis of humor and its reproduction in the target text, *simplification* in the comparison of texts based on the non-equivalence of registers or personal writing styles, etc.)

To place this communication strategy into a practical context, it might be helpful to look at the opening paragraph of Isaac Babel's story "Как это делалось в Одессе," and its two translations into English, "How It Was Done in Odessa," by Walter Morison and Andrew R. MacAndrew.[5] Fully acknowledging the atomistic nature of splitting the text into constituent elements, we present this analysis as a sample exercise that can be used in the study of the translation of any literary text. Our choice of the source text was based on the complex pragmatic structure of the narrative, and the subtle, ironic tone employed to deliver a whole range of implied, rather than directly communicated, ideological messages. In part, our selection was determined by the text's peculiar linguistic representation, based on stylistically different registers. These pragmatic and linguistic features of the story set additional challenges for translators and influence their preference for specific translation strategies.

(1) = Начал я.

— Реб Арье-Лейб, — сказал я старику, — поговорим о Бене Крике. Поговорим о молниеносном его начале и ужасном конце. Три тени загромождают пути моего воображения. Вот Фроим Грач. Сталь его поступков — разве не выдержит она сравнения с силой Короля? Вот Колька Паковский. Бешенство этого человека содержало в себе все, что нужно для того, чтобы властвовать. И неужели Хаим Дронг не сумел различить блеск новой звезды? Но почему же один Беня Крик взошел на вершину веревочной лестницы, а все остальные повисли на шатких ступенях? (Babel 1998: 307)

(2)   It was I then began.

"Reb Arye-Leib," I said to the old man, "let us talk of Benya Krik. Let us talk of his thunderclap beginning and his terrible end. Three black shadows block up the paths of my imagination. Here is the one-eyed Ephraim Rook. The russet steel of his actions, can it really not bear comparison with the strength of the King? Here is Nick Pakovsky. The simple-minded fury of that man held all that was necessary for him to wield power. And did not Haim Drong know how to distinguish the brilliance of the rising star? Why then did Benya Krik alone climb to the top of the rope ladder, while the rest hung swaying on the lower rungs?" (Babel 1955: 211–212)

(3)   I spoke first.

"Reb Arie-Leib," I said to the old man, "let us talk about Benya Krik. Let's talk about his meteoric rise and his ghastly end. Three silhouettes block my imagination. There's Froim Grach. Can't the steel of his deeds bear comparison with the strength of the 'King'? There's Kolia Pakovsky. That man's rage had in it all that is needed to wield power. And how is it possible that Haim Drong failed to recognize the blaze of the new star? Well, why was it, then, that Benya Krik alone climbed to the top of the rope ladder while the others were left hanging below on its shaky rungs?" (Babel 1993: 210)

Identifying the cultural context of the source text

Babel's Odessa stories are humorous laconic sketches portraying the life of the Jewish population in the Ukraine. His subtle psychological insights are based on a combination of the tragic and the comic, and his humor is influenced by regional folklore and anecdotes rendered in a colorful Russian dialect incorporating elements of Yiddish and Ukrainian.

It is well known that humor is perceived differently from one individual to another and that reactions to it vary among social and cultural groups. To perceive the comic elements in the opening lines of this story, the reader must be familiar with the marginal social status of the Jewish population in Russia at the beginning of the twentieth century and the particular poverty of Jews living in Moldavanka, a district in Odessa where the action in Babel's stories takes place. This implied cultural knowledge is important to an understanding of the irony of the situation, the incongruity between the reality of the characters' lives and its depiction through the point of view of the two narrators.

The composition of the story

The composition of "How It Was Done in Odessa" is that of a story within a story, a dialogue between two characters. The events are described through their point of view in the form of *skaz*,[6] a first-person narrative, popular in Russian literature, which imitates an oral, informal manner of discourse. This narrative device influences the manner of presentation of the events, and the use of vocabulary and syntax.[7] The language simultaneously serves two purposes: to express the referential meaning of the utterance and, indirectly, to characterize the producers of the speech act. The order in which the events are presented reflects the associative principle of thinking that is characteristic of unprepared, spontaneous oral discourse. Some facts and events are implied, rather than explicitly described in the narrative, since the participants in the dialogue have previous knowledge about the subject of their conversation and renew their discussion without bothering to introduce the reader to its details. This obviously requires more effort on the part of the readers to decode the information and understand the plot.

The evaluation of concepts by the narrator shifts the focus to the emotive meanings of words and the expressive function of syntax; ideological meanings are now formatted by the stylistic reference of the language. The humorous effect is based on the contrast between the content (the story of a petty Jewish gangster) and the form of the presentation (a heroic, legendary saga). The upside-down world of the story is revealed through its specific linguistic representation.

Linguistic representation of the ideological message in the source and target texts

The indirect, linguistically implicit communication subtly calls attention to stylistic shifts in semantics, and reminds the translator of the generally accepted hypothesis that the more language-bound implications are, the more difficult they are to reproduce in the target text. Already in the first paragraph of the source text, the proper names, used in their diminutive form Колька or replaced by a nickname Беня, signal a contrast with regard to the referential and the connotative meanings of the words Король, властвовать, сила, сталь, вершина (*King, to wield power, strength, steel, the summit*).

The contrast is intensified by the evidently Jewish origin of the characters, implied in the choice of their names, and the discussion of the possibility of their climbing to the top of the social ladder. This situation, easily recognized by the Russian reader as socially inconceivable, suggests irony, and provides a specific code for the interpretation of the source text: an attitude of doubt as to the truthfulness of the narrator's point of view and, as a result, an element of disbelief in the whole story.

This important onomastic feature is difficult to reproduce in the target text; the non-Russian origin of the names and their social connotation cannot be perceived immediately by the English reading audience. Both translators seem to be aware of this additional interpretative obstacle and attempt to resolve the matter through different translation techniques. Morison looks for direct equivalence at the level of vocabulary (Колька/*Nick*; Грач/*Rook*), but his selective translation of proper names (why not then Крик/*Outcry*; Паковский/ *Package*, etc.?) does not seem to be an effective device. The translator has correctly identified the invariables in this text unit, but has failed to reproduce their function, which is not based on the referential meaning of the proper names, but on their function in a complex socio-cultural context. On the other hand, MacAndrew obviously considers this loss in translation to be inevitable and makes up for it by putting the word "*King*" in quotation marks, thus suggesting its ironic meaning. The technique of *compensation* employed here by the translator seems to be more productive, for though it does not completely recover the information of the source text, it creates an additional signal in the target text, and helps to identify the account as ironic. Later in the story, when one of the characters is referred to as полтора жида, both translators replace the derogatory жид with the more neutral *Jew, Jew-and-a-Half.* In the original, the derogatory reference indirectly hints at widespread Russian anti-Semitism, while in the translation, it undergoes *normalization* to better fit the ethical norms of the receiving culture.

Contrast becomes the main stylistic device of the story and can be traced at all structural levels, from its composition to its linguistic code: the contrasting descriptions of the rich and the poor, the killer and the victim, and the obvious discrepancy between the more-than-ordinary plot and the high style of its presentation. Numerous rhetorical figures in the source text are adequately represented in both translations, contributing to the highly ornate style of the narrative and to the production of the ironic effect: the antitheses о молниеносном его начале и ужасном конце, *his thunderclap beginning and his terrible end* (Morison), *his meteoric rise and his ghastly end* (MacAndrew); the metaphors три тени загромождают пути моего воображения, *three black shadows block up the paths of my imagination* (Morison), *three silhouettes block my imagination* (MacAndrew); блеск новой звезды, *the brilliance of the rising star* (Morison), *the blaze of the new star* (MacAndrew); сталь его поступков, *the russet steel of his actions* (Morison), *the steel of his deeds* (MacAndrew). These few examples also show how Morison tends to use the technique of *explication* by adding new epithets into the target text: *black, russet.*

By the end of the paragraph, the author's irony becomes even more obvious in the simile that compares social climbing to a circus, with the social ladder turning into *the shaky rope ladder* on which the characters are hanging like acrobats. The epithet шаткие/*shaky*, reproduced only in the second target text, introduces the idea of instability as part of the general notion of Jewish displacement, which is humorously worded later in the story and constitutes an important ideological message in the Odessa cycle of Babel's stories.

At the syntactic level, the irony is sustained through the contrast between the poetic, rhythmically arranged sentences based on parallelism, rhetorical questions, and inversions and the ordinary, low subject of the conversation. The incongruity between the message and the intentionally inappropriate linguistic register is reproduced in both target texts through the equivalence of syntactic translation units.[8]

The register profile of the text and translation strategies

Throughout the story, neither vocabulary nor syntax is consistently poetic. The main narrator Arie-Leib constantly mixes registers of speech, which on the one hand, reveals his educational background and cultural incompetence, and on the other, creates the humorous effect of the story. This mixing of registers becomes an important invariant to be preserved in the target text. It already occurs in the opening paragraph, when the syntactic uniformity is broken up by the introduction of short colloquial sentences which create stylistic dissonance and cause arrhythmia in the generally poetic rhythm of the narrative: Вот Фроил Грач./Вот Колька Паковский. In the first translation, the colloquial nature of the utterance *Here is the one-eyed Ephraim Rook* is intensified by the expansion of the original sentence. The translator inserts the colloquial adjective *one-eyed*, which is used to characterize Grach only in the closing paragraph of the source text. The second translator marks the colloquial nature of these sentences by contracted verbal forms such as *there's*, and by adding several other contracted forms (*let's, can't*) into other sentences.

Colloquial and substandard elements of discourse are frequently used by Babel to describe the ethnic, social, and cultural background of his characters. They are represented in (1) the grammatically incorrect use of prepositions and (2) cases, (3) the introduction of jargon words, and (4) the violation of set expressions and phraseology:

(1)   и вог он погиб *через* глупость
(2)   Брось *этих глупостей*, Беня.
(3)   *Тикать с конторы*
(4)   перестанем размазывать *белую* кашу по *чистому* столу

The translators suggest the following:

	Morison	MacAndrew
(1)	had to meet a nonsensical death	he suddenly gets himself killed for no good reason
(2)	Give up this nonsense, Benya.	Quit fooling, Benya.
(3)	Let's scram	Let's get the hell out of here
(4)	stop smearing gruel over a clean table	let's stop messing up the tablecloth

Differences in the grammatical, lexical, and phraseological levels in the two languages make it difficult to seek direct equivalence in translation. This often results in numerous *simplifications* and stylistic losses in the target texts. In example (1), the violation of the grammatical norm in the source text is represented by a standard, stylistically neutral phrase by Morison, while MacAndrew preserves the colloquial tone of the phrase by means of compensation, expanding it, making it inappropriately 'wordy'. A similar difference in reflecting the substandard speech of the characters is evident in the translation of sentence (2). In example (3), both translators found stylistically relevant slang expressions. Less fortunate was the idiomatic collocation размазывать кашу по столу (4), equivalent to the English *to chew the fat*. In the original, the introduction of new elements into this colloquial set expression produces a humorous effect and is yet another signal of the character's 'non-Russianness.' Failure to identify this idiom as a translation unit is evident in both target texts.

In fact, the examples given above cover the most typical translation patterns which occur in the reproduction of substandard speech: non-equivalence in the choice of registers (Morison (1) and (2)); equivalence of registers based on substitution (MacAndrew (1) and (2)); lexical and stylistic equivalence (Morison and MacAndrew (3)); and semantic and stylistic loss (Morison and MacAndrew (4)).

Establishing formal equivalence by matching small, functionally significant text segments is an important exercise that shows that the correspondence between vocabulary registers of the source and target texts determines the balance between the text and its function and leads to the discussion of the more general issue of translation adequacy.[9] At the practical level of translation teaching, the analysis of contrastive linguistic layers becomes most helpful in identifying common grounds for text formation. Assuming that the functional specifics of the text rest with its idiolect, we would suggest exercises based on the contrastive analysis of registers in the source and the target texts as one of the important ways of assessing adequacy in translation.

Summary

Linguistic competence in both languages on the part of the translator is a necessary but not a sufficient condition for translation adequacy. Beyond the linguistic level, dual cultural competency is required, sufficient to achieve proper contextualization of the source and the target texts in their respective cultures. This includes, first of all, an understanding of the pragmatics of the source text, as revealed through its genre and register, and of the communicative and stylistic norms appropriate in the two cultures to the relevant type of discourse.

Even with a pragmatic text written in neutral language, it will often be necessary to transpose the material of the original to conform to the standards that apply to the corresponding communicative situation in the target culture. Such adjustments become even more indispensable with poetic texts in which stylistic expressiveness and distinctiveness form a prominent feature. These texts will often call for solutions that depend on the ingenuity of individual translators, which, of course, requires that they recognize the situations that allow for their inventiveness.

The paradigm of comparative text analysis described above is by no means all-inclusive, nor does it claim to cover all the points relevant to a discussion of literary translations. It is presented here as one of the many possibilities in teaching communicative competence, which in our understanding can be achieved only through a well-balanced combination of linguistic and cultural information introduced in a properly designed translation course. One must admit that, like any other methodology, the suggested strategy has its own limitations and cannot answer all the questions raised in the discipline. Only the integration of a plurality of approaches into instruction will provide the student with the necessary tools and perspectives for achieving truly adequate translation.

Notes

1. See Cook (1998) on the changing attitudes towards use of translation in language teaching.

2. This methodological principle is obvious in the textbook *Translating from English into Russian* (Radilova 1998), where the author catalogs the grammar patterns of the two languages as a guide to translation practice.

3. In his later works, Jakobson also defines the cardinal functions of language as "referential, emotive, conative, phatic, poetic and metalingual — and their different hierarchy in the diverse types of messages" (Jakobson 1959/1971a: 703).

4. Compare the narrowing down of its meaning to referential correspondence between SL and TL (Catford 1965: 50) and a very broad definition of 'equivalence' as "a commonsense term for describing the ideal relationship that the reader would expect to exist between an original and its translation" (Newman 1994: 4694).

5. Note also the publication in 2001 of *The Complete Works of Isaac Babel*, edited by Nathalie Babel and translated by Peter Constantine (New York: Norton).

6. This term was first introduced by Eikhenbaum in his analysis of Gogol's story *Shinel/The Overcoat* (Eikhenbaum 1919).

7. For a detailed discussion of the shifts in perspective in Russian literary narratives and their translation into English, see May (1994: 91B102).

8. The change in punctuation in the introduction of direct speech in the source and target paragraphs is based on *normalization* and can be used as a starting point for the discussion of the use of this translation technique in regard to syntax as well.

9. The assessment of translation quality is often connected with the theory of registers. Thus House builds his idea of the textual profile on register analysis and claims that "the degree to which... the [TT] textual profile does not match the ST's profile is the degree to which that TT is inadequate in quality" (House 1997: 50).

References

Babel, I. 1955. "How it was done in Odessa." In *The Collected Stories*, W. Morison (ed and trans), 211–222. New York: Criterion Books.

Babel, I. 1985. "How it was done in Odessa." A. MacAndrew (trans). In *The Portable Twentieth Century Russian Reader*, C. Brown (ed), 210–220. Harmondworth, Middlesex: Penguin Books.

Babel', I. 1998. "Kak eto delalos' v Odesse." In *Izbrannoe*, 307–318. Minsk: Sovremennoe slovo.

Baker, M. 1992. *In Other Words: A Coursebook on Translation*. London/New York: Routledge.

Bassnett, S., and Lefevere, A. 1990. *Translation, History and Culture*. London: Pinter.

Bassnett, S., and Lefevere, A. 1998. *Constructing Cultures. Essays on Literary Translation*. Clevedon/Philadelphia: Multilingual Matters.

Catford, J. C. 1965. *A Linguistic Theory of Translation: An Essay in Applied Linguistics*.

London: Oxford University Press.

Cook, G. 1998. "Use of translation in language teaching." In *Routledge Encyclopedia of Translation Studies*, M. Baker (ed), 117–120. London/New York: Routledge.

Crystal, D., and Davy, D. 1969. *Investigating English Style*. Bloomington/London: Indiana University Press.

Eikhenbaum, B. 1919. "Kak sdelana *Shinel'* Gogolia." In *Poetika: Sborniki po teorii poeticheskogo iazyka*. Vol. 3, 151–165. Petrograd: Gos. tipografiia Leshutkov per.

Frey, N. 1963. *The Well-Tempered Critic*. Bloomington, Indiana: Indiana University Press.

Gutt, E-A. 1998. "Pragmatic aspects of translation: Some relevance-theory observations." In *The Pragmatics of Translation*, L. Hickley (ed), 41–53. Clevedon/Philadelphia: Multilingual Matters.

Halliday, M. A. K. 1973. *Explorations in the Functions of Language*. New York/Oxford: Elsevier.

Hatim, B. 1997. *Communication Across Culture: Translation Theory and Contrastive Text Linguistics*. Exeter: Exeter University Press.

Hatim, B. 1998. "Text politeness: A semiotic regime for a more interactive pragmatics." In *The Pragmatics of Translation*, L. Hickley (ed), 72–102. Clevedon/Philadelphia: Multilingual Matters.

House, J. 1997. *Translation Quality Assessment: A Model Revisited*. Tübingen: Narr.

House, J. 1998. "Politeness and translation." In *The Pragmatics of Translation*, L. Hickley (ed), 54–71. Clevedon/Philadelphia: Multilingual Matters.

Jakobson, R. 1923. *O cheshskom stikhe*. Berlin: no publisher.

Jakobson, R. 1959/1971a. "Language in relation to other communication systems." In *Roman Jakobson Selected Writings II: Word and Language*, 697–708. The Hague/Paris: Mouton.

Jakobson, R. 1959/1971b. "On linguistic aspects of translation." In *Roman Jakobson Selected Writings II: Word and Language*, 260–266. The Hague/Paris: Mouton.

Koller, W. 1989. "Equivalence in translation theory." In *Readings in Translation Theory*, A. Chesterman (ed), 98–118. Helsinki: Oy Finn Lectura Ab.

Krings, H. P. 1986. *Was in den Köpfen von Übersetzern vorgeht. Eine empirische Untersuchung zur Struktur des Übersetzungsprozesses an fortgeschrittenen Französischlernern*. Tübingen: Narr.

Kussmaul, P. 1995. *Training the Translator*. Amsterdam/Philadelphia: Benjamins.

May, R. 1994. *The Translator in the Text. On Reading Russian Literature in English*. Evanston, Illinois: Northwestern University Press.

Nabokov, V. 1955. "Problems of translation: *Onegin* in English." *Partisan Review* 22 (4): 496–512. Reprinted: 1992. In *Theories of Translation: An Anthology of Essays from Dryden to Derrida*, R. Schutte and J. Biguenet (eds), 144–151. Chicago/London: University of Chicago Press.

Newman, A. 1980. *Mapping Translation Equivalence*. Leuven: Acco.

Newman, A. 1994. "Translation equivalence: Nature." In *The Encyclopedia of Language and Linguistics*. Vol. 9, R. E. Asher and J. M. Y. Simpson (eds), 4694–4700. Oxford/New York: Pergamon Press.

Nida, E. 1975. *Language Structure and Translation: Essays*. Stanford: Stanford University Press.

Obst, H. 2001. "Interpreter training in the United States." *The American Translators Associa-*

tion Chronicle XXX (2): 17–19, 65.

Radilova, S. 1998. *Translating from English into Russian.* Lanham/New York: University Press of America.

Rosental', D. E., and Telenkova, M. A. 1976. *Prakticheskaia stilistica russkogo iazyka.* Moskva: Prosveschenie.

Scherr B. P. 2000. "Eugene Onegin." In *Encyclopedia of Literary Translation into English,* O. Classe (ed), 1131–1133. London/Chicago: Fitzroy Dearborn Publishers.

Skrebnev, Yu. M. 1976. *Ocherk teorii stilistiki.* Gor'kii: Vysshaia shkola.

Sperber, D., and Wilson, D. 1995. *Relevance: Communication and Cognition.* Oxford: Blackwell.

3. Translation-related technologies

Towards a collaborative approach to corpus building in the translation classroom

Lynne Bowker

Introduction

Corpus use is growing in a range of language-related disciplines (e.g., lexicography, foreign language teaching/learning). Corpora are also gaining popularity in translation circles, where they can provide a wealth of examples that allow translators to see terms and expressions in context and thus glean valuable usage information. However, to date, many of the experiments with corpora in the translation classroom have focused on the *use* of existing corpora by students rather than on the *creation* of new corpora by students.[1] The reasons for this order of progression are logical. First, it makes sense to establish whether or not corpora seem to be beneficial as translation resources by experimenting with some existing corpora before investing a lot of time and energy in the development of new ones. Second, although many institutions now offer students quick and easy access to computers and electronic resources such as the World Wide Web and online databases, this was not always the case. In the not so distant past, students in the arts and humanities had limited access to computer labs and the Internet, and when access was available, it was often quite slow due to limited bandwidth.

The situation today is somewhat different: it has been clearly demonstrated that corpora can be valuable translation resources (e.g., Austermühl 2001; Bowker 1998, 2000; Bowker and Pearson 2002; Lindquist 1999; Pearson 1996; Tognini-Bonelli 2001; Zanettin 1998, 2001), and many students now have reasonable access to electronic resources that can be used for corpus compilation. The time is now ripe for further investigations into the advantages of having students construct their own corpora. The aim of this article is to present some of the experiences that led to the development of a collaborative approach to corpus building in the translation classroom. Essentially, the collaborative approach that will be described here is one that evolved gradually over several years, during which time a number of observations were made:

1. Students enjoy working with corpora and find them to be valuable translation resources.
2. A great number of existing corpora (e.g., British National Corpus, Bank of English, Mannheimer Korpus) are not suitable for many translation purposes because they deal largely with general language, whereas translation often deals with specialized language.
3. Translation corpora need to be targeted (i.e., designed and compiled for a particular task), which means that such corpora are not likely to be reused. Varantola (forthcoming) uses the term "disposable" to describe this type of corpus.
4. Because a new corpus must be created for every translation task, which in the case of translation classes may mean as often as every couple of weeks, students generally cannot afford to devote a great deal of time to the construction of individual corpora.
5. Given these time constraints, a collective effort can typically result in the production of a larger and more representative corpus than can an individual effort.

These points will be explored in more detail throughout this article, which reports on the evolution of corpus use and development in translation classes that I taught between the mid-1990s and the present day. The article begins by setting the scene with regard to the general situation and constraints in the translation classroom. This is followed by a summary of a number of experiments that I have conducted with corpus use in translation classes. The purpose of this summary is twofold: first, it will provide background information regarding the experiences that led to the eventual development of the collaborative approach to corpus building, and second, it may help others who are interested in using corpora with their own students to avoid making similar mistakes. As is often the case, some of these mistakes now seem glaringly obvious in hindsight; however, they did provide some valuable lessons that may benefit others. Following this summary, the actual collaborative approach to corpus building will be elucidated by outlining the strategy that was developed and discussing the results of its application. The article closes with some observations about the suitability of the World Wide Web as a resource for building translation corpora.

Setting the scene: The situation in the translation classroom

As noted above, the use of corpora is becoming common in a number of language-related disciplines; however, the needs of translators, and particularly translation students, are somewhat different than those of other language users. While many lexicographers and language learners work with general language, most translators tend to work in specialized domains (e.g., medicine, law, economics, science, technology) that have their own specialized sublanguages. Furthermore, many professional translators do not have the luxury of working within a single specialized domain — they must often be willing to take on jobs in a variety of fields, some of which may be relatively unfamiliar to them (McMillan 1987: 89; Teague 1993: 161; Wright 1987: 117). This professional reality is reflected in many translator-training programs. In order to expose students to a wide range of translational issues and thus properly prepare them for entering the translation profession, trainers must attempt to present students with a representative cross-section of subject areas and text types (Fraser 1996: 246; Snell-Hornby 1992: 17). Consequently, an undergraduate translation course with a scientific/technical specialization might cover subject matter ranging from engineering to computing to chemistry to medicine to geology, not to mention all the subfields of these broad-ranging disciplines. Furthermore, the text types could include product advertisements, user manuals, buyer's guides, technical reports, research papers, etc.

Given this situation, it is clear that many of the corpora that are currently available (e.g., British National Corpus) are not always appropriate for translation applications since they deal with general language and often comprise text types that are not relevant for many types of specialized translation (e.g., newspapers). This means that if translator trainers wish to use relevant corpora in the translation classroom, these corpora will need to be created from scratch — a challenging prospect, to say the least!

Experiments leading up to a collaborative approach to corpus building

Although this article focuses on the development of a collaborative approach to corpus building, it will be useful first to provide some background on how the collaborative approach evolved. I have been using corpora in translation classes regularly since the mid-1990s, and although some experiments have been more successful than others, they have all provided valuable insights into what does and does not "work" in a translation classroom setting. This cumulative experience led to a refinement and extension of my work with corpora, which has gradually evolved into the collaborative approach described farther down. Outlining some of these earlier experiences will not only provide some background but may also help others to avoid making some of the same mistakes. It should be noted that all the experiments outlined below were conducted in fourth-year undergraduate French-to-English technical translation classes; therefore, the comparable corpora were all in English since this was the target language.

Experiment 1: Building a "general specialized corpus"

When I first decided to introduce translation students to corpora, the computer facilities available to the students were not as advanced as they are today. There were relatively few computer labs, these labs did not allow unrestricted Internet access, and when Internet access was available, it was typically very slow. Therefore, for pragmatic reasons, it was necessary for me — the trainer — to compile any specialized corpora that were to be used in the classroom.

The course in question was a fourth-year undergraduate course in technical translation. By this point in their education, the students had already been exposed to a number of different subject fields (e.g., law, medicine), and the focus of the technical translation course was therefore restricted to a single broad theme: computing. At this time, I already had some limited experience creating corpora for use on a research project and therefore knew how much time and effort could go into the creation of a corpus. In order to minimize the amount of work required, I decided to build a single corpus that could be used for the duration of the semester.

Accordingly, I decided to loosely follow the model of a well-known existing general language corpus (the British National Corpus), and I set out to make a single corpus — a sort of "general specialized corpus" — that contained texts relevant to the subject field of computing. By searching the World Wide Web and consulting databases of electronic journals, I was able to compile a corpus totaling just over one million words. It was relatively unsophisticated in the sense that it did not contain any annotation (i.e., no syntactic or semantic tagging).

The corpus was posted on the central server and the students could access this corpus from the computer lab and could then manipulate it with the help of computerized tools known as corpus analysis tools (e.g., WordSmith Tools, MonoConc). Corpus analysis software lets users manipulate and display large volumes of information in a variety of useful ways. Such tools typically include at least a concordancer and a word lister. A concordancer retrieves all the occurrences of a particular search term and its immediate context and displays them in an easy-to-read format, while a word lister allows users to discover how many different words are in the corpus and how often each appears. The students had previously been trained to use these tools as part of another course. Further discussion of corpus processing techniques is beyond the scope of this article, but interested readers can refer to Bowker (2000) and Bowker and Pearson (2002) for a detailed description of some techniques that were used to extract translation-related information from comparable corpora.

The goal of creating a "general specialized corpus" had been achieved. All in all, the corpus represented a reasonable cross-section of computer-related subjects (e.g., operating systems, user interfaces, optical scanners, microprocessors, printers, artificial intelligence) and text types (e.g., product advertisements, product reviews, technical specifications, standards, installation guides). However, as it turned out, this corpus was not one that could be usefully applied in the classroom. Although the students were generally receptive to the idea of using a corpus, and they could, in principle, see the value of consulting such a resource, they found that, in practice, the "general specialized corpus" did not adequately meet their needs. The biggest problem with this corpus was that it had been compiled without direct reference to the specific texts that were to be translated. Even though a text may belong to a domain such as computing, it more than likely addresses a specific topic within that field. Similarly, although the field of computing can include a range of text types, any given text most likely conforms to only one text type.

Therefore, while the corpus turned out to be useful for some translations whose topic and text type were fortuitously included in the corpus, it was less helpful for others because not all subjects and text types had been covered. Moreover, because the corpus had been designed as a diverse rather than a targeted collection, it was rare for there to be more than a few texts on any given topic or of any given type; therefore, although the corpus contained over one million words, only a few texts were relevant at any given time, which meant that there were relatively few pertinent examples to which the students could refer. On a number of occasions, consulting the corpus actually turned out to be detrimental for some of the students. For instance, because the corpus contained a range of text types, a student might identify a term or expression in the corpus that referred to the correct concept, but whose register was too technical (e.g., "clock rate" instead of "speed") or too popularized (e.g., "shapeshifter" instead of "polymorphic virus") with respect to the target text in question. Similarly, because the corpus contained texts from a variety of subfields within the domain of computing, it was easy to confuse concepts that belonged to different subfields (e.g., "scanners" as opposed to "digitizers").

Experiment 2: Building a series of "targeted" comparable corpora

In hindsight, it is clear that the construction of a "general specialized corpus" was not appropriate for the intended application. Although such an approach might work for applications such as lexicography, where the aim is to cover the language used in a wide range of situations, the nature of translation is different — the translator is attempting to render the subject matter that is conveyed in a specific text. Therefore, in order for a resource to be useful for translating a particular text, it must take into account the specific characteristics of that text, such as subject matter, text type, purpose, and time period. In other words, the corpus must be *targeted*, rather than general; it must be tailored to match the specific characteristics of the text to be translated.

The following semester, this new approach of building a customized corpus for each text to be translated was implemented. It must be said that this was not really a radical idea since translators have been collecting and consulting collections of "comparable texts" for a long time (e.g., Schäffner 1998; Williams 1996).[2] Comparable texts are typically considered to be documents that have been produced independently in different languages, but which have the same communicative function as the source text. In other words, they are texts that have been written by specialists in the target language and that are of a similar text type, are from a similar time period, and deal with the same topic as the text to be translated. In the past, comparable texts have typically been collected in printed form, which has a number of drawbacks. First, the effort required to physically gather together a printed corpus often means spending hours at the library and/or photocopier. Then, once the corpus is gathered, additional hours must be spent manually consulting the texts, and this frequently entails reading large quantities of irrelevant material before stumbling upon a discussion of a pertinent point. Moreover, as observed by researchers such as Church et al. (1991: 116) and Meyer (1994: 9), relevant linguistic patterns can be difficult to detect when individual occurrences are spread over several pages or documents. Electronic corpora of comparable texts that can be processed using corpus analysis tools can help to overcome these drawbacks.

Since a new corpus was now to be created for each text that would be translated as part of the course, it was necessary to revisit the size criterion. Following some trial and error experimentation, as well as discussions with colleagues, it was decided to attempt to build corpora of between 20,000 and

50,000 words. The size varied somewhat depending on the subject matter and the text type in question as some types of texts were easier to obtain in electronic form than were others. Over the course of that semester, six different comparable corpora were compiled for the students to consult.

From the students' point of view, this exercise was a huge success: they liked working with corpora and found them to be worthwhile resources. However, I found the creation of so many corpora to be exhausting, which led me to rethink the approach once again.

Experiment 3: Getting the students to build individual corpora

Given the students' enthusiasm, it was important to keep the corpus-based approach as a central part of the class. Nevertheless, it was unrealistic to think that one person could maintain the pace of being the sole corpus creator. Maia (1997) provided inspiration for the decision to cast myself as a "facilitator" rather than a "provider" of information. This decision was reinforced by the fact that students were beginning to ask where they could find corpora to help them with their other translation courses (e.g., legal, economic, medical). Since it was clearly not feasible for me to create additional corpora in these subject fields, it seemed that the next logical step would be to teach the students how to compile their own corpora. After all, as pointed out by Manning (1996: 546), an important goal of teaching should be to make students independent of their teachers so that they can continue to learn long after they have left the classroom. In addition, the ability to create corpora would no doubt be a useful skill for them to have after they had graduated and were working as professional translators.

In my new role as facilitator, I made the students responsible for creating the corpora that they would use. We had several class discussions about corpus design criteria and about how to identify and evaluate potential sources. By this time, access to computer labs and the Internet was improving on campus, so students would be able to use resources such as the World Wide Web when building their corpora. The basic idea was that for each text to be translated, every student would build his or her own corpus and use it as a resource.

The students were initially keen, but as the semester progressed, their corpora became smaller and less well designed. It got to the point that some students would not bother to build corpora at all, while those who did often gathered only a handful of texts, many of which were not particularly well-chosen. We discussed the situation as a class and a number of points were raised. First, the students noted that although they liked to work with corpora and found them to be valuable resources, they had not fully appreciated the amount of time and effort that was required to compile a useful corpus. Second, as the semester progressed and they became bogged down in assignments and homework, they found that it was faster and easier simply to resort to a bilingual dictionary, rather than to compile a corpus. Finally, they acknowledged that, although they felt the quality of their translations suffered as a result of not consulting corpora, they simply did not have the necessary time to devote to corpus compilation.

The results of this attempt to have students individually compile corpora were somewhat disappointing, but rather than give up on the idea altogether, the class was interested in exploring other ways of approaching corpus compilation. One suggestion that was made was for students to take turns constructing corpora that the entire class could then consult. This idea was later dismissed as it was felt that it would be too much work for any one student to take on in any given week. However, this idea of sharing corpora did lead to further discussion, during which we hit upon the idea of adopting a more collaborative approach to corpus compilation: instead of each student compiling corpora individually, all members of the class would contribute to a common corpus. In this way, the compilation time required by any one student would be reduced, but the resulting corpus would be substantial enough to serve as a useful resource.

A collaborative approach to corpus building

In order to ensure that things ran smoothly during the collaborative exercise, it was necessary first to establish a number of guidelines or ground rules, and after some discussion an initial strategy was worked out. The strategy was then refined based on our experience over the course of the semester. This refined strategy is described below, and it addresses the following issues: (1) coordination, (2) number of texts contributed by each student per corpus, (3) quality of texts, (4) time frame, and (5) file format.

Coordination: In my continuing role as facilitator, I was determined not to end up being the sole person responsible for coordinating the compilation of each corpus. Therefore, it was decided that for each corpus, two students would act as the coordinators. The coordinator duties would rotate so that different students would get to act in this role over the course of the semester. Furthermore, it was decided that when students were acting as coordinators, they did not have to contribute texts to the corpus (but they still had to do the actual translation homework). Essentially, the coordinators were to act as a sort of clearinghouse. Students in the class would e-mail their texts to the coordinators, who would check for and eliminate duplications (i.e., cases where the same text had been submitted by multiple students).[3] The remaining texts would then be collated into a single corpus that would be posted on the class Web site, where it could be accessed by all the students.

Number of texts contributed by each student per corpus: It was agreed that each student in the class (with the exception of the coordinators) would try to identify three relevant texts that would make a good addition to the corpus. This number was considered to be a reasonable goal; however, it was not an absolute. If a student could only identify two suitable texts, these would still be welcome; likewise, if a student located four or five relevant texts, they could all be submitted.

At the time of this experiment, there were 22 students in the class, so the reasoning went as follows: if two students were to act as coordinators, that left 20 students to contribute to the corpus. If each student attempted to submit three texts, it was hoped that we would end up with a corpus of reasonable size. Even allowing for some duplication, we felt that we would likely end up with a corpus that was bigger than those corpora that individual students had previously compiled.

Quality of texts: The students agreed to put some time and care into selecting their three texts. It was noted that if everyone were to simply submit the texts corresponding to the first three hits that came up using a Web search engine, then there would be a lot of duplication and the texts might not be pertinent, which would limit the value of the corpus. This point is explored in more detail in the **Discussion** section below.

Time frame: It was noted that in order for the process to run smoothly, a reasonable amount of time had to be given for both the contributions and the coordination. It was agreed that each target text would be distributed three weeks in advance. Students would have one week to identify suitable texts and e-mail them to the coordinators. The coordinators would have one week to check for duplication, to amalgamate the texts into a corpus, and to post this corpus on the class Web site. All the students would then have one week to consult the corpus. Note that the students were free to begin working on their translation prior to being able to access the corpus, but once available, the corpus could be used to conduct further research or to verify or revise previous decisions.

File format: It was agreed that students would e-mail their contributions to the coordinators as attachments in plain text (ASCII) format. This decision was made for a number of reasons. First, it simplified the job of the coordinators as it meant that they did not have to worry about having access to different types of computers or software packages and they did not have to manipulate different file formats. Second, it ensured that the corpus would be in a format that could be manipulated by the corpus analysis software to which the students had access (i.e., WordSmith Tools). Finally, it also reduced the chances of spreading viruses.

Results of the collaborative corpus building exercise

Like the preceding experiments, the collaborative corpus-building exercise was conducted as part of a fourth-year technical translation course. In order to give some coherence to the course, the theme of "computer security" was selected and seven different source texts — each of a different text type and each focusing on a different subject relating to computer security — were chosen. Table 1 summarizes the corresponding comparable corpora that were compiled as part of the exercise.

Discussion

This section will outline strategies used by the students in selecting the texts and compiling the corpora; difficulties that were encountered and solutions used to overcome them will also be discussed. In addition, some general comments will be made on the suitability of the World Wide Web as a resource for building comparable corpora. As previously mentioned, specific details

Table 1. A brief description of the corpora produced as part of the collaborative corpus building exercise.

Subject	Text type	Texts submitted	Texts rejected	Texts/words in corpus
Passwords	FAQ Web page	58	35	23 texts / 40,600w
Antivirus programs	Instructional	78	22	56 texts / 170,919w
Encryption	Informative/popularized	74	19	55 texts / 216,522w
Firewalls	Buyer's guide	63	18	45 texts / 136,017w
Steganography	Product description	35	21	14 texts / 7,401w
Biometrics	Research article	29	17	12 texts / 69,651w
Cookies	Technical encyclopedia entry	41	19	22 texts / 11,754w

about techniques used to extract translation-related information from the corpora have already been detailed elsewhere in the literature (see Bowker 2000; Bowker and Pearson 2002) and so will not be repeated here.

The first corpus to be constructed dealt with "passwords", and the text type was a FAQ, which is a list of *Frequently Asked Questions* (and answers) about a given subject. FAQs are becoming an extremely popular and important feature of the Internet. Although they originated as a way to help new users learn the "rules" for using newsgroups, etc., one can now find FAQs on a wide range of popular topics. In total, the students submitted 58 texts for possible inclusion in the corpus; however, there was a high degree of duplication and the final corpus ended up containing only 23 texts.

A class discussion following the creation of this first corpus revealed that most students preferred to use the Web to identify comparable texts. Other resources, such as CD-ROMs and online databases, were available in the university library; however, many students had Internet access from home and found it more convenient to work from there. The preferred method of identifying texts for inclusion in the corpus was to read the source text and then select a potential subject key word to enter into a search engine. In the course of the discussion, it was revealed that most students used the AltaVista search engine, and many of them had not been very discerning when it came to selecting the three texts that they contributed — they often simply took the first three hits that came up. It was agreed that in order to identify a wider selection of texts for future corpora, students would have to make an effort to look beyond the first three hits. Moreover, we discussed the fact that different search engines index different Web sites, which means that the hits returned by one search engine may be different than those returned by another. Many students had not been aware of this fact and they were pleased to learn this as they felt it would prove useful not only for collaborative corpus building but also for their other research. We drew up a list of different search engines and meta-search engines and added the corresponding links to the class Web site. Students agreed to use a wider range of search engines when searching for comparable texts, and it was hoped that by doing this, there would be less duplication in future corpora.

The next three corpora were targeted to help translate an instructional text on "antivirus programs," a popularized informative text about "encryption," and a buyer's guide for "firewalls." In the world of computer security, these are all popular subjects and common text types, so there was a lot of information available. In particular, popularized informative texts are among the most common type of text on the Web, and many of the texts identified by the students were quite long, which elevated the word count of the encryption corpus considerably. Given that there were many texts to choose from, a number of students submitted more than three texts each. Moreover, the degree of duplication for these three corpora was reduced as a result of the students' efforts to use different search engines and to look beyond the first three hits.

The corpus on "steganography" was intended to help students translate a product description. Steganography is the act of hiding information, and there are software packages available that can allow users to place secret messages in unused or insignificant portions of files. These files can then be exchanged without the wrong people knowing what they really contain. Steganography is much less common than other security measures, such as encryption, and there are a limited number of products on the market. Consequently, the students found that there were fewer texts to choose from, with the result that only 35 texts were submitted, and of these, only 14 were retained. Of the texts that were rejected, many were duplicates; however, the coordinators also rejected a number of texts that were not of an appropriate text type. Given the relative scarcity of comparable texts, some of the students had submitted texts that were about steganography, but which were not product descriptions. Similar behavior has been observed by Pearson (2000: 237), who notes that translation students sometimes show poor judgment when sourcing terminology and phraseology from comparable texts. For example, they are often primarily concerned with identifying texts that deal with the subject matter in question, but they do not ensure that the texts they choose are comparable to the source text with respect to its other features, such as register, technicality and text type. In a class discussion, the matter was raised and it was emphasized that in order for a text to be "comparable," it had to take into account text type as well as subject matter.

The source text on biometrics was an extract from a research article. There were 29 comparable texts submitted, but only 12 of these were retained. However, since research articles tend to be long, the word count was still reasonably high. The main problem the students encountered was finding the relevant text type on the Web. Although there were a number of hits that looked promising, many of these links led to Web sites that required a paid subscription in order to gain full access to the contents of the site (e.g., online journals). This led to a discussion about other non-Web resources that may be useful for building corpora, including the *Computer Select* CD-ROM, which contains hundreds of computer-related publications ranging from the popularized (e.g., *PC Week*) to the more technical (e.g., *Communications of the ACM*). INSPEC abstracts and a variety of online journals that were part of the university's library collection (e.g., *Journal of Computer and System Sciences, Computing, Computer Communications, Information and Software Technology*) were also identified as sources that may be useful for future corpus building. Of course, it was noted that these resources are only available via paid subscription; however, as long as the students were registered at the university, they were able to use these resources freely. In addition, it was noted that, although students would rather work from home (hence their preference for consulting the Web rather than the library databases), it was not unreasonable to expect them to make an occasional trip to the library in order to consult more appropriate resources.

Finally, the source text on "cookies" consisted of an entry taken from a technical encyclopedia. Once again, there were relatively few submissions (41 texts), coupled with a high degree of duplication (only 22 texts were retained). This was because there are a limited number of electronic technical encyclopedias that could serve as comparable texts. Furthermore, it was observed that the entries in such encyclopedias tend to consist of short texts, which resulted in a relatively low word count for the corpus as a whole.

General observations about the Web as a resource for building comparable corpora

In addition to discussing particular problems that came up when creating specific corpora, the class also discussed a number of more general points, many of which concerned the nature of the Web and its suitability as a resource for building translation corpora. For example, it was noted that there are many texts on the Web that are of poor quality and which therefore do not make good translation resources. When asked to reflect on potential reasons for this poor quality, students came up with the following possibilities. First, they noted that anyone can post information on the Web, including non-experts, and Web documents are not always subject to an editing process in the same way that printed documents usually are. Furthermore, the Web is seen by many as an ephemeral resource; people are interested in communicating information, but unlike the case with printed documents, this information may not be preserved for long (i.e., a Web page can be revised, updated or removed very easily) and so people are less willing to invest much time or effort in formulating that information. In other words, many people feel that a Web page does not need to be elegant (or even grammatically correct!) as long as it adequately conveys the essential information.

Another comment focused on the types of texts that are commonly found on the Web. Given that the Web is most often used as a means of disseminating information to a non-expert audience, it contains primarily informative or instructional texts whose style, format, and content have been popularized. More specialized material and different text types can be accessed via the Web, but such information is often available only by paid subscription. This means that while the Web can be a valuable resource for constructing corpora that deal with popularized informative texts, it may prove less helpful for constructing corpora that must comprise other types of texts.

The very nature of the Web gave rise to two other observations. First, the idea behind hypertext is that people can jump from page to page to view associated information. Good Web design dictates that there should be a limited amount of information on each page so that people are not required to scroll unnecessarily; related pieces of information should be provided on separate pages with relevant links between them. When compiling a corpus from the Web, each page must be copied/saved separately and then later amalgamated into a corpus. Therefore, from a corpus builder's point of view, it would be preferable to have a single page containing a large quantity of information, as this page could be copied/saved in one operation, rather than having that same information spread over several pages, which would then need to be copied/saved separately. This basically means that good Web design is not conducive to easy corpus building! Second, the multimedia nature of the Web is another characteristic that is not always conducive to building text-based corpora. On a number of occasions, students rejected Web pages that would have been extremely useful sources of information but which could not easily be incorporated into a text-based corpus because their primary value resided in their graphical or audio content. This raises an important point: a corpus can be an invaluable resource, but it is not a panacea. There are many other complementary types of resources that can also provide helpful information, and these should not be ignored.

Finally, the sheer volume of information that is available on the Web made students aware of the importance of formulating queries carefully in order to focus on relevant material. As previously mentioned, students tended to read the source text first in order to get ideas for potential key words. These words were then entered into a search engine, and the resulting hits were examined for relevance as well as for ideas for other key words that could be used for further searches. In addition to key words that dealt with the subject matter, students also found that it could be useful to enter key words relating to the text type. For instance, a search using only the subject key word "cookie" returned many irrelevant texts such as recipes; however, a more carefully formulated search that combined subject and text type key words, such as *+cookie +computer +encyclopedia*, returned hits for entries for "cookie" in resources such as *The Grand Encyclopedia of Computer Terminology*, *TechEncyclopedia* and *PC Webopedia*. Other tricks, such as remembering to search for alternate spellings (e.g., encyclopedia/encyclopaedia) also helped to increase the number of relevant hits. In addition, as mentioned previously, the students found it useful to conduct a search using a variety of different search engines or a meta-search engine. Additional tips for effective Internet search strategies for translators can be found in Bergeron and Larsson (1999).

Concluding remarks

Overall, the collaborative corpus building exercise proved to be a worthwhile experience. The students demonstrated that they were eminently capable of working together to construct valuable translation resources, which they could then consult to identify relevant lexical, phraseological and stylistic information. Not surprisingly, of the seven collective corpora that were built, the larger ones, such those on antivirus programs and encryption, tended to contain a greater number of examples. Of more interest, however, is the fact that even the small corpora, such as those on steganography and cookies, contained useful information. This supports the point made by researchers such as Rogers and Ahmad (1994), who note that when working in specialized fields, it is not necessary to have the sort of multimillion word corpora that are typically required for general language work.

In addition to furnishing students with an opportunity to explore the merit of corpora as a translation resource, this exercise also provided a valuable opportunity for a shift in pedagogical strategy. The collaborative corpus-building exercise made it relatively easy for the trainer to take on the role of facilitator (rather than information provider), which in turn allowed the students to become independent learners and critical thinkers, who were encouraged to reflect on the characteristics of different text types and on the suitability of the World Wide Web as a translation resource. Acting as both contributors and coordinators, students learned to identify relevant features of texts and to be more discerning with regard to the appropriateness of a text (e.g., in terms of quality, text type, nature) for the task at hand.

The success of this exercise has prompted me to continue experimenting with collaborative corpus work and text typology in the translation classroom.

In particular, I am now planning to extend the exercise in order to have students create corpora that can be used in situations where the brief or *skopos* of the target text is not the same as that of the source text (e.g., an informative text that is to be translated as a persuasive text). In such cases, the students cannot merely examine the characteristics of the source text in order to find comparable target language texts; rather, they must reflect on the purpose or intention of the target text in order to come up with a list of features that will guide them in their search for suitable corpus material. It may prove even more interesting to have the students create several different corpora, each of which could be used to translate the same source text according to a different brief. As well as giving the students practice in both corpus construction and translation, such an exercise could be used to stimulate more theoretical discussions about functionalist approaches to translation (e.g., Nord 1997) or *skopos* theory (e.g., Vermeer 1989).

Notes

1. Exceptions include work carried out by Maia (1997) and Varantola (forthcoming), both of whom helped small groups of students create their own corpora for terminology- or translation-related applications.

2. In the past, translators often referred to such collections as "parallel texts"; however, in corpus linguistics circles, the terms "parallel texts" and "parallel corpora" are used to refer to a collection of source texts aligned with their translations, while "comparable texts" and "comparable corpora" refer to sets of texts that have been produced independently in different languages but which have the same communicative function. I have elected to use the corpus linguistics terminology, which is becoming increasingly prevalent.

3. A special e-mail account was set up for use by the coordinators for the duration of the collaborative corpus-building project so that students' personal e-mail accounts were not inundated with messages.

References

Austermühl, F. 2001. *Electronic Tools for Translators*. Manchester: St. Jerome.
Bergeron, M., and Larsson, S. 1999. "Internet search strategies for translators." *ATA Chronicle* 28 (7): 22–25.
Bowker, L. 1998. "Using specialized monolingual native-language corpora as a translation resource: A pilot study." *Meta* 43 (4): 631–651.
Bowker, L. 2000. "Towards a methodology for exploiting specialized target language corpora as translation resources." *International Journal of Corpus Linguistics* 5 (1): 17–52.
Bowker, L., and Pearson J. 2002. *Working with Specialized Language: A Practical Guide to Using Corpora*. London: Routledge.

Church, K., Gale, W., Hanks, P., and Hindle, D. 1991. "Using statistics in lexical analysis." In *Lexical Acquisition: Exploiting Online Resources to Build a Lexicon*, U. Zernik (ed), 115–164. Englewood Cliffs, NJ: Lawrence Erlbaum Associates.

Fraser, J. 1996. "Professional versus student behaviour." In *Teaching Translation and Interpreting 3: New Horizons*, C. Dollerup and V. Appel (eds), 243–250. Amsterdam/Philadelphia: John Benjamins.

Lindquist, H. 1999. "Electronic corpora as tools for translation." In *Word, Text, Translation: Liber Amicorum for Peter Newmark*, G. Anderman and M. Rogers (eds), 179–189. Clevedon, UK: Multilingual Matters.

Maia, B. 1997. "Making corpora — A learning process" In *Proceedings of the International Conference on Corpus Use and Learning to Translate*. Online.

Manning, A. 1996. "A classroom-bound approach to the meaning of translation quality assessment." In *Translation and Meaning (Part 3)*, B. Lewandowska-Tomaszczyk and M. Thelen (eds), 541–548. Maastricht: Universitaire Pers Maastricht.

McMillan, E. N. 1987. "Recruitment and retention of staff and freelance translators: Experience at one international agency." In *Translation Excellence: Assessment, Achievement, Maintenance*, M. G. Rose (ed), 87–92. Binghamton: SUNY.

Meyer, I. 1994. "Linguistic strategies and computer aids for knowledge engineering in terminology." *Terminology Update* 27 (4): 6–10.

Nord, C. 1997. *Translating as a Purposeful Activity: Functionalist Approaches Explained.* Manchester: St. Jerome.

Pearson, J. 1996. "Electronic texts and concordances in the translation classroom." *Teanga* 16: 85–95.

Pearson, J. 2000. "Surfing the Internet: Teaching students to choose their texts wisely." In *Rethinking Language Pedagogy from a Corpus Perspective*, L. Burnard and T. McEnery (eds), 235–239. Frankfurt: Peter Lang.

Rogers, M., and Ahmad, K. 1994. "Computerised terminology for translators: The role of text." In *Applications and Implications of Current LSP Research, Vol. II*, M. Brekke, O. Andersen, T. Dahl and J. Myking (eds), 840–851. Norway: Fagbokforlaget.

Schäffner, C. 1998. "Parallel texts in translation." In *Unity in Diversity? Current Trends in Translation Studies*, L. Bowker, M. Cronin, D. Kenny and J. Pearson (eds), 83–90. Manchester: St. Jerome.

Snell-Hornby, M. 1992. "The professional translator of tomorrow: Language specialist or all-round expert?" In *Teaching Translation and Interpreting: Training, Talent and Experience*, C. Dollerup and A. Loddegaard (eds), 9–22. Amsterdam/Philadelphia: John Benjamins.

Teague, B. 1993. "'Retooling' as an adaptive skill for translators." In *Scientific and Technical Translation*, S. E. Wright and L. D. Wright, Jr. (eds), 161–172. Amsterdam/Philadelphia: John Benjamins.

Tognini-Bonelli, E. 2001. *Corpus Linguistics at Work.* Amsterdam/Philadelphia: John Benjamins.

Varantola, K. Forthcoming. "Translators and disposable corpora." In *Corpora and Translator Education*, F. Zanettin, S. Bernardini and D. Stewart (eds). Manchester: St. Jerome.

Vermeer, H. J. 1989. "Skopos and commission in translational action." In *Readings in Translation Theory*, A. Chesterman (ed), 173–187. Helsinki: Oy Finn Lectura Ab.

Williams, I. A. 1996. "A translator's reference needs: Dictionaries or parallel texts?" *Target* 8 (2): 275–299.

Wright, S. E. 1987. "Translation excellence in the private sector." In *Translation Excellence: Assessment, Achievement, Maintenance,* M. G. Rose (ed), 113–124. Binghamton: SUNY.

Zanettin, F. 1998. "Bilingual comparable corpora and the training of translators." *Meta* 43(4): 616–630.

Zanettin, F. 2001. "Swimming in words: corpora, translation and language learning." In *Learning with Corpora,* G. Aston (ed), 177–197. Bologna/Houston: CLUEB/Athelstan.

Task-based instruction
and the new technology

Training translators for the modern
language industry

Geoffrey S. Koby and Brian James Baer

Introduction

Until the mid 1980s, when personal computers began to transform the language industry, translation skills were typically passed on to future translators by an experienced teacher/mentor who would demonstrate the methods of translation by example. According to this pedagogical approach, described by Jean-René Ladmiral as the *performance magistrale*, a student's translation would be evaluated against the instructor's "master text" (1977). Donald Kiraly describes the traditional translation classroom as organized around "a single behaviorist principle: One learns how to translate by translating" (1995: 7). While this may have produced a certain number of competent "solitary" translators, it is an approach that, like the grammar-translation method of foreign language teaching, accommodates a limited variety of learning styles and fails, for the most part, to address the extralinguistic qualities that are increasingly prized within the contemporary language industry, such as flexibility, creativity, resourcefulness, professionalism, and the ability to work in teams.

Gregory Shreve (2000) has described the translation industry as an ecosystem in which change in any one area necessarily impacts all others. It is certainly the case that the evolution of the contemporary language industry poses a number of challenges to translation pedagogy in terms of both content and methodology. Technological innovation has significantly expanded the range and the nature of texts for translation, the number and complexity of tools available to assist the translator, and the variety of avenues for translators to carry out research on terminology, parallel texts, and background information. Increasing demand for translation, fueled in part by the technology boom, has produced changes in the professional landscape of the translator as well, as is evident in the creation of, or increased demand for, certain types of language professional, such as localizer, project manager, and terminologist. This has also had its effect on the translator's work environment. The translator today often finds him/herself part of a team, a situation that requires teamwork, flexibility, and well-developed communication skills, qualities that were far less important to the "solitary" translator.

These changes in the translation ecosystem represent real challenges to translator training. The *performance magistrale* is increasingly inappropriate to the training of the contemporary language professional, who is expected to have a variety of extra-linguistic skills that are typically not addressed by those traditional methodologies. Moreover, research in the field of pedagogy suggests the relative ineffectiveness of those methodologies when compared to pedagogical approaches based on Cognitive Theory. In the first section, we explore the various ways in which new technology has affected the translator's task. We then focus on pedagogical initiatives, in particular Task-Based Instruction (TBI), that may be more effective in training today's language professionals, proposing some principles for incorporating TBI within a translator training curriculum. Finally, we offer a number of task-based learning modules for use in teaching software localization.

Technologization

Over the last 25 years, the development of powerful computers and related technologies has significantly altered the landscape of document production. Increasing technologization has expanded the scope of translation pedagogy by creating new text types for translation that challenge in fundamental ways the traditional concept of what constitutes a text. The method of presenting information on the World Wide Web, for example, represents a new kind of text. There, the traditional concept of a text has given way to hypertext linking, which allows a "text" to be composed of many different, interrelated paragraphs or "screens" of information that can be accessed in any order. Cognitively, this requires translators to develop a sense of the way text components are interrelated, prior to or during translation; technically, it means that the translator must be able to deal with HyperText Markup Language — HTML — either directly or by using technological tools.

At the same time, software is being localized simultaneously into multiple languages. Localization involves, among other things, the translation of menu items, dialog boxes, on-line help, and "strings" of text — words, phrases, sentences, and paragraphs that appear during use of the software. For the translator, these texts for translation are typically provided out of context (i.e., collections of help files, strings, etc.). Here again, the translator is faced with the cognitive task of constructing coherence and cohesion for textual elements that appear to have none. The translator must also be aware of extralinguistic elements that may or may not be culture-specific, such as icons, graphics, color schemes, or layout. Moreover, the translator must have the technical tools and skills to open and translate the text — without inadvertently deleting important software codes — to resize visual elements to fit the text, and to edit visual elements (icons, graphics) to fit the target culture.

As large companies have attempted to deal with an enormous volume of information in multiple languages, they have been forced to find ways to efficiently store, retrieve, and reuse this information. Solutions to this problem involve organizing the information as unique self-contained units of content that can be stored separately, assembled into longer texts to serve the various needs of different end users, and updated as needed. For the translator, this means that an initial translation may involve a longer, coherent text, but when changes are made, only the changed units are sent out for translation. As more information is stored in this way, less context will be available to the translator. Shreve comments, "As the extreme differentiation of text types continues, it will become more and more difficult for translators to understand the essential character of the new texts they are transforming" (2000: 222). Therefore, translators must develop skill in constructing cohesion and coherence from the elements presented.

The increase in the volume and diversity of text types for translation has naturally led to an expansion of the skills expected of a translator, and in some cases has produced new language-related professions, such as bilingual editor, multimedia designer, research and information specialist, cultural assessor, multicultural software designer, software localizer, terminologist, or project manager (Shreve 2000: 228). The explosion in document production, globalization, and the concomitant need for intercultural communication has increased demand for translation to a point where computer tools — both general purpose tools and special purpose translation tools — are needed and have been developed to deal with this volume of work.

By tools, we mean *software applications* — as it is generally assumed that translators now use computers. Already in 1994, Alan Melby noted, "Over the past 10 years, the issue of whether or not a translator should use a computer has largely been replaced by the issue of what kind of computer hardware and software to acquire in order to best succeed in the translation market" (127). Although one might assume that it should not be our task to teach basic software applications (and given the amount of time we have in a class, the assumption is justified), it is by no means the case that students enter a translation program with appropriately extensive skills in such basic computer tasks as word processing or even Web browsing. Therefore, even though we may only teach the specialized tools, we must be aware that students may have fundamental conceptual problems and lack know-how at a more basic level.

Specialized software tools for translation are many and varied, and change rapidly. Some of the software tools that we must teach include CD-ROM dictionaries, the use of online databases, terminology management systems, computer-assisted translation (CAT) tools, localization tools, and desktop publishing software. When teaching such tools, our fundamental pedagogical goal must be the acquisition of conceptual knowledge. Given that the specific operating principles of the tool will change (often in a matter of months), students need to learn the conceptual principles underlying each tool, so that they are able to look beyond differences in the interface to find the basic similarities. At the same time, students must learn the actual operation of at least one full-featured software tool in each category. This represents a general pedagogical paradigm shift and challenge, since learning a tool properly involves a large amount of hands-on experience at the computer with a teacher or facilitator available when problems are encountered. Below, we will briefly examine these specialized tools in order of increasing complexity, and the specific pedagogical challenges involved with each one.

The new technology

At this time, a *CD-ROM dictionary* is most often simply an edition of a paper dictionary that has been converted to the new format, with greater or lesser degrees of success. Even so, CD-ROM versions of dictionaries change the way that the information they contain can be accessed. Advantages of electronic dictionaries include speed of lookup, the ability to search using truncated word forms or to search the text of an entry for a specific word, the option of having multiple definitions open in multiple windows simultaneously (useful when trying to find precisely the right word from a number of similar options), and the ability to paste directly into a translation. Beyond the usual challenges linked to the use of dictionaries, we find (1) a lack of serendipity (related words that would be found on a page may not appear in the results of a search), (2) a tendency among students to accept what is seen on a screen as valid information without verification (also found with paper dictionaries), and perhaps (3) screen clutter — many applications need to be open at the same time while translating.

Another widely used tool is an *online database*, any repository of information that is accessible to users through the World Wide Web. These databases are accessible in standard ways using standard browsers, and therefore present few technological issues. Instead, the challenge is one teachers across disciplines face with increasing frequency: students assume that what they find on the Web is correct without considering the authority and reliability of the source. For example, students assigned to find parallel texts or terminology in English will often cite Web pages located on a site ending in .de (Germany) or .fr (France) as being representative of authentic English usage. In addition, students are increasingly relying on the World Wide Web as their only source of information, disregarding paper sources that would require them to walk to the library. Since students prefer to access no-cost sites, the reliability and particularly the scope of coverage of these freely accessible databases often leaves a great deal to be desired.

A third, more complex tool is a *terminology management system,* "a computer application designed for documenting and managing terminology." Terminology is "the set of all the terms that are specific to a special subject field, a group of persons, or a single individual" and "the discipline whose object is the systematic study of the monolingual or multilingual designation of concepts pertaining to domains of human activity..." (Delisle et al. 1999: 186). Thus a terminology management system is a software tool that allows users to store their own terminology for a particular domain or domains. Some of these software applications permit flexible entry of a broad range of information in addition to simple term-term equivalences (such as parts of speech, usage information, contexts, etc.), creation of hyperlinks between related terms, and consistency enforcement across data categories. Like many software applications today, this kind of tool makes it possible for a broad range of users to adapt the software to their specific needs. Here, the conceptual challenge involves the fact that students are often unable to recognize items that are part of a terminology, that is, "The set of all the terms that are specific to a special subject field, a group of persons, or a single individual" (Delisle et al. 1999: 186). Terminology management system software has been misused by students who simply insert a term for every word they do not know in a source text (thus reflecting their level of L2 competence) and do not supply any of the relevant ancillary information.

The fourth and most complex tool involves *computer-assisted translation*, which is "a mode of translation where the human translator creates a text using a computer program designed to support the translation process" (Delisle et al. 1999: 126). Computer-assisted translation systems generally include some form of translation memory. Translation memory is "a computer program that stores and aligns previously translated source texts and their respective target texts in machine-readable form and matches new texts for translation to previous solutions in order to reuse previous translations" (190). Challenges for pedagogy here involve construction of a sufficiently large database of translated segments to actually demonstrate the software, finding suitable texts for translation within this domain, and, again, teaching students how to evaluate texts provided or suggested by the computer. (See also Bowker's contribution in this volume.)

Last, *desktop publishing software* is not actually a translation tool *per se*, but rather, as the name suggests, a publishing tool. Nevertheless, as the language industry has shifted from being merely a provider of translated texts to a provider of multilingual publishing solutions, knowledge of at least one desktop publishing system is becoming a useful if not a necessary component of translator knowledge.

Pedagogical responses to technologization

In a computerized translation classroom or lab, the overarching goal is to enable students to acquire both declarative knowledge (i.e., specific technical skills in an application) and procedural knowledge (i.e., the ability to recognize and contextualize technical issues within a conceptual framework) to enable them to work effectively in an increasingly technologized translation industry, and to deal with change proactively through their understanding of the nature and underlying principles of the technology. Maria-Luisa Arias-Mareno describes the distinction between declarative and procedural forms of knowledge in the following way: "*Declarative knowledge* is explicit and conscious and involves 'knowing what' (facts, rules). In contrast, *procedural knowledge* consists of 'knowing how' using cognitive strategies and procedures to solve problems" (1999: 338). For example, one can visit the ATA website on the Internet and use a search engine to select individual translators from the database; yet without understanding the underlying principles of Boolean logic, the search is likely to produce misleading results — too many or too few "hits." Along the same lines, knowing how to resize boxes and align text in a localization application such as Catalyst represents memorized knowledge. Conceptually, however, it is much more important to understand the metaphor underlying such actions, i.e., that a gray box on the screen represents an object that can contain other objects, such as outlines, divider lines, check boxes, text boxes, etc., each of which is itself an object. Once the concept has been acquired, the student can encounter any such object in any software environment and, knowing that it can be manipulated in particular ways, need only discover how these manipulations are implemented in this particular software application.

Over the last twenty years, we have seen the development of a number of learner-centered pedagogical approaches based in Cognitive Theory that might help translator trainers avoid the temptation to dispense declarative knowledge regarding the use of technology — of the "press this button first" variety — within a traditional *performance magistrale*. Task-Based Instruction (TBI) is one such methodology. Developed for the teaching of foreign languages, it is based not on Skinner's behavioral theory, but on the theory of cognitive processing elaborated by Bloom. In his now famous taxonomy, Bloom delineated six different cognitive processes and organized them hierarchically from the least to the most complex: memorization, understanding, application, analysis, synthesis, evaluation. Arguing that behaviorist approaches to language instruction based largely on repetition and drills engaged only the lowest levels of cognitive processing, methodologists following Bloom developed TBI in order to "bring the real world into the classroom" in such a way that "language form is learned through language use," not through explicit explanations of grammatical forms and functions (Krahnke 1987: 57, 58).

This shift in focus initiated a major re-thinking of traditional classroom activities insofar as:

> From an interactionist perspective, most classroom activities or instruments for data collection are not an efficient means to assist language learning in the classroom or to study the processes of L2 comprehension and interlanguage modification, as they do not guarantee the conditions for goal-oriented or negotiated interaction in which learners can take an active role. Instead, they require learners to comply with goals they have had no part in setting. Their opportunities to work toward collective or individual goals are blocked, as teachers and researchers control both the questions that are asked and the responses that are expected. Opportunities for learners to negotiate meaning or exchange information are also limited since information flows in only one direction — from answer-supplying learner to question-asking teacher or researcher. (Pica, Kanagy, Falodun 1993: 10)

Although Anita Csölle and Krisztina Károly are generally correct in saying the "despite the recent welcome of the task-based approach to language instruction, the term 'task' lacks a unified, generally accepted definition" (1998: 1), there are several features of the instructional task that distinguish it from other classroom activities such as substitution drills or role-playing. An effective language learning task aims to motivate students to acquire language forms in order to perform in a real world language event that engages higher-level cognitive processing. "Learner-centered tasks," explains Robert Davis, "are designed to give participants 'a social or personal reason to speak,' such that their production is 'potentially interesting to the participants,' to use the terminology of Pattison" (Davis 1997: 270). As James Lee puts it:

> While there is not yet complete agreement on how to construct task-based activities, the consensus is that task-based activities engage the language learner in purposeful language use for which the language is the *means to an end*. (1995: 445, italics added)

Krahnke also insists that the goal of the language-learning task be "non-instructional" (1987: 57), that is, the goal should be related to the student's real-life needs and activities. The student is therefore directly invested in the goal of the task. "In an academic setting," Krahnke explains, "students might work on a paper or report that is actually needed for a content-area class. Beginning students might tackle the process of applying for a program or job, obtaining the forms and information necessary to complete the process" (58).

Pica, Kanagy and Falodun summarize the fundamental shift in methodology represented by TBI, when they write that "a task is not an action carried out on task participants; rather, a task is an activity which participants, themselves, must carry out" (1993: 2). Other essential characteristics of a task as described by Krahnke include: a process of informational manipulation and development; the acquisition of informational content that the language learner did not have at the beginning of the task; the application of the higher-order cognitive processes of evaluation, selection, combination, modification or supplementation. Lee makes a similar point that a task should involve the expression, interpretation, and negotiation of meaning (1995: 445). David Nunan, too, emphasized the higher-level cognitive processing involved in the completion of an effectively designed task:

> [A task is] a piece of classroom work which involves learners in comprehending, manipulating, producing or interacting in the target language while their attention is principally focused on meaning rather than form. (1989: 10)

In addition to producing greater communicative proficiency, the benefits of Task-Based Instruction may include: enhanced motivation, insofar as the task relates to the real life of the students; enhanced self-confidence in students who are able to accomplish a real-world task; enhanced L2 proficiency in adult learners; and enhanced cultural literacy (Leaver and Stryker 1989: 272–3). Moreover, task-based language learning, when organized as group work, "can help to bridge the gap between what Moorjani and Field (1988) have identified as an inherent mismatch between teachers' and students' preferences for 'functional, global-type explanations and oral modes of communication" (Davis 1997: 268).

The task can be easily adapted for the teaching of technology-related translation topics so as to ensure that (1) the classroom is learner-centered, (2) classroom activity involves higher-level cognitive processing, and (3) classroom activity is based on real-world knowledge and actual professional situations and events. After providing the necessary materials for completion of the task as well as pre-task exercises, readings, and/or discussion, the teacher would serve as a facilitator in the classroom, guiding students in the completion of the task. In addition to learning how to use new technology, TBI in the translation classroom can challenge students to think about the implications of technological innovations on text-types, job descriptions, and translation tools, and may offer the additional benefit of improving professional self-image, professional behavior, teamwork, flexibility and resourcefulness.

It should be noted that difficulties involved with task-based instruction in the translation classroom, particularly and largely issues of implementation, are similar to those in the language classroom. As Brian Baer and Theresa Minick point out, "in order for these teaching approaches to be successful, special teacher training is necessary, as well as a great deal of creativity and initiative on the part of the teacher" (1999: 2). While simulation of real-world professional situations and events can be challenging from a pedagogical point of view, the advisory board for the new Certificate Program in Localization at the University of Washington recognized its importance by including it in their goals: "Model student projects after those in the real world. Exercises derive from situations encountered by localizers in the field and are designed to *facilitate problem-solving skills* directly related to the daily work of localization professionals" (Irmler 2001: 22, italics added).

Taking task-based instruction into a localization classroom can be challenging to the teacher used to preparing and presenting lectures and having students do exercises based on the information he/she imparts. However, since classroom time presents an opportunity "to activate and apply comprehension and production processes" (Pica, Kanagy, Falodun 1993: 2) through student-student and student-teacher interaction, it is too valuable to spend in lecturing. Instead, information can be provided through reading assignments, so that class time can be spent on tasks that engage higher-level cognitive processing, which in turn produces more effective learning. Moreover, task-based instruction allows the teacher to address a variety of competences that are essential to effective localization and that may go unaddressed in a traditional classroom. Cornelia Groethuysen, for example, notes that, in addition to linguistic and technical competence, localizers must possess social and organizational competence, which she describes as "many competencies ... efficient communication ... exact planning and transparent communication rules...", as well as pragmatic competence, or the ability "to work efficiently with the various programs and tools that make up the increasingly complex modern translator workplace" (2001: 18). In the following section, we will present examples of ways in which task-based instruction can be brought into the translation/ localization classroom.

Teaching localization through tasks

In this section, we propose a number of tasks that can be incorporated into an introductory course on language localization. *Localization* is defined by the Localisation Industry Standards Association (LISA) as "the process of modifying products or services to account for differences in distinct markets" (Fry 2000: 35). The implicit assumption here is that most localization is *software* localization, although other products can also be localized. For translators, localization usually means using software tools to translate the textual elements found in a software package into another language, without "breaking the code" by deleting or changing control or formatting codes. The challenge to translation pedagogy is both conceptual and textual: the way in which text is stored and used in software programs makes software localization texts differ in important ways from conventional texts. Students are faced with the challenge not only of translating text fragments that appear to lack context, but also of understanding where the text comes from, where and when it will appear to the user, and how to ensure that all of the text in a program is translated. The latest localization tools are highly sophisticated, allowing translators to work on textual items while keeping them from inadvertently modifying the software code, but the problems of textual cohesion and coherence remain.

We choose a course on localization for the presentation of a task-based syllabus for a number of reasons. First, there is an urgent need for localizers in the language industry, which puts pressure on translator training programs to "churn out" localizers as soon as possible. This need is illustrated by a search on the IT website *dice.com* in March 2002, which showed 3,894 job listings containing the words "localization" and "Japanese" (Wright 2002). In such situations, pedagogy is often ignored in favor of a straightforward presentation of the declarative knowledge involved in the localization of software. Second, the obvious real-world application of localization skills is an invitation to TBI.

The course can be organized around a major, semester-long localization project using authentic materials. In order to make it as similar to the real world as possible, teams of students can be assigned to localize a project into their working language. (In a multi-language classroom, the source project can be in English or the *lingua franca* of the institution in question; students localize out of the central language into French, Spanish, German, etc.) The students can be instructed to treat the assignment as if they were working in a translation company. The teacher prepares a translation brief (if desired, lacking some key information that students would be expected to notice and request, see below) and students take on the various roles of project manager, translator, proofreader, revisor, client contact, etc., with the teacher now acting as a mentor as well as simulating the client. The goal is both to create a final localized version of the software and to present it to the class in a professional manner. In the final summative presentation, the other students have the opportunity to evaluate (critique) the job of localization and the presentation, since they have all worked on the same software. This format may also expose students to various issues that arise in connection with the different languages into which the software was localized.

Many tasks could be assigned to activate and practice skills of analysis, synthesis, and evaluation. In the translation/localization classroom, these could involve translation briefs, the text types involved in localization, quality control/quality assurance, localization of non-linguistic objects/aspects, and presentation of the project at the end of the semester. Possible goals may include developing an awareness of the actual situation in the translation industry, teamwork skills, independence, confidence (translator self-image), professionalism, and, of course, a deeper and broader understanding of the issues and concepts involved in translation and localization. However, while development of specific skills in a range of specific software applications may be one of the goals of a course, the goal of an in-class task will always be more effective learning through activation of higher-order cognitive processing. Once the issues and concepts have been actively grasped by the learner in task-based instruction, the application skills can be practiced at home — through follow-up exercises, etc.

The tasks presented below are elaborated through a slightly modified version of Nunan's model of the task. Nunan proposes six components essential to the design of a classroom task. As paraphrased by Davis, they are: "a goal, input 'text' (verbal or nonverbal), an activity derived from the input, specified teacher role and student role, and the setting" (Davis 270). For each task, we elaborate: the goal(s) of the task; pre-task reading and/or exercises; input; activity; output; teacher role; learner role; setting.

The **Task** describes the overarching theme or topic of the activity. The **Goal(s) of the task** are the specific learning objectives to be achieved by this task. The **Pre-task exercise** involves work (readings, discussions, summaries) preliminary to the activity that may (1) provide students with background knowledge, filling in incomplete schemata, (2) stimulate thought on a given topic, (3) prepare students for classroom discussion. These pre-task activities can be done either at home or in class and should raise conceptual issues that will allow students to engage higher-level cognitive processing in the completion of the activity. **Input** refers to the materials (authentic texts) provided to the students so that they can carry out the activity. The **Activity** refers to the structured, goal-oriented activities that occur within the classroom to facilitate learning, while the **Output** is a product that organizes the results of the activity — preferably in the form of a real-world communicative act (an e-mail, a business letter, a PowerPoint presentation). The **Teacher role** indicates the teacher's mode of participation in the classroom during completion of the task (discussion leader, facilitator, mentor), while the **Learner role** indicates the context in which students perform the task (individually, in pairs, groups, etc.). Finally, the **Setting** designates where the task activity occurs (traditional classroom, computer lab, etc.).

Task: Translation Briefs

Translation briefs (or assignments) represent the product specifications for any translation job. In the actual practice of freelance translators, the translation brief is often quite scanty, i.e., "I have 3200 words of German text that I need by Monday, it's some kind of legal text." Students, however, should be made aware of what information is necessary in order to carry out a translation responsibly.

Goal: To learn the features of the ideal translation brief versus typical briefs in industry practice, to analyze briefs, and to acquire the skills and knowledge necessary to evaluate and respond in a professional manner to actual translation briefs.

Pre-task exercise: Readings should focus on the "situatedness" of the translated text, e.g., the necessity of taking into consideration the nature and the needs of the L2 audience. In the next class period, students would discuss their readings and generate questions that could be asked about any translation brief (e.g., language pair, source use, source audience, target use, target audience).

Input: A number of actual translation briefs, assignment sheets, and assignment e-mails, preferably related to localization.

Activity: Based on the readings, students formulate the information that should be contained in an ideal brief. They then examine the actual briefs provided, comparing them to the ideal brief, and note what desired information is lacking in each of the briefs. Finally, the students summarize (synthesize) their results for the class.

Output: A business e-mail to the client, requesting additional information for one of the briefs.

Teacher role: Facilitator.

Learner role: Participant in group work.

Setting: Classroom.

Task: Text Types in Localization

Goal: Acquire understanding of text types in localization and how they differ from traditional text types.

Pre-task exercise: Read and discuss Chapter 3 of Bert Esselink's *Practical Guide to Localization* (2000) on the various types and formats of files that are localized.

Input: Excerpts of various text types found in localization (e.g., menu items, help text, messages), as well as more traditional text types in the same domain, such as computer software manuals.

Activity: Analyze and synthesize the significant differences (lack of context, strings and help paragraphs potentially translated in isolation, particularly in large projects) and similarities (importance of terminological accuracy and consistency).

Output: PowerPoint presentation on localization text types for client education.

Teacher role: Discussion facilitator.

Student role: Discussion partner.

Setting: Classroom.

Task: Localization of Non-Linguistic Content (Cultural Issues)

It is usually necessary to localize not only the text of a software application, but also its non-linguistic content. Graphics, pictures, icons, and even color schemes can have different meanings and thus have a different (sometimes negative) impact in different cultures.

Goal: To become aware of, analyze, and evaluate various images, as well as to acquire the ability to manipulate such objects.

Pre-task exercise: Readings and discussion might focus on the culture-specific and historically determined value attributed to such universal categories as color and shape (cf. Umberto Eco, *Art and Beauty in the Middle Ages*) or to certain commonplace items (cf. the film *The Gods Must Be Crazy*).

Input: Students are provided with a variety of images and with Esselink's description of the cultural specificity of computer images (34).

Activity: Students would run the software for the current project, browsing for culturally charged items, analyze the items for neutral, potentially offensive or misleading content, and suggest alternatives.

Output: A table, where one column shows culturally charged images, another column lists the culture(s) in which each image is charged, a third describes the problem, and a fourth column lists possible alternative images, providing them if available.

Teacher role: Discussion facilitator.

Student role: Cultural expert, discussion partner.

Setting: Localization classroom.

Task: Localization of Non-Linguistic Content (Technical Issues)

Goal: Learn to access and edit or replace images.

Pre-task exercise: Read product descriptions of various image editors and discuss their advantages and disadvantages.

Input: An introduction to the software in question. A tutorial demonstrating the program, and the program itself.

Activity: Students work in pairs at computers, working through software to learn to access and edit or replace images. Students work together in order to facilitate higher-order processing: the student not at the keyboard can function as an advisor to the other, enabling them to discover on their own how to open an image, make modifications, replacements, etc. Potentially, information gaps that may exist will be filled by the other student, enabling peer-to-peer learning.

Output: Localized image file.

Teacher role: Facilitator, roaming the computer lab to assist students.

Student role: Computer learner, discussion partner.

Setting: Computer lab.

Task: Quality Assessment

Goal: Acquire a deeper knowledge and understanding of what translation quality is and how it is maintained.

Pre-task exercise: Read a variety of quality evaluation tools, such as the American Translators Association grading scale or the SAE J2450 Translation Quality Metric. Discuss the applicability of these tools to the localization product (see also Arango-Keeth and Koby in this volume).

Input: Actual localized product information or software.

Activity: The task would involve discussion, analysis, and evaluation of short excerpts of translations of various quality.

Output: Quality assessment report.

Setting: Classroom.

Task: Presenting a Localized Product

Goal: Make a professional presentation of a localized product.

Pre-task exercise: Discuss effective public-speaking techniques, use of presentation software, culture-specific aspects of professional behavior.

Input: A checklist of criteria for evaluation of effective presentations, and the product that has been localized over the course of the semester.

Activity: Students present localized software to the class in a professional manner.

Output: An outline of the presentation and any presentation software files used.

Teacher Role: Simulated client.

Student Role: Simulated localization provider, client.

Setting: Conference room.

Other tasks might involve the style guides referred to in Kosaka and Itagaki in this volume, issues in project management, terminology management, etc.

Conclusion

We believe that the task-based exercises presented in this article are an effective method of addressing student needs to acquire the skills and information necessary to be a competent translator in today's increasingly technologized language industry. While instructors may be tempted simply to provide students with the declarative knowledge necessary to operate a given software application, tasks such as those elaborated above may help them to create more learner-centered classrooms, conducive to the acquisition of the cognitive and theoretical background necessary to be more effective, thoughtful translators who understand the conceptual foundations of their craft.

References

Arias-Mareno, M.-L. 1999. "What? Teach translation?" In *Proceedings of the 40th Annual Conference of the American Translators Association*. Alexandria, Virginia: American Translators Association.

Baer, B., and Minick, T. 1999. "Task-based instruction and the Internet: Overcoming the obstacles." In *Perspectives in Foreign Language Teaching, Volume XII*. [Proceedings of the Twenty-Third Annual Conference on the Teaching of Foreign Languages and Literatures, Youngstown State University, October 8–9, 1999]. J. Sarkissian (ed), 1–7. Youngstown, OH: Youngstown State University.

Csölle, A., and Károly, K. 1998. "Learning from errors: A task-based approach." *NovELTy: A Journal of English Language Teaching and Cultural Studies in Hungary.* 5.3. Online.

Davis, R. L. 1997. "Group work is NOT busy work: Maximizing success of group work in the L2 classroom." *Foreign Language Annals* 30.2: 265–279.

Delisle, J., Lee-Jahnke, H., and Cormier, M. C. (eds). 1999. *Terminologie de la traduction/ Translation Terminology/Terminología de la traducción/Terminologie der Übersetzung.*

FIT Monograph Series 1. Amsterdam: Benjamins.

Eco, U. 2002. *Art and Beauty in the Middle Ages.* Bredin, H. (trans). New Haven: Yale UP.

Esselink, B. 2000. *A Practical Guide to Localization.* Language International World Directory 4. Amsterdam: Benjamins.

Gods Must Be Crazy, The. 1981. Dir. Uys, J. Fox Home Entertainment.

Groethuysen, C. 2001. "Real-life training for translators: Software localization and technical documentation at the Sprachen- und Dolmetscher Institut München." *Language International* 13 (4): 16–19.

Fry, D. 2000. *Localization Industry Primer.* Féchy, Switzerland: Localisation Industry Standards Association (LISA).

Irmler, U. 2001. "The University of Washington presents a new certificate program in localization." *Language International* 13 (2): 20–22.

Kiraly, D. C. 1995. *Pathways to Translation: Pedagogy and Process.* Translation Studies 3. Kent, OH: Kent State UP.

Krahnke, K. 1987. *Approaches to Syllabus Design for Foreign Language Teaching.* New York: Prentice-Hall.

Ladmiral, J.-R. 1977. "La traduction dans le cadre de l'institution pédagogique." *Die Neueren Sprachen* 76: 489–516.

Leaver, B. L., and Stryker, S. B. 1989. "Content-based instruction for foreign language classrooms." *Foreign Language Annals* 22.3: 269–275.

Lee, J. F. 1995. "Using task-based activities to restructure class discussions." *Foreign Language Annals* 28.3: 437–446.

Melby, A. 1994. "The translator workstation." In *Professional Issues for Translators and Interpreters* (American Translators Association Scholarly Monograph Series, Volume VII), D. L. Hammond (ed), 127–147. Amsterdam/Philadelphia: John Benjamins.

Nunan, D. 1989. *Designing Tasks for the Communicative Classroom.* Cambridge: Cambridge UP.

Pica, T., Kanagy, R., and Falodun, J. 1993. "Choosing and using communication tasks for second language instruction." In *Tasks and Language Learning: Integrating Theory and Practice*, G. Crookes and S. M. Gass (eds), 9–34. Philadelphia: Multilingual Matters.

Shreve, G. M. 2000. "Translation at the millennium: Prospects for the evolution of a profession." In *Paradigmenwechsel in der Translation. Festschrift für Albrecht Neubert zum 70. Geburtstag*, P. A. Schmitt (ed), 217–234. Tübingen: Stauffenburg Verlag.

Wright, S. E. 2002. "Market-oriented translation pedagogy." Presentation at the First Conference of the American Translation Studies Association, Kent State University, March 2002.

Building a curriculum
for Japanese localization translators

Revisiting translation issues
in the era of new technologies

Takashi Kosaka and Masaki Itagaki

Introduction

After several decades of development, localization has established itself as a successful industry worldwide, and the translation industry as a whole has benefited. Defined as "the process of creating or adapting an information product for use in a specific target country or specific target market" (Hoft 1995: 11), localization involves both technical and linguistic adaptation. An original product must be modified to create a functionally equivalent product that meets the business and technical standards of the target country. An increasing number of translation agencies are engaged in localization projects, requiring them to hire such diversified personnel as localization engineers, localization translators, localization linguists, and terminologists. It is not surprising then that many graduates of U.S. translation schools are being hired to work in the translation departments of software manufacturers.

Translators of the new generation may function as more than mere transformers of language. Unlike some traditional translators, localizers also act as intercultural communicators, working across the boundaries between translation and other professional activities, e.g., marketing, business consultancy, and engineering; the field of the translator now extends into all of these areas.

Unfortunately, there are not enough translator training programs to meet the growing demand for localizers. At present, skills are transferred from individual translators to their colleagues and are often acquired through trial and error. Some companies and individual consultants, however, have begun to develop localization training programs that may serve as models for academic programs.

This article describes a course offered at the Monterey Institute of International Studies (MIIS) in English>Japanese localization of graphical and text information embedded in a product's interface. The first half of this paper makes use of the methodology of auto-ethnography. It is a personal recollection of Takashi Kosaka's experience as a new teacher of translation and localization. Academic research in cross-cultural communication has made increasing use of the method of auto-ethnography (e.g., Geist 1999, Gonzalez et al. 1997, and Cooper 2000) and although it is at times subjected to severe scrutiny due to its apparent departure from the scientific approach to data analysis, we firmly believe that narrative, the use of the personal story — namely auto-ethnography — provides us with special insight into the experience of those who are left out or marginalized within the dominant discourse, in this case, the localizer.

The second half of this paper explains language-specific localization courses offered through the MIIS Japanese program and summarizes the Do's and Don'ts of English to Japanese localization within the areas of documentation, software, and Web localization.

Three specific questions will be explored in this paper. First, what attitude did, and now do, translation students and educators have toward localization education? Second, what kinds of courses and exercises can be offered for Japanese localization translators? Third, what guidelines should be taught to students of Japanese localization?

A localizer in the classroom

In August 1997, I — Takashi Kosaka — was hired as an Assistant Professor at MIIS in Monterey, California. MIIS offers a unique educational model centered around language education. The language of the student's area of expertise determines the field of study. For example, the study of Korean diplomacy includes content in the fields of both English and Korean. A major in Japanese translation requires the study of both English>Japanese translation and Japanese>English translation (along with spoken Japanese and spoken English). The target language is the foundation on which the student's field of study is built.

My first encounter with translation education came at the translation examination, where I was stunned to discover that all of the students had to handwrite their translations for the exam. By then computers were all but required for translation. I knew that I was going to teach translation to graduate students, not beginners, so why should I have to waste everyone's time teaching exam strategy for handwritten translation? Never having submitted handwritten translations to my clients, I was unable to answer this question.

When I met the students in my first class, I was immediately struck by their reaction to localization. I vividly recall that I literally lost my voice for a moment or two after I heard this comment from one of my students: "I hate localization. I never want to work in the localization industry." Negative reactions against localization were most common among Japanese students, who comprised the majority of the Japanese program. Japanese students usually exceed 80% of the student body every year.

I was not prepared to offer a course on localization translation that would require me to work with students who showed an almost allergic reaction toward computers. Over the last few years, however, I've seen a decline in the harsh reactions of students to localization. These days, students tend to control their reactions, knowing that it is localization that will most likely get them a job in the U.S. It has been the case for the past several years that approximately 95% of translation job openings are in the localization industry. Moreover, because Japanese students are unable to work as freelance translators due to their visa restrictions, localization is the surest way for those who desire to remain and to work in the U.S. to do so.

I had worked for IBM Japan as a systems engineer before I came to the U.S. Since systems engineers work as a team, skills that are necessary for systems engineering include interpersonal communication with customers, interface design, implementation, coding, testing, and follow-up. Systems engineering covers basic phases of project management. What does this summary have to do with localization? It includes almost everything I needed as a background to become a localization trainer. I regained my confidence and started thinking about how I could approach teaching localization translation to my students.

Pedagogy for localization education

While the list of localization trainers and courses has been growing longer, it is still short when compared with the demand for localization translators. Obviously, it is preferable for an individual who has experience in localization to teach localization. Unfortunately, many traditional translator trainers have little background as in-house translators. Since earlier localization projects were often carried out in-house, freelance translators have been least exposed to the localization process. Moreover, salaries for in-house translators are relatively high, normally higher than those of translator trainers. There is therefore no economic incentive for an in-house translator to become a translator trainer; the only incentive would be the pleasure of teaching itself.

We feel that the subject of localization provides sufficient content to justify a separate semester-long course in localization for translators. Most translator trainers, however, tend to regard localization as the new kid on the block. They sometimes diminish its importance and even try to deny that it is an essential subject at a translation school. Their mindset seems to be that localization is no more than translation, and they prefer to teach translation issues in a traditional way and in a traditional context. According to this logic, localization translation can be accommodated within the existing translation curriculum without assigning units specifically to its study. Citing research findings of the Localization Education Initiative Taskforce (LEIT), Altanero (1999) points out that very few schools offer courses pertaining to localization. At MIIS, however, courses on software localization, terminology management, and project management have been in existence for a number of years now.

Given this current level of translator trainer knowledge, we must conclude that not only students but also teachers ought to study the localization process in order to familiarize themselves with the subject. Students are sometimes much more familiar with and more skillful with computers than their teachers. On-line faculty development is one possible solution to promoting understanding of localization and computer literacy among faculty members.

In localization education, there has been a paradigm shift from constructivist to social constructivist practices in translation pedagogy, as advocated by Kiraly (2000). A traditional transmission approach emphasizes a one-to-many transmission of knowledge, and, in translation studies, knowledge and translation skills have been traditionally transmitted from teachers to students. If students were living in a society where access to information were blocked, or if a teacher had to give lectures to a large audience, this approach might be necessary. However, it may not be best suited to a society where information and skill sets are constantly developing and changing.

Moreover, when student knowledge sometimes outstrips that of teachers, pedagogy needs to be reassessed accordingly. Localization education is a case in point. The increasing demand for localization courses and the lack of qualified localization trainers demands new solutions. Social constructivism, by which aggregate knowledge and skills are created out of the collaboration between students and teachers, may offer a remedy.

Course description

Building a curriculum for localization at MIIS proved to be a difficult task, as students were already taking so many required courses, such as Basic Translation Exercises into Japanese, Translation of Economic and Commercial Text into Japanese, Translation of Scientific and Technical Text into Japanese, Translation of Political and Legal Text into Japanese, and Advanced Translation Seminar. Each course has its own unique purpose and provides students with useful skills and opportunities to discuss issues related to each topic. It would be burdensome to add additional course requirements and teaching responsibilities.

Creating a localization curriculum is also difficult because the localization industry and its processes are always in a state of flux. Localization is in an early stage, with manufacturers still developing and testing their localization workflows. New tools have also emerged and have been applied to the workflow. Sun MicroSystems and MIIS jointly established the Global Resource Center to promote streamlining localization processes, integrating memory tools, Control Language, and Machine Translation technology.

In 1997, there was no course pertaining to localization and I could not spare the time then to design such a course. Now, with help from an external resource, MIIS has managed to put together a software localization course, which is a required course for translation majors across all language programs. Language-specific issues are left to other courses, because there simply isn't enough time to explore such issues. (The exception is the inevitable issue of double-byte encoding in localization into Asian languages.) Because few instructors are capable of evaluating the linguistic aspects of localization, it is necessary for each language program to coordinate to fill in the gaps. Localization training is only complete when language-specific issues are discussed.

It is for this reason that only linguistic issues pertinent to Japanese localization are introduced here. Because no extra course units can be afforded, the Japanese Department chose to present localization translation issues in Scientific and Technical Translation in the second semester and in the Advanced Seminar in the fourth semester. The former course deals with scientific topics, including the basics of computers, and the latter course has flexibility in terms of its course content. According to the 2001 school year calendar, a total of twenty instructional hours were devoted to localization translation in both the fall and spring semesters of the second year. This figure includes hands-on training with translation memory tools, which students first encounter in a class on computer-assisted translation offered the previous semester.

Given the time constraints, it is important to choose topics wisely, and to identify students' skill levels. Let us reiterate that these localization segments are not intended to provide an introduction to localization processes; instead, they attempt to provide additional opportunities for translators who already possess basic knowledge of localization and wish to learn more about the linguistic aspects of Japanese localization. These segments should be entitled "localization for Japanese translators." Business aspects of localization, as well as general concepts, are omitted from the course content.

Three major components of Japanese localization are documentation (on-line help, manuals), software localization, and Web localization. The content and methods of each component will be described below, although each segment can be easily expanded as a separate two-unit course. A maximum of 20 hours is devoted to exercises and discussion of language-specific issues.

1.   Documentation

A documentation exercise provides students with an opportunity to create their own translation style guides. A style guide specifies the markup and design requirements for a publication. Almost all localization companies have their own style guides for both interface and documentation translation, but few translators have actually created an original guide from scratch. Most of them use the *Microsoft Manual of Style for Technical Publications*, the *de facto* translation style guide of the industry. While following the instructions of style sheets can be tedious, creating a style sheet can be demanding and intellectually stimulating. Moreover, new graduates in the job market as well as current students have reacted positively to the task. At a job interview, a student was asked whether or not she was familiar with any translation style guides and had actually translated a document following one. She answered that she knew style guides, but hadn't used one, although she had created an original translation style guide of her own.

Students are encouraged to analyze available style sheets and already published Japanese manuals. Without any guidance, students are easily lost and feel frustrated. Students present their 5–6 page style sheet every week for three consecutive weeks. Three weeks appears to be an appropriate length of time to spend on this style sheet project.

In order to evenly divide the discussion time among presenters, students select from among many topics, which means that not all topics are discussed in the course. A table of contents containing all topics covered in an actual style sheet is shown in Fig. 1. About 10 students in each session present different topics, so that a variety of topics are automatically covered. After each presentation, the style guide is discussed and opinions from both peers and the instructor are exchanged. Finalized style guides amount to about 20–25 pages. Again, only portions that interest each presenter are explained in detail.

Katakana
Parentheses ([], <>,「」)
Connective (and, but, however, when)
Infinitive verbs (To do ...)
Auxiliary verbs (can, should, may, could, must, will)
Common expressions (See Figure 1.)

Figure 1. Table of Contents of translation style guide

2. Use of memory tools

Memory and terminology management tools are a vital part of documentation localization. As collaborative translation is the norm in localization, no translator can arbitrarily decide his or her own terminologies and styles. A style sheet and terminology management standards are a necessity, since inconsistent terminology and translation style can double or triple the cost of documentation localization.

Nevertheless, the use of such tools does not necessarily reduce project costs. For example, the cost cannot be reduced by introducing such tools in the middle of a project. If translators were to begin their tasks without fixing styles and terminologies, the memory would contain useless and sometimes misleading information. Such a failure might be due to the often hectic schedule during the beginning phase of a localization project. However, when used properly, memory and terminology management tools can greatly reduce costs. (In the localization course, students do not use computer-assisted translation (CAT) tools, since there is a parallel CAT course running in the same semester.)

3. Software localization

A software localization exercise can be extremely monotonous unless students are motivated and clearly understand the overall localization processes. An interface localization exercise such as described here should be carried out with an understanding of the wider context in which a specific interface is developed. For example, most software screens are comprised of menu/task bars with each item represented by one or two words. Except for the on-line help system and messages that consist of complete sentences, the context necessary for translation is largely absent and the meanings of words are embedded in the lost context, which can be retrieved only when one is actually in the process of using the software. The main task for a software translator is to reconstruct the context from a list of words that are displayed in spreadsheet form in software localization tools. Ideally, the actual software application can be available to the translators, so that they may refer to the interface whenever necessary.

4.   Memory tool

In contrast to the overwhelming number of general translation memory tools available on the market, standard software localization tools do not exist. Because software localization is embedded in the software development environment, software vendors create their own tools to localize their products. Memory tools may often share common functions, but the interfaces of the software localization tools developed by each company are largely unique. Learning how to use tools, then, is not the main purpose of the software localization exercise. Instead, students use the tools to deal with typical issues in localization.

In our software localization exercise, students are provided with *The Handbook of Software Localization* (1999), co-authored by the authors, and asked to localize three screens using a tool developed by one of the authors. These screens are simplified versions of those found in the actual software. The handbook has been adopted in the Advanced Translation Seminar course because it explicates relevant aspects of software localization, including software, documentation, visuals, project management, and terminology management unique to Japanese localization.

The tool is user-friendly, requiring only a minimum number of steps. Students first view an original screen in English to understand the context in which the interface is built. Next, students display a translation screen in order to input their translation into a spreadsheet-like file, translating English words by inserting equivalent words in Japanese. When the translation is completed, they press the "Switch" button to display a screen with their own translation embedded in it. On the translation screen, they can switch between source and target language, allowing them to check their work.

Studying the screen prior to and during translation is the most critical aspect of software localization. In reality, however, few translators are given this opportunity because products are not usually available. Translators are often in a rush to translate a file, and do not carefully analyze the interface when products do become available.

Our tool provides some real pedagogical benefits. First, students' tasks become more interactive. They can easily switch back and forth between English and Japanese screens. Recompilation of source code is time-consuming and is only necessary for those who need to understand technical localization processes. While students are well advised to familiarize themselves with such processes, it is not a requirement for localization translators who are only responsible for the linguistic aspects of localization. Our tool eliminates such recompilation processes related to software localization.

Second, the tool preserves the context in which the original application was built. Three screens were adopted from actual accounting software screens. Students need to know the function of the application before they start translating. The program is carefully planned so that students have already been exposed to basic accounting knowledge. They have taken economic translation in their second semester, and have translated one page of text from the manual for this application in the same semester as their assignment. No one in the class feels a stranger to the software when they begin work on this localization exercise in their third semester. Having completed the exercise, they feel confident, because they have localized semi-real screens into their own native language. Screens used in an exercise should ideally come from a real application in the real world.

In addition, students have already become acquainted with a basic business model through a brief lecture in the second semester. Knowledge of the application plays an important role in translation in general and in software localization in particular. However, it is impossible to familiarize oneself with an infinite number of applications. In a basic course like this, students can be exposed to a standard business application rather than to a very specific industry-unique application. The localization industry takes into account the business model when it determines whether an application is worth being localized (Thibodeau 2000: 30). The business model, which is usually the input of an Enterprise Resource Planning (ERP) application, is the most appropriate application to teach within the context of business translation. Modules of the business model include ordering, purchasing, accounts payable/receivable, inventory, general ledger, delivery, and payment management. Once the decision to use this type of software has been made, the next step is to create a course that uses materials from the above contexts that are extremely useful for learning ERP applications.

5.   Web analysis

It is advantageous for students studying Web localization to understand how to evaluate the quality of a Web page interface. Although they are not Web page designers, they are the ones who first review and assess localized Web pages. Original Web page designers can receive more meaningful feedback from translators if translators themselves are familiar with Web design issues.

For example, "i-mode" requires a unique interface different from the ordinary Web interface. I-mode has become a social phenomenon in Japan, where the number of i-mode users has reached 20 million (*Yomiuri Newspaper* March 13 2001). I-mode can only display text-based information using a special interface, which is basically a cellular phone panel. If a company wants to target i-mode users when they market their Web products in Japan, they ought to take into account the technical restrictions of i-mode as well.

Translators can function not just as bilingual people who change the source language into the target language, but as marketing advisers in Web and software localization. They can identify functions that cannot be used in their own countries and need to be modified, e.g., calendar and measurement modules, and they can also advise as to whether localized Web pages have a professional appearance according to the standards of the target country. Simple modifications involving font sizes and typefaces can be an issue in Web localization. The details of these Web localization issues will be explained below.

6.   Web localization exercise

There are two kinds of exercises in Web localization — those at the macro and the micro levels. The macro-level exercise consists of content analysis, while the micro-level exercise is an actual translation using an HTML editor. The macro-level exercise involves content analysis of documentation (on-line help, message, manual) localization, which necessitates that students analyze how a manual is structured as a text. The micro-level exercise is an actual translation of the manual.

In the macro-level Web exercise, students are given an assignment to cross-analyze Web pages published in English with those published in Japanese. The purpose of this assignment is to understand the content and writing style of Web pages, in particular, culture-specific aspects. Content and industries are evenly divided so that there is no overlap among students. The specific items to be analyzed are up to each student; a student may choose to work on writing styles or may decide to compare overall content between the English and Japanese Web pages. The students present their opinions of the high quality Web pages — in other words, marketable pages — which can be invaluable input for Web design consultants.

In the micro-level exercise, students choose their own Web pages to translate. In such an exercise, students use Trados® TagEditor® to localize Web pages of their choice. Because the ideal way to increase students' motivation is for them to work on an actual Web localization project, localization of an online Ocean Report prepared by the U.S. Department of Commerce and editing/proofreading of the MIIS school website have been carried out in the course. In the former project, students volunteered to play different roles. There was one project manager, one terminologist, four editors, and seven translators. The instructor filled in as a localization engineer. Though some students, particularly the project manager and the editors, were initially overwhelmed with the difficulty of the project, it turned out to be a meaningful and successful experience for both students and the instructor. It is worth noting that the terminologist on the project, who had a background in biology, played a key role in building a high quality terminology list based on her research. Actual projects like these can provide the most realistic exercise materials, but an instructor has to pay special attention when designing the overall curriculum, including schedule changes and handling a worst-case scenario.

Discussion

After all these school assignments have been completed, students graduate from school and work as localization translators in the real market. Suddenly, they are responsible for real world assignments. At school, they are penalized if they are not able to finish and turn in their assignments by the due date. Even in a worst-case scenario, however, the penalty is that their grade for that one assignment is reduced by one grade point (e.g., from A minus to B plus). Their overall grade would not be significantly affected by their failure to turn in one assignment on time. In the real world, they might be severely reprimanded by their supervisor if they cannot meet their goals. It may adversely affect their performance evaluation, which directly affects their salary. Issues of time and quality management loom large when students take on real localization projects.

The authors would like to reiterate that localization translators are in a good position to transform the role of translation and act as intercultural mediators (Katan 1999). For documentation, translators can actively engage in the creation of appropriate writing styles to ensure that manuals are user-friendly in the target language. For software localization, translators can act as intercultural business consultants to provide developers with proper business models in each country. For Web localization, translators can function as marketing/interface advisers to evaluate the appropriateness of localized Web pages.

In real-life localization, a translator has to acquire an understanding of both the overall process of localization, as well as the technical issues related to the specific localization translation. The translator's job description may imply that the work involved is simply to translate the source language in one text format into the target language in the same format. If the boundary between translators and engineers is clearly defined, this job description may be strictly observed. However, this is often not the case. Translators are frequently expected to cross the boundary between the two job descriptions to enable a smooth transition of the localized product from one department to another. Esselink argues that translators should work in an environment more like that of software developers (1999: 29), in which case a wider range of choices would open up for translators who would like to play cross-functional roles.

Experience has shown that to play a cross-functional role, a translator need not have all that much non-linguistic, technical knowledge. Even common-sense advice from a foreign language speaker can solve serious language-related engineering problems. In the following section, we will discuss several practical issues that translators ought to know in order to handle multi-task translating of Japanese software and Web localization.

While in principle, translators should never be involved in any technical problems in software localization, the reality is that software engineers almost always face problems that force them to seek help from Japanese translators: "Why are all the double-byte characters garbled?" "What makes the text truncated?" "Why does the screen show all those funny squares?" Actually, none of the above questions is part of a translator's job *per se.*

However, few companies can afford to employ Japanese-expert engineers, even though language-specific issues slow down the localization and quality assurance processes. Many of these issues arise from mere linguistic trifles that translators can easily point out. A little knowledge concerning Japanese software development and computing could help non-Japanese engineers avoid such troubles, and minor help from Japanese colleagues can accelerate the localization process.

Below, we will discuss some fundamental technical issues in Japanese software localization.

A. *Encoding Japanese characters*
Character encoding is a convention used for displaying characters on screens. The most widely-used encoding in Japanese is "Shift JIS" on the MS Windows

and Macintosh platforms, and "EUC-JP" in the Unix environment. When Japanese characters get garbled — known as "moji-bake" — it is often a problem of encoding. Understanding character encoding and trying to solve encoding issues is beyond the scope of this paper. Nevertheless, there is one thing a translator might want to remember: there are many encoding schemes in Japanese. This knowledge is beneficial for those who work on Web translation. For example, suppose that the platform is Windows and the assignment is to translate one English HTML page. After translating all of the text in the file, the file may be simply returned as it is. It is saved with the".html" extension, and opened in a browser. The Japanese text will then be displayed as all garbage characters as shown in Figure 2.

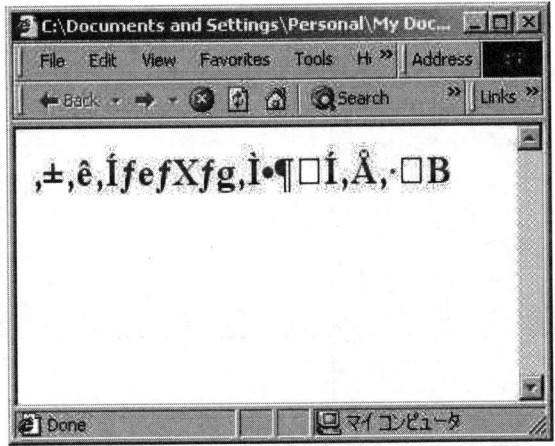

Figure 2. All Japanese characters turned into garbage

When an HTML source is opened for an English Web page, there is often a tag called META as shown in Figure 3.

```
<HTML>
<HEAD>
<META HTTP-EQUIV="Content-Type" CONTENT="text/html; charset=iso-8859-1">
</HEAD>
<BODY>
<H2>これはテストの翻訳文章です。</H2>
</BODY>
</HTML>
```

Figure 3   a META tag

When an HTML file is translated and saved using an editor, the editor uses the system encoding as a default, which is "Shift JIS" for Windows. However, the Web page's META tag specifies "iso-8859–1," which is "Latin 1" for ASCII (see Figure 3). A browser reads the META tag information to display all of the characters with ASCII, which of course cannot display Japanese Shift-JIS characters. Fortunately, the encoding defect does not really break characters. When "Shift JIS" is selected from a display-encoding menu in the browser view option, it displays Japanese correctly as in Figure 4.

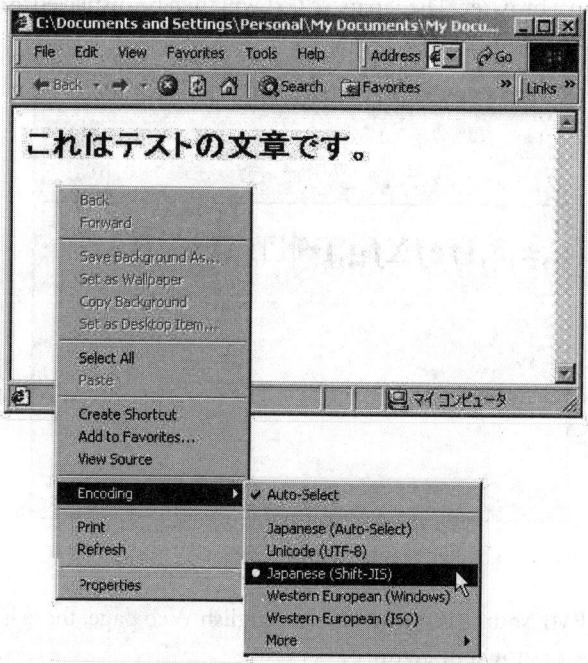

Figure 4. Changing browser encoding

Nevertheless, Web page localization cannot be complete without correct encoding information in HTML. A translator has to place an appropriate Japanese encoding keyword, which is "Shift JIS," as follows:

<META HTTP-EQUIV="Content-Type" CONTENT="text/html; charset=**Shift JIS**">

Although "moji-bake" problems have nothing to do with translation, engineers tend to doubt the quality and reliability of the translation when they encounter character problems.

B. *Double-byte Japanese terms*

After software is compiled with the Japanese translation, character type does not really matter, because it is turned into bits. One byte, or eight bits, is required to represent a single placeholder for one ASCII character, such as a letter of the alphabet; eight-bit encoding can only contain up to 256 character variations. Double-byte encoding, that is, sixteen bits, can handle up to 65,536 characters, and is required for all Chinese, Japanese, and Korean languages (commonly abbreviated as CJK). The number of characters that belong to these languages exceeds the maximum capacity of one byte. The Japanese Kanji set, for instance, which was borrowed from Chinese and adopted as Japanese characters, includes approximately 50,000 different characters, with 100,000 variations altogether if other non-standard Kanji are counted. In addition, Simplified Chinese, Traditional Chinese, and Korean have their own "Kanji" (or Han) sets. As a result, 65,536 characters is not really sufficient to handle all existing Asian characters.

Although non-Japanese engineers at least know about the distinction between single byte and double byte, many of them still subscribe to the "double-byte myth."

> *Myth No. 1: A Japanese translation text is always double in size and length compared with the English original.*

To illustrate the fallacy of this myth, the following example shows the difference in byte length between English and Japanese terms for "address."

[Text]	[Byte length]
Address	7 bytes (7 characters)
住所	4 bytes (2 characters)

In terms of byte size, the Japanese text is about 40% shorter than the English original. However, this sample figure does not predict translation length in general. No one knows whether the number of characters in a Japanese translation will be larger or smaller until the text is translated. Similarly, display-pitch size is almost impossible to predict in Japanese. As shown in Figure 5, glyph display size depends entirely on which font is used with what point size.

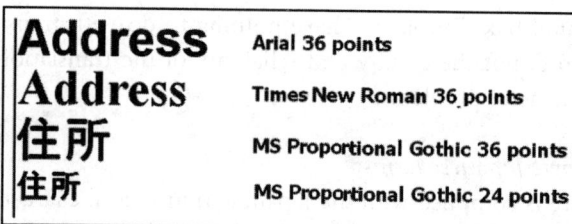

Figure 5. Variations of fonts and points

Another likely question from the engineer would be, "How much extra space should I leave for Japanese text on a software interface?" Suppose that the engineer is creating a form shown in Figure 6.

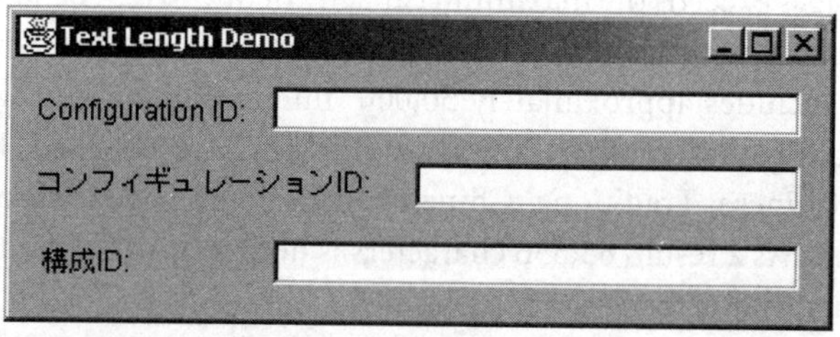

Figure 6. Label texts on a form

The English label text, "Configuration ID," fits in the first line. Buying into Myth No. 1, the engineer allows some extra space for translated text, because s/he believes that the Japanese text tends to be longer than the English original. But the length of the Japanese text changes depending on the character type. For example, when "configuration" is translated with phonetic Katakana characters as the second line, it requires more space, but when Japanese Kanji characters are used for "configuration," the length is much shorter than the English word.

Predicting the length of Japanese text is a perilous enterprise. The best advice would be for engineers to allocate components in graphical interfaces so that virtually any size text could be accommodated (see Figure 7).

Figure 7. Desirable text component allocation

Placing the text above an input box leaves ample space on its right side. The engineer does not have to worry about space shortage and truncation. While engineers may at first resist this approach to interface design, they will soon understand that it is preferable to deal with text truncation issues in the QA process.

Myth No. 2: A Japanese character is always double byte.

False. Many engineers have asked if the size for a telephone number in Japan should be doubled. First, it seemed as if they were asking whether Japanese telephone numbers contained more digits than country codes and area codes, but they were actually assuming that numeric characters in Japanese also used double bytes. There is a double-byte number or double-byte alphabet in Japanese, but double-byte alphanumeric characters are seldom used to represent Japanese telephone numbers.

C. *Unicode and Japanese*

Myth No. 3: Unicode makes all system development easy and makes everyone happy.

Unicode is a single encoding scheme that aims at accommodating all the character sets in most languages. As Unicode is based on a 16-bit (or 2 byte) encoding scheme, it can contain up to 65,536 characters. As was mentioned above, the number appears to be large, but it still cannot contain all the different Asian characters.

Unicode simplifies the internationalization process in system development, but implementation of Unicode still requires some additional effort. First of all, Unicode adopts a rule to preserve consistency with current language-specific encoding, which is called the "Source Separation Rule." With this rule, the same code point can represent two different glyphs depending on their language attributes: "Japanese Unicode" and "Chinese Unicode." When a system handles Unicode text, it must first differentiate the Unicode language. Second, unless Unicode is used in the entire system, some process must be used to handle encoding conversion between Unicode and Japanese-specific encoding. For example, if for some reason a Japanese Windows client interface cannot handle Unicode, all the characters incoming from a Unicode-compliant server-side system must be converted from Unicode to Shift JIS. However, if the system is open to another platform, the conversion could be from Unicode to EUC-JP. In that case, the system always has to detect the local encoding system before any data is processed for clients. It should be apparent from this that it is not an easy process. Translators do not have to send a warning to developers on this point. However, when Unicode-euphoric engineers say that Unicode can solve any language problem, they should be re-educated as soon as possible.

D. *Moji-bake*

Japanese characters become garbled primarily for two reasons. One is that a non-Japanese font is specified, and the other is that the character codes themselves are corrupted. If it is a font issue, all characters are displayed as the same "garbage," such as dots, squares, and question marks. This shows that the system misunderstands the characters "equally" and means that the characters themselves are still valid. All that is needed is to change the font specification, which is fairly easy to do. This is "benign moji-bake."

However, characters may turn into randomly displayed single-byte characters, as in the following:

[Ì,¤,è,fi,Í,Á,«,è,Æ,Œ©,¦,é,æ,¤,É,È,Á,Ä,«,½□]

If this happens on a Web page, one has the option to change the encoding. However, if this happens on a software interface, all of the Japanese characters have been corrupted. The problem may have been caused by programming logic that can only handle single-byte characters. This type of "malignant moji-bake" requires special attention on the part of engineers.

E. *Word-break issues*

"Japanese doesn't use a space to separate words." This fact, which is trivial to a Japanese translator, often comes as a big surprise to an engineer. Furthermore, knowing that there is no word-breaking space in Japanese, an engineer may jump to the conclusion that all double-byte languages handle spaces the same way. In fact, Chinese does not use a space, while Korean does use a space just like English.

When programmers manipulate strings to automatically break between words, they make extensive use of complex logic. For example, sometimes a program has to split terms into two separate lines due to limited width on an interface, as shown in Table 1.

Table 1. Sample word-break in English

[Original term]	⇒	[Two-line display]
Initial value		Initial value

To do term decomposition, programmers simply find a space to split words across two lines. However, that logic will not work for Japanese (Table 2).

Table 2. Sample word-break in Japanese

[Original term]	⇒	[Two-line display]
初期設定値		初期
		設定値

An engineer may ask, "How then did you split it into two parts?" The logic is not simple. First, it is necessary to tokenize the term into minimum meaningful units, such as (初期), (設定), (値). Next, taking into consideration alignment balance in the length of each line, the engineer must figure out a split point. Studying Japanese morphological analysis would be helpful, if the engineer is willing to make the effort. Most engineers would give up at this point and start to remodel the interface to keep the string on one line.

F. *Backslash and Yen mark*

Most of the ASCII characters are shared in Shift JIS encoding, which means "A" in ASCII is also "A" in Shift JIS. However, the yen mark (¥) in Shift JIS is assigned to the same code point as a backslash (\) in ASCII, because ASCII does not contain the yen mark. Korean has the same situation with its won mark, while the Chinese encoding sets have a backslash. This issue is not very serious, but naïve engineers might easily panic.

There is no way for program logic to take this difference into account. When the logic is written to search for a backslash in an English environment, it behaves as a search for a yen mark in a Japanese platform. Looking at yen marks everywhere in the database, engineers could blame the translators. Under such circumstances, the ability to explain the problem makes a big difference. Localization translators might want to keep in mind that one little piece of information like this can make a major difference in the localization process.

One should be aware that such knowledge will soon be a must for the localization translator. In the real world, more and more technical translators have equipped themselves with engineering experience to distinguish them-selves from traditional translators. As computer and network technology be-comes more complicated, localization and translation agencies face an increase in the number and variety of technical problems. In the realm of Web localiza-tion, a certain level of knowledge about database and Web programming is definitely required for Web translation as more dynamic websites become more widespread. Localization agencies do not want to be burdened with teaching translators the rudiments of HTML. What they are looking for are translators who can handle Web translation without any problems and so contribute to translation efficiency. Moreover, clients are also looking for technically savvy translators. Many companies have noticed a significant hidden cost in using agencies and so try to bypass them. The authors refer to this as "T2C (translator-to-client) shift." Particularly in the supply-chain business world, companies have realized significant cost savings through business-to-business (B2B) and business-to-customer (B2C) transactions. These approaches can also be applied to the translation process. Translators are not able to deal with a T2C framework, however, without sufficient technical knowledge.

Conclusion

Building a curriculum for localization translation presents a number of difficulties. First, translators' knowledge and skill levels vary. Second, an overwhelming amount of technical information exists in the market, i.e., programming languages, networks, databases, system design, hardware structure, to name just a few. Third, the localization process is always in flux, with everyone attempting to streamline its processes. Fourth, current translator trainers cannot keep up with the rapid development of the industry nor do they generally possess more than limited knowledge and experience in localization. Having said this, it is clear that simple transmission of basic translation skills in a traditional translation context from instructors to students cannot serve the purpose of creating an effective learning environment for localization translators.

We would like to underscore the fact that the necessary and essential skill for the translator is the skill of translation, not technical knowledge. An effective way to train localization translators to meet the demands of the market is to determine an appropriate level of minimum technical knowledge required by the localization translator and then to create an environment in which students and instructors can work collaboratively to construct that knowledge in a semi-real work environment. Criteria for inclusion of material in a course should reflect actual market demand. To this end, we encourage collaboration among engineers, translators, and translator trainers at a micro level, and software manufacturers, localization agencies, and schools at a macro level, in the creation of a market-driven training curriculum for localization translators. For traditional translator trainers, this will be a challenging task, but it will provide an invaluable opportunity for them to revisit traditional translation issues in the new technical environment called localization.

References

Altanero, T. 1999. "Building a curriculum for localization: Austin Community College takes the first steps toward a training program in partnership with industry." *Multilingual Computing and Technology* 11(8): 35–36.

Bacak, W. W. 1999. "Boom time for translators." *Language International* 11(5): 34–35.

Cooper, P. 2000. "Twists and turns: An autoethnography." *Human Communication* 3(1): 85–96.

Esselink, B. 1999. "The end of translation as we know it: An industry watcher speculates on translation post-Y2K." *Language International* 11(6): 28–30.

Geist, P. 1999. "Surreal illusions, genuine realities: Disenchantment and renewal in the academy — Introduction." *Communication Theory* 9(4): 365–376.

Gonzalez, A., Houston, M., and Chen, V. (eds). 1997. *Our Voices: Essays in Culture, Ethnicity, and Communication.* Los Angeles, California: Roxbury Publishing Company.

Hoft, N. L. 1995. *International Technical Communication.* New York: John Wiley & Sons, Inc.

I-mode 2000 mannin toppa. [I-mode users exceed 20 million.] 2001. *Yomiuri Newspaper,* March 13, 2001, 2.

Itagaki, M., Kosaka, T., and Ono, Y. 1999. *Software Localization Jissen Handbook* [The Handbook of Software Localization]. Tokyo: Software Research Center.

Katan, D. 1999. *Translating Cultures: An Introduction for Translators, Interpreters and Mediators.* Manchester/United Kingdom: St. Jerome Publishing.

Kiraly, D. 2000. *A Social Constructivist Approach to Translator Education: Empowerment from Theory to Practice.* Manchester/United Kingdom: St. Jerome Publishing.

Thibodeau, R. P. 2000. "Translating for success: How MapInfo created a localization process that cut cost and time." *Language International* 12(2): 30–33, 44.

Contributors

Fanny Arango-Keeth is an Assistant Professor of Spanish at Mansfield University of Pennsylvania. Her research interests include corpora-based translation instruction and literary translation.

Brian James Baer is an Associate Professor of Russian and a faculty member in the Institute of Applied Linguistics at Kent State University, where he teaches undergraduate and graduate courses in the theory and practice of translation. He is presently completing an anthology of Russian writings on translation.

Lynne Bowker is currently an Assistant Professor at the School of Translation and Interpretation of the University of Ottawa (Canada). Her teaching and research interests include translation technology and corpus linguistics. She is the author of *Computer-Aided Translation Technology: A Practical Introduction* (2002) and co-author of *Working with Specialized Language: A Practical Guide to Using Corpora* (2002).

Sonia Colina is an Associate Professor of Linguistics and Translation at Arizona State University where she teaches in the Translation Certificate Program. In addition to her recent book on teacher training, *Translation Teaching From Research to the Classroom* (2003), she has published articles on various aspects of translation pedagogy in journals such as *Target, The Translator* and *Babel.*

Alexander Gross has been translating and writing about translation since 1965. He has taught courses on translation and lectured on translation history for the New York University Translation Studies Program.

Jonathan T. Hine Jr. is a freelance translator. He has done postgraduate work in project management and translator education. His current research interests include the evaluation of translator education. He currently teaches technical translation and text revision at James Madison University in Virginia.

Masaki Itagaki is an adjunct faculty member at the Graduate School of Translation and Interpretation at the Monterey Institute of International Studies. He has worked as a technical translator at J. D. Edwards World Source Company, where he is presently employed as a linguistic engineer. His latest publication is a co-authored book, *Talking Technical Turkey* (2002).

Julie E. Johnson is an Assistant Professor at the Monterey Institute of International Studies, where she teaches courses in French-to-English translation. She is a conference interpreter and published translator specializing in corporate law, advanced technologies, and telecommunications. She is a former director of the American Translators Association.

Donald C. Kiraly is a member of the faculty of the School of Applied Linguistics and Cultural Studies at the University of Mainz in Germersheim, Germany, where he is involved in the training of professional translators. His research to date has been focused on various aspects of translator education. His publications include *Pathways to Translation* (1995) and *A Social Constructivist Approach to Translator Education* (2000).

Geoffrey S. Koby is an Associate Professor of German (Translation) and a faculty member in the Institute of Applied Linguistics at Kent State University, where he teaches undergraduate and graduate courses in translation and coordinates the Bachelor of Science in Translation program. He edited and co-translated Hans P. Krings's *Repairing Texts: Empirical Investigations of Machine Translation Post-Editing Processes* (2001).

Takashi Kosaka is an Assistant Professor at the Graduate School of Translation and Interpretation at the Monterey Institute of International Studies. Prior to teaching, he was a technical translator at J. D. Edwards World Source Company. His latest publication is *Translation of Scientific and Technical Texts into Japanese* (2002).

Carol S. Maier is a Professor of Spanish at Kent State University, where she teaches courses on translation. Her current projects include essays about the theory and pedagogy of literary translation and translations of work by Rosa Chacel and Severo Sarduy.

Natalia Olshanskaya is an Assistant Professor of Russian at Kenyon College in Ohio. She worked in the USSR as a translator and has taught courses on the theory and practice of translation at Odessa University (Ukraine) and at the College of William and Mary (USA). She has published numerous articles on comparative stylistics and translation.

Judy Wakabayashi worked as a professional translator in Japan before completing a Ph.D. on Japanese-English translation. She taught Japanese-English translation at an Australian university for 15 years before recently taking up a position as Associate Professor of Japanese translation at Kent State University.

Index